GENDER IN HISTORY

Series editors:
Lynn Abrams, Cordelia Beattie, Pam Sharpe and Penny Summerfield

The expansion of research into the history of women and gender since the 1970s has changed the face of history. Using the insights of feminist theory and of historians of women, gender historians have explored the configuration in the past of gender identities and relations between the sexes. They have also investigated the history of sexuality and family relations, and analysed ideas and ideals of masculinity and femininity. Yet gender history has not abandoned the original, inspirational project of women's history: to recover and reveal the lived experience of women in the past and the present.

The series Gender in History provides a forum for these developments. Its historical coverage extends from the medieval to the modern periods, and its geographical scope encompasses not only Europe and North America but all corners of the globe. The series aims to investigate the social and cultural constructions of gender in historical sources, as well as the gendering of historical discourse itself. It embraces both detailed case studies of specific regions or periods and broader treatments of major themes. Gender in History books are designed to meet the needs of both scholars and students working in this dynamic area of historical research.

Women, dowries and agency

Manchester University Press

OTHER RECENT BOOKS
IN THE SERIES

Love, intimacy and power: marital relationships in Scotland, 1650–1850
Katie Barclay
(Winner of the 2012 Women's History Network Book Prize)

Modern women on trial: sexual transgression in the age of the flapper
Lucy Bland

Modern motherhood: women and family in England, c. 1945-2000
Angela Davis

Jewish women in Europe in the Middle Ages: a quiet revolution
Simha Goldin

The shadow of marriage: singleness in England, 1914–60
Katherine Holden

Women, travel and identity: Journeys by rail and sea, 1870-1940
Emma Robinson-Tomsett

Imagining Caribbean womanhood: race, nation and beauty contests, 1929–70
Rochelle Rowe

Infidel feminism: secularism, religion and women's emancipation, England 1830-1914
Laura Schwartz

Being boys: working-class masculinities and leisure
Melanie Tebbutt

Queen and country: Same sex desire in the British Armed Forces, 1939–45
Emma Vickers

The 'perpetual fair': gender, disorder and urban amusement in eighteenth-century London
Anne Wohlcke

WOMEN, DOWRIES AND AGENCY
MARRIAGE IN FIFTEENTH-CENTURY VALENCIA

⇌ Dana Wessell Lightfoot ⇌

Manchester University Press

Copyright © Dana Wessell Lightfoot 2013

The right of Dana Wessell Lightfoot to be identified as the author of this work has been asserted by her in accordance with the Copyright, Designs and Patents Act 1988.

Published by Manchester University Press
Altrincham Street, Manchester M1 7JA, UK
www.manchesteruniversitypress.co.uk

British Library Cataloguing-in-Publication Data is available

Library of Congress Cataloging-in-Publication Data is available

ISBN 978 1 5261 0665 0 *paperback*

First published by Manchester University Press in hardback 2013
This edition first published 2016

The publisher has no responsibility for the persistence or accuracy of URLs for any external or third-party internet websites referred to in this book, and does not guarantee that any content on such websites is, or will remain, accurate or appropriate.

Printed by Lightning Source

To Milli Wessell, Eryka Wessell
and Doris Wessell

Contents

LIST OF TABLES	*page*	viii
ACKNOWLEDGEMENTS		ix
MAP OF VALENCIA AND THE *HORTA*		xi
Introduction		1
1 The making of marriage in fifteenth-century Valencia: canon law, civil law and community opinion		14
2 Marital alliances and the choice of spouse		43
3 Marital property of labouring-status wives		65
4 *Germanía* contracts: the exception to the rule		97
5 Earning the dowry: domestic service and donations		112
6 The right to property: dowry restitution in fifteenth-century Valencia		151
Conclusion		189
APPENDIX		192
BIBLIOGRAPHY		199
INDEX		215

Tables

2.1	Central actors in labouring-status marriage contracts, 1420–39	page 44
2.2	Artisan marriage alliances, 1420–39	50
3.1	Size of artisan dowries, 1420–39	66
3.2	Size of *llaurador* dowries, 1420–39	70
3.3	Type of artisan and *llaurador* dotal assets, 1420–39	74
5.1	Marital donation in *donationes inter vivos* and testaments, 1420–39	124
5.2	Marital donation in dowry contracts, 1420–39	125
6.1	Reasons for dowry restitution, 1420–39	153
6.2	Background of plaintiffs in dowry restitution cases, 1420–39	159
6.3	Relationship of witnesses to plaintiffs/defendants in dowry restitution cases, 1420–39	164

Acknowledgements

During the completion of this book, I was fortunate to have the support of an amazing group of advisers, colleagues, family and friends. First and foremost, I would like to thank Dr Mark Meyerson and Dr Barbara Todd whose guidance over the years has helped me to become a better historian. From the University of Toronto, I would also like to thank Dr Nick Terpstra, Dr Jill Ross and Dr Natalie Zemon Davis. My research in Valencia was conducted with the help of the staff at the Archivo del Reino de Valencia and the Archivo de Protocolos del Patriarca de Valencia. I am grateful for their aid in searching out the numerous documents on which this book is based.

Portions of this book have appeared in the following articles: 'Family Interests? Women's Power: The Absence of Family in Dowry Restitution Cases in Fifteenth-Century Valencia', *Women's History Review*, 15(4) (2006), pp. 211–220 (www.tandfonline.com); 'The Projects of Marriage: Spousal Choice, Dowries and Domestic Service in Early Fifteenth-Century Valencia', *Viator*, 40(1) (2009), pp. 333–353; and 'The Power to Divide? *Germanía* Marriage Contracts in Early Fifteenth-Century Valencia', in Jutta Gisela Sperling and Shona Kelly Wray (eds), *Across the Religious Divide: Women, Property, and Law in the Wider Mediterranean (c.1300–1800)* (New York: Routledge), pp. 109–121.

This book was funded in part by a University Research Initiative Grant from the University of Texas at El Paso (UTEP). I would also like to acknowledge the support of my former colleagues at UTEP, especially Cheryl Martin, Sandy McGee Deutsch, Yolanda Leyva and Julia Schiavone Camacho. While I was at UTEP, I was a member of a cross-discipline chapter reading group and am thankful for all the comments on my work provided by Joshua Fan, Adam Arenson, Matt Desing, Keith Erekson and Lee Ann Westman. In my new position at the University of Northern British Columbia, I am grateful for the support of my colleagues Jacqueline Holler, Jonathan Swainger and Ted Binnema.

Researching and writing can be a solitary experience and so I am ever thankful for the friendship and support of those who dragged me away from the computer as well as those who discussed and debated many aspects of this book with me: Matthew Naysmith, Lindsay Richardson, Kim Stanford, Joy Henderson, Greg Downs, Kelly Fogg, Krista Hearty, Becky Young, Mike Lightbody, Carol Bell, Catherine Carstairs, Dave Saad, Martha Bajec, Quentin Blasingame, Sarah Coles, Devi Krieger, Dave Hay, Chris Meissner, Amanda DeGraff, Ted Cooper, Stacey Sowards, Richard Pineda, Marion Rohrleitner, Jamie Smith Houghton, Joanna Carraway, Alan Bell and Seymour. I must give special acknowledgement and thanks to my collaborator in research and teaching, and my closest friend, Alexandra Guerson, without whose support and friendship I'm not sure this book would ever be finished. I look forward to our future collaborations together!

For their encouragement and love, I would like to thank my family: Wayne Wessell, Milli Wessell, Eryka Wessell, Doris Wessell, Debbie and Bob Lightfoot,

ACKNOWLEDGEMENTS

Neil Lightfoot, Michelle Lightfoot and Jasmine Lightfoot.

Finally, there are no words to convey the depth of my gratitude to my husband Rob Lightfoot and our daughter Piper. I am truly thankful for their love, support and understanding during the completion of this book.

Map of Valencia and the *Horta*

Introduction

In late September 1434, a suit of dowry restitution was brought before the civil justice in the city of Valencia on behalf of Teresa Dauder, the wife of a barber. In her petition, Teresa claimed that her husband Tomàs had fallen into debt and penury, and had alienated part of her dowry without permission. For these reasons, Teresa sought to have her dowry immediately restored, in order to protect its financial integrity. Four witnesses testified on Teresa's behalf, including her former mistress and three neighbours of the couple. According to their testimony, in the five years since Teresa and Tomàs were married, he had 'caused many and diverse debts … owed money to many people and had fallen into penury'.[1] In the end, the justice was convinced by the arguments put forth on Teresa's behalf, and ordered Tomàs to return her property.

In many ways, Teresa Dauder was typical of lower-status wives in late medieval Valencia. As a teenager, she had immigrated to the city from her natal town of Sogorb to work as a servant in the home of Maria and Francesc Oviet. After seven years of service, Teresa had earned twenty-five pounds, which she added to a ten-pound gift from her master Francesc, and a five-pound donation from her father, to create the forty-pound dowry which she donated to Tomàs Dauder at the time of their marriage. Her natal family was not present at Teresa and Tomàs's nuptial celebrations, but her employers, the Oviets, played the parental role and hosted a feast for the couple in their home. Once married, Teresa and Tomàs set up their own household using her dotal assets as an economic foundation. But, within five years of marriage, Teresa was before the court, demanding that Tomàs return the dowry, the administration of which he had been entrusted.

Teresa Dauder's story, as told through the civil court records relating her suit of dowry restitution, exemplifies the central argument of this book: that labouring-status wives such as Teresa were able to exercise agency not only in the projects of marriage, choosing a spouse and gathering dotal assets, but also in controlling this property after they wed. Although the prevailing legal code in Valencia, the *Furs*, appeared to give wives little authority over these assets, they were still able to negotiate a measure of control. In these actions, labouring-status wives exercised agency by protecting their marital goods from harm, utilizing legal statutes to their own advantage. The key factors in this argument are the immigrant and labouring-status background of these women. Like Teresa, many had immigrated to Valencia on their own, from smaller towns and villages throughout the kingdom of Valencia, as well as from Castile, Catalonia and Aragon. In doing so, these women moved outside of their natal families' sphere of influence, making them less embedded and subject to the authority of their kin relations. Second, artisan and *llaurador* women (wives/daughters of small farmers who lived in the city of Valencia or the surrounding countryside) often married after their fathers were deceased. These women married later than women of elite status. They made their marital choices independently, as over three-quarters of labouring-status men did not reach the age of 50.[2] Lastly, artisan and *llaurador* women such as Teresa worked themselves, most often as servants, to generate the necessary funds for their dowries. All three of these factors gave wives of this status greater agency than elite women in contracting their marriages, providing dotal assets and challenging their husbands' authority over this property in dowry restitution cases. Without the influence of their natal families in making marital decisions, these wives were able to act independently in controlling their marital property, negotiating the structures of patriarchy to their advantage.

Yet this agency must be viewed as limited for a number of reasons. As Rebecca Winer has argued, 'no woman [in pre-modern Europe] made her choices alone'.[3] On the one hand, women such as Teresa Dauder lived in a patriarchal system that, regardless of social class, defined them as mentally, physically and morally weaker than men. Thus each woman was circumscribed in her actions by a society that saw her as unfit to make her own decisions and so she was 'continually negotiating a system of gender … that she could never control'.[4] Women's agency in this context was therefore shaped by societal norms as defined by legal statutes, theological texts, religious leaders, legislators, judges and political leaders. At the same time, Winer's point can be taken literally, in that kinship and community ties meant that all women were embedded in social networks of various kinds. Elite Valencian women were members of extended marital and natal kin groups, both within the city of Valencia and the wider kingdom of which it was a part. For labouring-status women, familial ties may have been less evident, as many of them were immigrants. These women nevertheless developed strong neighbourhood networks as well as connections through guilds and other economic bodies.

Legal constraints could also create limitations for a labouring-status woman's control of her marital assets. While the *Furs* recognized that a woman's marital property was solely owned by her, it gave complete administrative control of it to her husband for the duration of their marriage. A wife was able to challenge her husband's legal authority over these assets if she felt their financial integrity was being threatened, and the justices almost always supported these claims; however, a woman's ability to regain control of this property once it had been awarded to her is uncertain as there is evidence that in some cases, women had difficulty doing so. Additionally, the *Furs* only worked to protect those women that married under the prevailing marital property system based on dowries. Women who chose, for a variety of reasons, to utilize a second regime, known as the *germanía*, had little recourse to protect the assets which they brought to their marriages. While the *germanía* system has been described by historians as giving greater equality to women in marriage than the dotal regime, as it proposed a strictly equal division of conjugal assets at the dissolution of the marriage, the lack of legal recognition and protection for wives under it has led me to question its perceived egalitarianism.

Not only did labouring-status married women face some limitations in their exercise of agency, they were also subject to certain negative consequences. While the lack of natal kin present in the city of Valencia may have given immigrant women greater freedom in their marital choices, it also left them without a support network if they were faced with difficult situations, such as economic hardship or abuse at the hands of their husbands and employers. Eventually labouring-status women were able to utilize systems of support created with friends and neighbours for aid in dealing with such problems, but these connections took time to develop. In the meantime, immigrant women could be placed in very precarious situations.

Furthermore, although being of labouring-status certainly gave these women some agency, particularly in terms of controlling their marital property, this went hand in hand with desperation. The dowry money that many of them earned as servants rarely exceeded twenty-five pounds, funds obtained after as many as ten years of labour. Living in the household in which they worked, female servants, some from the age of 7 or 8, worked long days with little leisure time.[5] For some servants, the families they worked for replaced their blood kin and, in such situations, these young women were treated as quasi-daughters by their masters and mistresses. For others, their subordinate position as servant left them open to abuse, both physical and sexual, at the hands of their employers, leaving them, in the end, even more vulnerable and desperate.[6]

Widows, more than any other group of women in the medieval period, demonstrate the double-edged nature of agency.[7] On the one hand, widows were legally independent, able to conclude contracts and conduct business entirely on their own. In possession of the dowry and counter-gift, and often holding usufruct rights to their deceased husbands' property, widows could be prosperous and therefore exercise a great deal of agency. On the other hand, widows often represented the poorest sections of medieval society and were the most common recipients of charity. Indeed it was believed that widows had an unquestioned entitlement to poor relief.[8]

To a large extent, social status determined a woman's experience after her husband had died. Isabelle Chabot and Christiane Klapisch-Zuber have argued that higher-status widows were often helpless victims in clashes between their natal and marital families who each wanted control of their persons and property.[9] While these kinds of struggles likely took place among higher-status families throughout southern Europe, elite widows were also able to live with a certain amount of economic autonomy, if they were in possession of their dowries and other property, and were not subject to familial pressures.[10] This was not necessarily the case for labouring-status widows. Even if they were able to regain their dotal assets from a previous marriage with relative ease (and evidence from Valencia and other areas of Europe demonstrates that this could be problematic), their dowries were often not worth enough to support themselves and any surviving children they had. Frequently, widows retained usufruct rights over their deceased husbands' goods, but, as their spouses were labouring-status men, this property may not have amounted to much. Some lower-status widows were able to turn to their families for help, but those that were immigrants did not have such support networks. Friends and neighbours likely aided these women in the short term, but to survive, many of them remarried. All in all, for wives of labouring-status, whether *donzellas* or widows, agency did not always come without negative repercussions. My argument therefore is for limited or constrained agency, by which I mean that labouring-status women were able to create some manoeuvrability for themselves within the patriarchal structures of late medieval Valencia, using the frameworks available to them to exercise some self-determination in their marital choices.

Women, marriage and property in southern Europe

The historiography of women, marriage and property in southern Europe has traditionally focused on the experiences of elite women, especially those living within the Italian city states of Florence and Venice. These scholars emphasize the central role of families in choosing a spouse, gathering dowry assets and controlling this property once the marital union was created; however, historians such as Christiane Klapisch-Zuber, Julius Kirshner, Thomas Kuehn, Diane Owen Hughes and Stanley Chojnacki debate the question of how much 'independence of action, influence and self-determination'[11] elite women had in their marital choices. For example, Diane Owen Hughes has argued that men used the rights they held over women to assert or compete for status, using a daughter's dowry to make alliances for the family.[12] Christiane Klapisch-Zuber also presents wives as pawns in the hands of their husbands and fathers, remarking that they were viewed as merely 'an object of trade.'[13]

While Stanley Chojnacki has explored the ways in which urban patricians controlled spousal choices for their daughters, using marriage to cement important political alliances, he also argues against portraying elite women as entirely controlled by the patriarchal structures of medieval and early modern European society. The work of Julius Kirshner and Thomas Kuehn has demonstrated how the wives and daughters of elite men were able to work within Roman law, judicial institutions and marriage as actors for their own rights, particularly in terms of their marital property. Yet, at the same time, these scholars still present elite women as embedded within kinship relations, working to protect family interests in their legal actions.

For Spain, growing interest in women's history has produced some work by Spanish and Catalan scholars, mining rich archival material to detail the lives of women in the medieval period in various ways.[14] Like scholars whose research focuses on Italy, Spanish and Catalan historians highlight both women's independence *and* lack of self-determination in marriage. For English-language scholars of medieval Iberia, Heath Dillard's *Daughters of the Reconquest: Women in Castilian Town Society, 1100–1300* demonstrates how legal codes provided urban women with agency in marital relationships; however, her foundational study does not consider the practice of law in any way and thus does not comment on whether or not wives in the frontier towns of high medieval Castile were able to utilize these legal statutes successfully.

Analysing how the law 'categorized and defined' women in the late thirteenth and early fourteenth centuries, Marie Kelleher's *The Measure of Woman: Law and Female Identity in the Crown of Aragon* goes beyond the examination of legal codes to look at how women actively participated in 'the formation of the legal culture that sketched out the boundaries of their lives'.[15] Much like I am in this book, Kelleher is interested in exploring the spaces within the patriarchal system of law where some women were able to negotiate status for themselves. In doing so, Kelleher discusses topics such as sexual transgression and violence as well as a chapter on women and property. She argues that in pursuing legal cases against their husbands or their husbands' families, wives were subject to gendered legal assumptions which greatly affected how they could present themselves before the law; thus these women were not necessarily vulnerable victims but 'legal actors developing strategies to preserve the household property in ways that actively engaged with broader legal ideas about women.'[16] Kelleher's book raises many important questions about how women interact with and utilize the law, both adhering to gender norms while simultaneously searching for areas within legal practice that allow them a measure of independent legal identity and authority.

Due to the nature of her sources, Kelleher is not able to infer much about the social status of the women who participate in the legal cases which form the backbone of her book.[17] The civil prosecutions and criminal inquests from late thirteenth- and early fourteenth-century Crown of Aragon rarely indicate a woman's background, beyond her position as wife, widow or daughter of a certain man.[18] This study of women, marriage and property in the early fifteenth century is not affected by such limitations, as my sources allow me to identify the socio-economic background of the women who utilized both notaries and the civil courts of late medieval Valencia. In doing so, it is clear that socio-economic status and immigration greatly influenced women's marital strategies, providing labouring-status women with the ability to act on their own behalf in choosing spouses, gathering marital assets and protecting that property once married.

Use of agency theory

Although often utilized by historians to characterize the actions of those deemed powerless in the past, agency theory is inherently problematic in many ways. Most notably, the concept of agency carries with it distinct tones of resistance by the subjugated and contained within it, is the idea that agents should have the ability to effect some changes on the societies where they live, that is, to transform, to some degree, the dominant structures in which they are embedded.[19] In reference to the experiences of labouring-status wives in late medieval Valencia, at no time is the idea of resisting hegemony, resisting the dominant social group, resisting patriarchy, present. There is no evidence that these women were attempting to fight explicitly or implicitly against the hegemonic patriarchal constructs that defined them as mentally, physically and morally weaker than men. One cannot argue, therefore, that artisan and *llaurador* wives were transforming late medieval notions of marriage, or even patriarchy. As Judith

Bennett has argued, medieval society should be viewed as a 'patriarchal equilibrium' because wives may have gained short-term benefits, getting their dowries restored to them in civil court for example, but over the long term, their status remained the same.[20]

Labouring-status wives cannot be described as attempting to resist and change patriarchy, but they can be seen as manoeuvring within the structures of it for their own advantages. As Sherry Ortner has explored, theories of agency encompass more than simply the binary of dominance and resistance. While this definition of agency is questionable in considering the experiences of labouring-status wives in late medieval Valencia, Ortner's 'agency of intentions' works quite well for a consideration of how these women negotiated within these patriarchal structures. 'Agency of intentions' consists of 'culturally constituted' projects, purposes and desires that infuse life with meaning and purpose.[21] The agent seeks to accomplish these projects within a framework of social structures in which they are already embedded.[22] Ortner argues that such projects can be used as a method of empowerment or for constructing identity.[23] This conception of agency is more apparent for labouring-status women in late medieval Valencia if we consider the act of marriage and the garnering and protection of dotal assets as culturally constituted projects.

Late medieval society viewed marriage as the ultimate goal for all women, if they could not join a convent. Numerous didactic manuals, such as Francesc Eiximenis's *Lo llibre de les dones*, conceptualized the structure of women's lives around marriage, viewing them as 'maids, wives and widows'.[24] Such prescriptive literature never discussed women's lives outside of this trinity as it upholds the argument that the purpose in life of all women was to marry and produce children. Popular preachers frequently expounded upon similar themes in their sermons. For example, in a sermon from 1412, Vicent Ferrer told the story of a woman who, seeing another man gift his wife with two dresses, asked her own husband for one, crying 'I brought as good of a dowry as she did'. Her husband insists that they have no money to pay for such things, but she bothers day and night until he capitulates, financially ruining himself in the process. Ferrer ends his sermon with St Paul's admonition that the man was to be head of his wife, not ruled by her.[25] In this sermon, Ferrer's fictional wife insists that the dowry she brought entitles her to gifts, such as the dress, from her husband. In another homily, concerning nuptials, the preacher rails against weddings and the sins they encourage, stating at one point that 'women think of the dowry and say: How much has that bride brought as dowry?'.[26] Ferrer utilizes this comment to demonstrate the sin of avarice that is inherent in nuptial celebrations, but both sermons raise important links between a woman and her dowry in late medieval Valencian society. Reflecting the realities of the world in which he lived, Ferrer's sermons identified a woman's value with the assets she brought to marriage.

Due to their labouring-status and immigrant background, women such as Teresa Dauder exercised agency in fulfilling the marital projects of choosing a spouse and garnering the necessary dotal funds, as well as protecting these assets once married. As the families of these women were not often present in the city of Valencia, and their fathers were likely deceased, they had influence over their choice of spouse. Unlike the dowries of elite women which were donated largely by family, those of labouring-status women came from a variety of sources, often including income they earned themselves. Evidence from the civil court demonstrates that these women were more than willing to protect their dotal property before the courts if their husbands attempted to diminish it in any way. Labouring-status women in late medieval Valencia negotiated a variety of opportunities to create honourable and viable marriages. Networks of friends, neighbours and employers were used to the fullest extent in order to form successful marital households in the absence of blood kin. Due to their lower socio-economic status, these women were able to foster particular kinds of connections not available to elite brides who were closely supervised by their families. Labouring-status women therefore can be seen as exercising 'agency of intentions', as choosing a spouse, the accumulation of one's own dotal assets and protecting this property from harm are projects accomplished within the framework of medieval social structures that defined these women as married, or to be married. This form of agency is much more subtle than 'agency of power', but it still infuses the lives of these women with meaning and purpose that is closely tied to the development of their own identities.

Sources and chapters

This study is based on hundreds of notarial and court records held in the *Archivo del Reino de Valencia* (ARV) and the *Archivo de Protocolos de Patriarca de Valencia* (APPV). I examined twenty years of notarial instruments from 1419 to 1439, including: 367 dotal contracts, 88 *germanía* contracts, 94 *donationes inter vivos* (donation contracts), 190 testaments, 61 domestic service contracts, 84 *apochas* (receipts) as well as approximately 25 miscellaneous notarial contracts (apprenticeship, dowry return, transfer of usufruct, etc.). I have also examined 220 cases of dowry restitution from the court of the civil justice (Justícia Civil) and 50 cases from the court of the governor (Gobernació) from 1420 to 1439. For both courts, my analysis is based on all extant cases of dowry restitution involving still-living husbands. Both the records of the tribunal of the Justícia Civil and that of the Gobernació contain numerous suits of dowry restitution involving widows suing the executors of their husbands' estates to have their dotal property returned. My concern in this book, however, was solely with those suits brought by wives against their husbands.

The search for dowries in notarial records, in particular, has limited somewhat my sample of contracts beyond those dealing directly with marriage. I therefore did not examine in any detail property transactions and other types of business contracts concluded by women which may have involved dotal and non-dotal assets. In terms of dowry restitution, the lack of extant church court records for the bishopric of Valencia has left me unable to examine what happened to couples once a wife's dowry had been restored to her. In the conclusion, I speculate on the consequences of dowry restitution, but I cannot make any concrete arguments as to the effects that these kinds of cases would have had on a couple's marriage.

The six chapters of this book are organized to follow the journey of a labouring-status woman in late medieval Valencia as she negotiated the projects of marriage and then utilized the legal system to protect these assets once marriage went wrong. It begins by looking at the city of Valencia in the fifteenth century and the experiences of immigrants as they arrive in this urban centre. The second part of this chapter sets the theoretical framework for marriage in late medieval Valencia by considering what made marriages valid in the eyes of the canon law, civil law and community opinion. It explores canonical legal strictures regarding marriage in the medieval period and then more specifically looks at synodal legislation from the bishopric of Valencia. The next section of this chapter focuses on the civil contract drawn up between a couple, and examines the secular legal precepts that governed marital property. Lastly, this chapter analyses the social definitions of a marital union using witness testimony from dowry restitution cases. These criteria both complemented and differed from those defined by canon and secular laws.

Chapter 2 examines the marital choices of artisan and *llaurador* women in late medieval Valencia and argues that because of their socio-economic and immigrant background, labouring-status women exercised agency in the first 'project of marriage': choosing a spouse. Some of these women were influenced by family members in their marital decisions. For others, the lack of familial presence in Valencia, and the fact that many of their fathers were deceased, had an impact on the ability of labouring-status women to make their own spousal choices. At the same time, these women were influenced by friends, neighbours and employers. While families looked for marriage alliances that could augment their economic resources and cement social ties within neighbourhood and guild structures, these factors were also considerations for women themselves as they sought husbands with whom they could create economically and socially viable households.

The economic aspect of marriage is the focus of Chapter 3, looking specifically at the amount and type of property given as dowry and how this varied according to economic, familial and marital background. Women of labouring-status largely had dowries that were valued at twenty to forty pounds, consisting primarily of cash, household goods and jewellery; however, widowhood and the loss of a father could affect these patterns, in both a negative and positive manner. Legally, Valencian wives had no control of this property while married, as their husbands held administrative rights. Husbands also controlled the *creix*, given to women in exchange for their virginity. My evidence demonstrates that the type of property women received as marital assets was similar across socio-economic status in many ways, as it consisted largely of moveable goods but elite women tended to bring more investments as part of their dowries while labouring-status women's assets were primarily cash, household goods and jewellery.

Chapter 4 moves away from the dotal regime to explore another system of marital assigns utilized in late medieval Valencian society, known as *germanía*. This regime stipulated that all of a couple's assets would be held together as a conjugal fund for the duration of the marriage. When one member of the couple died, the survivor received half of the assets, with the other half devolved upon their children. If there were no offspring, the survivor received the entirety of the fund. This type of marriage contract was not formally recognized by the *Furs*, although a large minority of lower-status Valencian women utilized this system. Historians have argued that women who married under a regime such as the *germanía* had greater equality in marriage; however, this chapter argues that the absence of legal protection could place these wives in difficult situations.

Labouring-status women who married in late medieval Valencia gathered their marital assets in two ways: earning them through work or receiving them from outside donors. Chapter 5 explores the methods by which these women earned their marital property, looking at how artisan and *llaurador* women provided their own dowries and share of the conjugal fund from income earned through service and bequests prior to marriage. While families were often closely involved in marital property donation, by no means were they exclusively so. Immigration had a great effect on how labouring-status women earned their dowries as, in the absence of family, these women turned to other means to generate such assets. The evidence therefore suggests that labouring-status women retained a great deal of agency in cobbling together the assets needed to marry according to their status. Men who married under the dotal and *germanía* systems also received marital donations. The types and sources of these gifts reflected, rather than challenged, gendered notions of property as they supported inheritance trends prevalent in late medieval Valencia.

The final chapter of this book uses evidence from the court of the civil justice and the court of the governor to examine wives' claims against their husbands for the restitution of their dowries. It begins by looking at the laws allowing for dowry restitution as well as the ways in which the courts functioned in these suits. The chapter then turns to an examination of the cases themselves, looking in depth at labouring-status women as instigators of these suits and the types of evidence they utilized to prove them. The vast majority of witnesses that testified in dowry restitution cases were neighbours, indicating the impact that immigration had on definitions of kin in late medieval Valencia. Dowry restitution cases present the greatest evidence of women's agency in protecting their marital assets from errant husbands. Although the law restricted the access of wives to this property while married, dowry restitution provided women with a method to negotiate patriarchal structures such as this to their advantage.

The key factor in my argument about married women's access to and control of marital property in early fifteenth-century Valencia is socio-economic status. As labouring-status women, they were affected by patterns of immigration, lack of living fathers and work, issues which never had an impact on the lives of elite women in the same manner. Considerations such as these have allowed me to examine the ways in which artisan and *llaurador* wives in late medieval Valencia worked within legal and social norms to protect and maintain their marital assets, in particular their dowries, which were so integral to their own identities. By negotiating these normative patriarchal structures, labouring-status wives were able to generate some agency for themselves in a society which defined them solely in terms of their husbands and families. In the chapters that follow, I will explore these negotiations, looking at the choices that artisan and *llaurador* wives made in conferring and protecting their marital property.

Notes

1 Archivo del Reino de Valencia (hereafter ARV) Justícia Civil Peticiones 3723 m. 14, f. 8r. sig. f. 35r. a 38v. (30 September 1434).
2 Antoni Furió, *Història del País Valencià* (Valencia: Edicions Alfons el Magnànim, 1995), p. 192.
3 Rebecca Lynn Winer, *Women, Wealth and Community in Perpignan, c.1250–1300: Christians, Jews, and Enslaved Muslims in a Medieval Mediterranean Town* (Burlington, VT: Ashgate, 2006), p. 4.
4 *Ibid.*
5 María Teresa López Beltrán, 'La accesibilidad de la mujer al mundo laboral: El servicio domestico en Málaga a finales de la Edad Media', in *Estudios históricos y literarios sobre la mujer medieval* (Malaga: Diputacion Provincial, Servicio de Publicaciones, 1990), p. 133.
6 For a discussion of the sexual tension that could exist between female servants and employers, see Christiane Klapisch-Zuber, 'Women Servants in Florence during the Fourteenth and Fifteenth Centuries', in Barbara Hanawalt (ed)., *Women and Work in Preindustrial Europe* (Bloomington: Indiana University Press, 1986), pp. 72–73; Dennis Romano, *Housecraft and Statecraft: Domestic Service in Renaissance Venice, 1400–1600* (Baltimore: Johns Hopkins University Press, 1997), pp. 52–53; p. 213.
7 Scholars of medieval Valencia have yet to explore the experience of widows in any detail. For other areas in the Crown of Aragon, see Equip Broida (Olga Bravo Ortega, Pilar Gallego Garces, Margarida González i Betlinski, Montserrat Marsiñach i Tirvio, Nuria Muñoz i Soria, Anna Rubio i Rodon, Elisa Varela Rodriguez and Teresa-María Vinyoles), 'La viudez ¿triste o feliz estado? (Las últimas voluntades de los barceloneses en torno al 1400)', in C. Segura Graiño (ed.), *Las mujeres en las ciudades medievales* (Seminario de Estudios de la Mujer, Universidad Autonóma de Madrid: Madrid, 1984); María García-Herrero, 'Capitulo X: Las Viudas de Zaragoza', in *Las mujeres en Zaragoza en el siglo XV* (Zaragoza: Ayuntamiento de Zaragoza, 1990), vol. I, pp. 317–377; María García-Herrero, 'Viudedad foral y viudas Aragonesas a finales de la edad media', *Hispania: Revista Espanola de Historia*, 184 (1993), pp. 431–450; María Isabel Pérez de Tudela y Velasco, 'La condición de la viuda en el medievo castellano-leonés', in *Las mujeres en las ciudades medievales*, pp. 87–108.
8 Sandra Cavallo and Lyndan Warner, 'Introduction', in Sandra Cavallo and Lyndan Warner (eds), *Widowhood in Medieval and Early Modern Europe* (New York: Longman, 1999), p. 23; Agustín Rubio Vela, *Pobreza, enfermedad y asistencia hospitalaria en Valencia del siglo XIV* (Valencia: Institución Alfonso el Magnánimo, 1984), p. 14.
9 Isabelle Chabot, 'Lineage Strategies and the Control of Widows in Renaissance Florence', in Cavallo and Warner, *Widowhood in Medieval and Early Modern Europe*, pp. 127–144; Christiane Klapisch-Zuber, 'The "Cruel Mother": Maternity, Widowhood, and Dowry in Florence in the Fourteenth and Fifteenth Centuries', in *Women, Family and Ritual in Renaissance Italy* (Chicago: University of Chicago Press, 1985), pp. 117–131.
10 For example, see the work of Stanley Chojnacki on patrician widows in Venice; 'Getting Back the Dowry', in *Women and Men in Renaissance Venice: Twelve Essays on Patrician Living* (Baltimore: Johns Hopkins University Press, 2000), pp. 95–111.
11 Jennifer Carpenter and Sally-Beth MacLean, 'Introduction', *Power of the Weak: Studies*

on Medieval Women (Chicago: University of Illinois Press, 1995), pp. xi–xix; p. xv.

12 Diane Owen Hughes, 'From Brideprice to Dowry in Mediterranean Europe', in Marion A. Kaplan (ed.), *The Marriage Bargain: Women and Dowries in European History* (New York: Haworth Press, 1984), p. 43.

13 Christiane Klapisch-Zuber, 'Zacharias or the Ousted Father: Nuptial Rituals in Tuscany from Giotto to the Council of Trent', in *Women, Family and Ritual in Renaissance Italy*, p. 67.

14 Teresa-Maria Vinyoles, *Les barcelonines a les darreries de l'Edat Mitjana (1370–1410)* (Barcelona: Fundació Salvador Vives Casajuana, 1976); María Francisca Gámez Montalvo, *Régimen jurídico de la mujer en la familia castellana medieval* (Granada: Editorial Comares, 1998); Jaume Codina, *Contractes de matrimoni al Delta del Llobregat (XIV a XIX)* (Barcelona: Fundació Noguera, 1997); García-Herrero, *Las mujeres en Zaragoza en el siglo XV*.

15 Marie A. Kelleher, *The Measure of Woman: Law and Female Identity in the Crown of Aragon* (Philadelphia: University of Pennsylvania Press, 2011), p. 1.

16 Ibid., pp. 78–80.

17 Ibid., p. 8.

18 Ibid.

19 William H. Sewell, Jr, 'A Theory of Structure: Duality, Agency and Transformation', *American Journal of Sociology*, 98(1) (July 1992), p. 20. For a recent discussion of the agency debate, see Cornelia Hughes Dayton, 'Rethinking Agency, Recovering Voices', *American Historical Review*, 109(3) (June 2004), p. 827. Dayton is responding to two articles contained in a previous issue of the *American Historical Review* by Caroline Castiglione and Giovanna Benadusi. Both shy away from using the term 'agency' in their discussions of the efforts of peasants in eighteenth-century Rome and servant women in seventeenth-century Arezzo to exert their wills upon the dominant group in their respective societies. See Castiglione, 'Adversarial Literacy: How Peasant Politics Influenced Noble Governing of the Roman Countryside during the Early Modern Period', pp. 783–804; Benadusi, 'Investing the Riches of the Poor', pp. 805–826.

20 Judith M. Bennett, 'Theoretical Issues: Confronting Continuity', *Journal of Women's History*, 9(3) (autumn 1997), p. 74 and *History Matters: Patriarchy and the Challenge of Feminism* (Philadelphia: University of Pennsylvania Press, 2006), pp. 54–81.

21 Sherry Ortner, 'Specifying Agency: The Comaroffs and Their Critics', *Interventions* 3(1) (2001), p. 79.

22 Ibid., p. 80.

23 Ibid., p. 81.

24 See Francesc Eiximenis, *Lo llibre de les dones: Volums I i II* (Barcelona: Biblioteca Torres Amat, 1981).

25 Vicent Ferrer, *Sermons: volum segon*, ed. Josep Sanchis Sivera (Barcelona: Editorial Barcino, 1934), pp. 42–43.

26 Vicent Ferrer, *Sermons: volum cinquè*, ed. Gret Schib (Barcelona: Editorial Barcino, 1984), p. 8.

1

The making of marriage in fifteenth-century Valencia: canon law, civil law and community opinion

When Teresa Dauder arrived in Valencia at the age of 12 to work as a servant in the Oviets' household, she came to a city on the rise. The fifteenth century has been described by historians as the 'Golden Age' for the city of Valencia. Culturally, this century was characterized by the artistic and literary splendour of writers such as Ausiàs March and Jaume Roig. Economically, its manufacturing and commercial activity flourished as Valencia became a central port in the Mediterranean trade routes. Politically, it came to dominate the kingdom of which it was the capital, as nobles and urban patricians consolidated their power. During the course of the fifteenth century, Valencia became the centre of the Crown of Aragon, the wider polity of which it was a part, as it entered a period of prosperity while other cities in the Crown were on the decline.[1] The city reached its zenith in the latter half of the century, but the first fifty years saw important developments in manufacturing and commerce as well as demographic expansion that provided it with the population necessary to flourish.

Conquered from the Muslims by Jaume I in 1238, the city of Valencia and its surrounding *horta*[2] soon came to be the power centre of Jaume's newly created kingdom. Concerned not to have limitations placed on his power as in his other domains of Aragon and Catalonia, Jaume made Valencia autonomous and independent with its own distinct kingdom-wide legal code, the *Furs*. Most of those who settled in Valencia were from Catalonia and Aragon, but the kingdom gradually became Catalanized, both culturally and linguistically.[3] Up until the end of the fourteenth century, the city had numerous Muslims and Jews living within it, making Valencia one of the most religiously and culturally plural cities in the Crown of Aragon. The thriving Jewish community was 2,500 strong but the pogroms which swept across the Iberian peninsula in 1391 decimated it, leaving Valencia with only *conversos*, Jews who had converted to

Christianity, some of them by force.[4] Over the course of the fifteenth century, Valencia became the dominant urban centre in the Crown of Aragon, eclipsing Barcelona. Although Barcelona had predominated in the fourteenth century, the hundred years that followed were not kind to the city. A disastrous civil war fought between royalists supporting the recently installed Castilian Trastamara dynasty and the patricians of Barcelona facilitated the decline of the city and allowed the rise of Valencia, both the city and the kingdom, in comparison.[5] This was especially true in economic terms, as the city of Valencia took over the role of the central port of the Crown of Aragon from Barcelona.[6]

Valencia's ascent to its position of power in the fifteenth century began in the post-Black Death period of the late fourteenth century. Although the city experienced its share of difficulties in this period due to plague, famine, drought and war, these were offset by a dynamic population and economy that was fuelled by immigration.[7] Indeed Valencia did not experience the same kind of recession as Catalonia and many other European countries after 1348. The city's recovery from the disasters of the Black Death and its repercussions was quick and within twenty-five years, the population was growing again at an even faster rate, despite repeated waves of plague, famines, droughts, the flooding of the city four times by the river Turia from 1356 to 1403 and even an earthquake in 1396.[8] Valencia's population almost doubled from 1355 to 1418, and grew again by one-third from 1418 to 1489.[9] By the end of the fifteenth century, 45,000 people lived within its walls, with a further 20,000 to 25,000 in the surrounding countryside.[10] This demographic expansion is even more extraordinary since Valencia experienced 28 epidemics from 1400 to 1512, with 7,200 deaths in 1439, 11,000 in 1450 and another 12,000 nine years later.[11]

As the centre of government, manufacturing and commerce, the city dominated the entire kingdom and it acted as a magnet for those seeking to improve their fortunes. Those who came to Valencia were from across the Iberian peninsula, as well as from other parts of Europe, most notably Italy. They were attracted to the city's economic dynamism, a condition that was not transferred to the kingdom as a whole. Fifty per cent of those that immigrated to the city of Valencia were from other areas in the kingdom. So, while its population exploded, other regions experienced severe demographic decline. The northern part of the kingdom faced the greatest losses in population, while the south increased in opposition. For example, the town of Morella, located in the extreme north of the kingdom, went from a population of 2,898 hearths in 1418 to 254 in 1469. Overall, by the middle of the fifteenth century, the north and central part of the kingdom lost 40 to 50 per cent of its population.[12]

Legally, when the new immigrants arrived in the city of Valencia, they were to appear before the justice and the *jurats*[13] of the city, swearing to uphold the obligations of a resident.[14] This oath meant that they had to keep the city's laws and pay certain taxes. They also had to indicate whether or not they were going to be a true resident by establishing their household in the city. Now deemed a *vehi* (resident), the scribe of the municipal council would record the day and year that the immigrant was received as a resident, and the name of the parish and street where he or she lived. If the *vehi* or *vehina* wanted to move, he or she would have to come before the justice and *jurats* again to request permission to do so.[15] All of these regulations were designed to allow the municipal council to keep track of the city's residents, therefore making it easier for them to collect taxes. Immigrants who did not keep their obligations as promised on arrival could lose their residency rights. Both the monarchy and the municipal *consell* established methods of investigating newcomers and instituting penalties for those who did not uphold their responsibilities.[16]

Despite these regulations, huge numbers of individuals and families who immigrated to Valencia did not go through this process, making it impossible to discern accurately just how many people actually moved to the city during this period. This group of immigrants were largely journeymen artisans, *llauradors*[17] and labourers, attracted by better conditions and increasing economic opportunities. Women also moved to Valencia, either on their own as domestic servants, or with their husbands and families. Immigration such as this helped to fuel the expansion of industrial activity and manufacturing in the city.[18] Neighbourhoods saw a constant flux of activity, as artisans and *llauradors* moved in and out, trying to improve their economic lot. As the city's economy was based on commerce, artisanal industry and agricultural production, those of labouring-status had numerous economic opportunities.

Although Valencian artisans were engaged in a variety of trades, the city's three main industries were ironwork, leatherwork and textiles. Cloth production was central and the city became a leading producer of medium-quality cloth.[19] Fullers, carders, weavers, dyers, tailors but most of all wooldressers made up a large percentage of the artisans plying their trade in the city. There were also great numbers of blacksmiths, shoemakers, cobblers and tanners of various kinds. Over the course of the fifteenth century, artisanal trades became increasingly specialized with trades like tanners being broken down into more specific categories such as *blanquers*, *asaonadors* and *aluders*.[20] Production was based on the family workshop, headed by a master artisan and powered by the work of journeymen and apprentices. Wives often worked alongside their husbands or performed other economic tasks to help keep their households afloat.[21] In certain types of production, such as cloth making, rural workers were hired by merchants to do piecework, although this practice was discouraged by master and journeymen artisans.[22]

Trades in Valencia were organized and regulated by confraternities, or guilds, which became increasingly elitist as the fifteenth century progressed. When Jaume I first conquered Valencia from the Muslims in the early thirteenth century, he forbade the establishment of guild structures out of concern that the presence of such organizations would create problems of social order.[23] In 1329, this prohibition was lifted and within three years, twenty confraternities organized by trade were reorganized or introduced; however, it was not until the mid-fifteenth century that these organizations developed into true guilds.[24] While initially masters and journeymen of particular trades had their own separate corporations, by the mid-fifteenth century, these had been combined into a single guild. For example, in 1380, the wooldresser guild was divided between journeymen attached to the parish of Holy Trinity and masters, connected to that of the Archangel Michael. Within a hundred years, these two corporations were combined into one, with their ordinances approved by the municipal council.[25] The group of families of master status in each guild was solidified during the fifteenth century, and journeymen who were not related by blood were rarely able to join their ranks.

Although Valencian women were able to join guilds on their own, their participation and movement within these corporations was circumscribed. It was rare for a woman to become a master, except as a widow and female artisans who practised trades different from their husbands tended to cluster in low-skilled, low-paid crafts connected to the textile trade such as spinning and carding.[26] While we do see some girls signing apprenticeship contracts,[27] they were not necessarily allowed to complete the exams which would move them up to journeyman status. The exclusion of women from higher-status trades and guild positions in Valencia is not surprising, given the political roles that guilds played in the city. Unlike other cities in southern Europe during the late medieval period, master artisans served as municipal councillors.[28] Women's position within the guild structures of fifteenth-century Valencia was therefore largely as the wives of masters and journeymen, participating in the social and charitable activities of the corporations but not necessarily the economic aspects. This does not mean that women were not involved in artisanal production in Valencia during this time but that they were often working outside of guild regulations or alongside their husbands and fathers in family workshops.

In Barcelona, the situation for women's participation in guilds was comparable to Valencia. In some cases, women (often widows) were able to run workshops, especially in the clothing and textile trades.[29] Although women worked as apprentices in many trades, their rights to practise those crafts and move up through the ranks of a guild varied. For example, the guild of the linen weavers allowed women to complete their exams and have full membership in the corporation. In contrast, the guild of the coral workers forbade women from teaching apprentices without a formal licence which could only be obtained with special dispensation.[30] Elsewhere in the Iberian peninsula, women's access to and participation in guilds varied a great deal. In some areas, despite working as apprentices within particular trades, women were forbidden from completing exams, as they were not allowed to become journeymen or masters.[31] The experience of women in the Crown of Aragon and Castile was similar to the rest of the Mediterranean world in this period. As guilds developed over the course of the fifteenth century, regulations regarding women's work became stricter, often pushing them into low-paid, low-skilled and low-status trades, a trend that was common across Europe in the late medieval period.[32]

In terms of agricultural production, most land in the *horta* of Valencia was used to produce commercial crops such as sugar cane, linen, vegetables and rice, with an increasing amount of wheat.[33] The *llauradors* who farmed this land rented it by various forms, largely from noble families and members of the urban patriciate who were eager to turn themselves into a rentier class. The two main forms of landholding were emphyteusis and leasehold. A *llaurador* who held his land by emphyteutic tenure was able to sell, transfer or alienate his parcels and paid a yearly rent to his landlord. Leaseholds were usually terms of three to four years, where a *llaurador* handed over half of his cultivation to the landlord.[34] While both were utilized, emphyteusis was by far the more common as landlords preferred to receive their rents in cash. Numerous *llauradors* immigrated to the *horta* seeking better farming conditions. The rich coastal lands located just outside the city drew *llauradors* who abandoned marginal farmlands, many of which were located in the northern regions of the kingdom.[35] Although they all worked the land in various types of agricultural production, there were great differences among peasant families. Some *llauradors* did extremely well and were able to purchase the land they farmed outright. Others scraped by with subsistence-level production and still others were forced to work as day labourers to make ends meet. Like artisans, *llauradors* had their own confraternal organizations, with corporations attached to four separate parishes in the city, reflecting the large number of *llauradors* living there.³⁶ Such associations were similar to those created by *llauradors* elsewhere in the Iberian peninsula. For example, farmers in rural and urban areas of Castile developed confraternities that functioned like craft guilds by regulating the market, settling internal disputes and providing representation in conflicts with other groups and individuals.³⁷ The confraternities of *llauradors* in Valencia performed similar functions, providing them with a social, political and economic collective voice in the city.

While some *llauradors* chose to live in one of the many villages located in the *horta*, others resided within the city walls, going out each day to work their plots of land. This is just one example of the clear interrelationship that existed between the city and the surrounding countryside. Other examples include the increasing number of city dwellers that owned land in the *horta*, the sale of agricultural products in the urban market, *llauradors* working as day labourers and the movement of girls and boys into the city to take up positions as domestic servants and apprentices. Each of these connections demonstrates the strong links that developed between Valencia and the surrounding *horta* region over which it held jurisdiction.

Over the course of the fifteenth century, more and more citizens of Valencia came to own land in the *horta*. Wealthy artisans bought land and rented it out for profit. Artisans of more modest means owned land that they either rented to *llauradors* or farmed themselves, usually devoting one or two days a week to cultivation. But the main players in the Valencian land market were the *ciutadans honrats* or honoured citizens. These were the richest merchants, master artisans and professions who monopolized municipal offices and consolidated their political power through intermarriage and associations with the lower nobility.³⁸ Many *honrats*, eager to distance themselves from their occupations as merchants and master artisans, began to buy estates in the countryside, mimicking noble culture. Their goal was to become a rentier class and thus they rented out this property to *llauradors*, many of whom were immigrants. Paulino Iradiel has argued that this gobbling up of land by the *honrats* led to the consolidation of rural property into the hands of fewer and fewer people, pushing out the small freehold farmers and leading to peasant indebtedness as many *llauradors* became tenant farmers, paying a cash rent rather than owning the land they farmed.³⁹

The increasing involvement of *honrats* in the Valencian land market, as well as the migration of *llauradors* to the region, led to a profound and prolonged reorganization of the agrarian system in the mid-fifteenth century. Irrigation systems which were first implemented in the region under the Muslims, were expanded and other techniques such as crop rotation were implemented. New kinds of cultivation were introduced that could be sold for great profit, such as sugar cane and, increasingly, the agricultural goods of the *horta* region were produced for commercial reasons.[40] This shift in cultivation (which also included the expansion of wheat production) cemented ties between the city and countryside as many of these crops were sold in Valencia's market. Some were used to feed the ever-growing population and others were crucial in helping to expand the city's industries, in particular, the textile sector.

Changes in the land market, coupled with the increasing division of plots due to Valencia's partible inheritance practices, created numerous economic problems for *llauradors*. When added to plagues, famine and other disasters of the late medieval period, many *llauradors* were forced to look for additional work in order to help sustain their families.[41] Although the surviving documentation makes it difficult to determine what kinds of work *llauradors* performed alongside agricultural production, it is evident that many found work in the city as day labourers. As the city's economy was growing consistently, employment opportunities were numerous, especially with the large number of building projects taking place in the course of the fifteenth century. Huge undertakings such as the Torres de Quart (completed 1444), the Torres de Serranos (completed 1400), the Cathedral (begun in 1262 with work continuing into the early modern period) and La Lonja (built by Valencia's silk merchants and completed in 1483) are just a few of the many building projects going on in the city during the late medieval period which required large amounts of unskilled labour.

It was not only *llauradors* who went to the city in search of work, but also their children. Due to economic necessity, many peasant families arranged apprenticeships with artisans for their sons and domestic service positions for their daughters. Indeed poor children throughout late medieval Europe entered into the labour market at a young age, hoping to improve their own and their families' fortunes. Almost three-quarters of the apprentices and domestic servants in Valencia came from outside of the city, and many of them were from *llaurador* families in the *horta*.[42] Joan Sanxo, a *llaurador* from Xerica in the Valencian *horta* concluded an apprenticeship contract with the wooldresser Joan Enyego of Valencia for his son Joanet, age 8, in 1433. This agreement stated that Enyego was to teach Joanet his trade and provide the boy with '*obs*', the necessities of life (food, clothing and shelter) for nine years.[43] Domestic service contracts from Valencia were similar, such as one from 1437 in which the *llaurador* Michael Vicent of Quart handed over control of his daughter Johaneta, aged 11, to *honrada* Ursola, the widow of *honrat* Berenguer Cortes of Valencia. This contract was to last for seven years and instead of learning a trade, Joaneta earned a salary of twenty pounds, paid when the agreement had been fulfilled.[44]

Joanet Sanxo and Johaneta Vicent are two of the thousands of children who migrated from the *horta* region to Valencia to work as apprentices and domestic servants in the late medieval period. In many cases, these children remained in the city after their contracts were completed, marrying Valencian spouses and establishing new urban households. Young women who moved to Valencia for these reasons and either stayed in the city to marry or returned to their natal villages in the *horta* form the core of this book. This kind of migration was crucial in helping Valencia to expand its population and retain its economic predominance in the fifteenth century.

For both artisans and *llauradors*, marriage was an essential institution for establishing a permanent household in late medieval Valencia. A wife's dowry was used as the economic foundation of the newly created union, and the couple's combined income supported the household. Marriage created important economic and social alliances between kin groups, friends and neighbours. Those who wished to marry in early fifteenth-century Valencia did so within the framework of canon and secular legal precepts. The church regulated the spiritual nature of these unions, while the *Furs* governed the civil aspects of marriage, particularly regarding the marital assets of wives. At the local level, neighbours, friends and family had their own markers that determined the validity of a marital union. In order to fully understand the role that marriage played in the lives of labouring-status women, we need to explore how this institution was shaped by the laws and norms that regulated it. The remainder of this chapter will consider what made a marriage valid in the eyes of the church, the law and society in fifteenth-century Valencia. Although each of these structures had different criteria for determining the validity of a marital union, there was also a great deal of intersection, demonstrating the close relationship between religion, law and social norms in this period.

Marriage in canon law

Based on the myriad of laws compiled by Gratian in his *Decretum* of 1140, the late medieval Catholic Church held that marriage was both a spiritual and physical union. It was initiated through words of consent, spoken freely by the couple with affection, and perfected by consummation through carnal copulation.[45] These two acts together created the sacrament of marriage, which canon law held was indissoluble.[46] While both consent and consummation were considered necessary to have a full and complete union, in the manner of 'two in one flesh' as described in the Gospels, canon law of the late medieval period stressed that marriage was founded on the free consent of the couple. This emphasis differed from secular law which recognized the need for the bride and groom's consent, but also highlighted parental approval. According to canon law, parents had no control over their children's choice of spouse, despite the fact that marriage was vitally important to the fortunes of their families. In Valencia, the *Furs* presented both aspects of consent, mandating that parents could not force their daughters to marry against their will while simultaneously allowing parents to disinherit disobedient daughters who refused to marry the man of their choice.[47] In fact, the *Furs* explicitly stated that a woman must have the consent of her father, or with her father dead, her mother, to marry.[48] Any woman who married against her parents' wishes was viewed as rebellious and therefore disinheritance was justified.[49]

While the Catholic Church maintained that free consent of the couple alone formed a legitimate union, it did stress that this consent must be given publicly, in front of witnesses, preferably including a priest. Clandestine marriage was a great concern for the church which wanted to ensure that all marriages were publicly recognized and legitimated. Greater emphasis was placed on the solemnization of marriages by priests in parish churches, with members of the community present as witnesses. The church's goal was to prevent bigamy, and laws were enacted that stipulated excommunication for those that married secretly. In Valencia, the *Furs* went one step further, making clandestine marriage a capital crime in 1342.[50]

Despite concerns that marriages be celebrated publicly by parish priests, there was no general church legislation detailing exactly how nuptial ceremonies should be performed, beyond the insistence that these unions take place in a church, and before a priest and witnesses. Instead, local synodal legislation determined nuptial practices. Such was the case in Valencia where regulations passed by bishops provided priests with explicit directions for performing marriage ceremonies, complete with the exact vows that should be exchanged by the couple. Legislation from 22 October 1258 stated that the priest receive the wedding ring to be given to the bride, having the groom repeat, 'I [name] take you [name] as wife and I give myself over to you as a legal husband'. Next, the groom took the ring from the priest and placed it on the fourth finger of his bride saying, 'In the name of the Father and of the Son and of the Holy Spirit, amen'. The bride performed the same actions and the marriage was contracted.[51]

By providing explicit directions for its priests regarding marriage ceremonies, the Valencian church was ensuring that all its followers understood this was not just a union between a man and a woman but also between the couple and God, Christ and the Catholic Church. It also guaranteed that all marriages in Valencia were performed in the correct, legally and religiously valid way. While overall church legislation mandated that all marriages should be blessed by a priest, usually at the door of the church, in Spain these blessings took place inside the church building, in front of the altar. The parish priest was to announce the impending marriage for eight days prior to the ceremony, urging his congregation to come forth if they knew of any possible impediment to the union. If no one objected, the couple was able to marry after the eighth day.[52] This public celebration of marriage was seen as essential, and legislation from the thirteenth century threatened couples who did not marry publicly, in front of a priest and numerous witnesses, asserting that if they did not 'many bad things will happen'.[53] The reason given in the legislation for this threat was that 'any bad thing hates the light'[54] and therefore if a marriage was to be good, it must be celebrated in the light. If not, the union was doomed from the start.

Despite their desire for marriages to be celebrated publicly, church officials were greatly concerned about popular festivities such as wedding feasts. For example, Vicent Ferrer expounded upon the church's views regarding these celebrations in his sermon 'Concerning Nuptials', preached near the end of his life. He began by telling the story of the wedding at Cana and then used this biblical example to speak about weddings and the sins they encourage. Ferrer warned his audience that weddings contained 'all the mortal sins'.[55] For example, the sin of pride was committed by guests in their vanity at being well dressed. This iniquity was then compounded when the same people looked scornfully at those less fortunate in their fashion sense. According to Ferrer, the Devil loved weddings because the guests and bridal party gorged themselves on food and drink, and thus emboldened were provoked into name-calling and violence. The Dominican even claimed that many people were killed at wedding feasts, in particular the groom, in an attempt to demonstrate the serious nature of these offences to God.[56] In this strong condemnation of wedding celebrations, ecclesiastical ideals clashed with secular social views that held the wedding feast as an integral part of creating the new marital union. But in their desire to solemnize and sacralize marriage, church authorities wanted stress placed on the religious nature of a marital union rather than its social and secular implications.

Marriage in secular law

While by the late medieval period, marriages were regularly solemnized by priests in their parish churches, it was the exchange of property that the general public saw as central in forming new conjugal unions. It is essential to remember that medieval Spanish society viewed marriage as a contract which involved obligations on both sides. These obligations were usually economic and concerned the property brought into the marriage by the bride and groom. Marriage contracts served as a means to regulate marital property, clearly defining the amount and type of goods contributed as well as who was to provide them. But these contracts also give clues as to the influence that family could have in creating new unions. In some cases, most often for women of labouring-status, family members simply indicated their consent to the union but sometimes blood kin, most notably fathers, provided the assets that made up the all-important dowry.

In Valencia, marriage contracts were drawn up by a notary. For couples who were of higher status, this took place in the family home of the bride at the time of the couple's betrothal. Spanish engagement ceremonies blended the sacral with the secular, as the couple first swore on the Cross, the Gospels and other sacred objects. They then kissed the Cross and the notary placed their hands together and had the couple seal the agreement with a public kiss on the mouth.[57] On the same day, the notary would draw up the formal contract of marriage which indicated the exchange of property that was to take place between the couple. This kind of elaborate ceremony was only practised by families of higher status for whom the official acknowledgement of the new union was important in announcing the alliance formed between the two families.

For those of labouring-status, the series of events that created a union was quite different as they may not have even had blood kin present in the city. Instead they brought friends, neighbours and former employers with them to visit a notary in order to have a contract of marriage drawn up. For example, on 11 September 1429, Johana the daughter of the deceased Angelini Bonifaci of Italy concluded a contract of marriage with the baker Pere Boraç of Valencia. Acting as witness to the couple's agreement was the silversmith Jaume Pereç, Johana's former employer.[58] Many other couples went alone to the notary's place of business. Acting as witnesses to their marriage contracts were other people waiting to use the notary's services. These witnesses were often of the same or similar background to the couple as particular notaries tended to serve specific neighbourhoods. Numerous clients of the notary Martí Doto were like Maria, the daughter of the deceased Martí Ferran of Valencia who concluded a marriage contract with the *llaurador* Berenguer Oçura of Quart in 1421. Two other *llauradors* of Quart acted as witnesses to this agreement and subsequent documents in Doto's register reveal these men were present at the notary's to make use of his services themselves.[59]

After concluding these secular contracts, labouring-status couples then exchanged consent and had their unions solemnized before their local parish church. Evidence for these actions comes from dowry restitution cases where petitions always state that the couple had celebrated and solemnized their marriage 'en faç esglesia'. For example, in her petition of 1421, Johana Spital stated that 'her marriage was made and confirmed and solemnized before the holy mother church and after consummated through carnal copulation.'[60] As mentioned earlier, it was the couple's exchange of present consent, followed by consummation, that legally created the marital union between them, according to canon law.

Couples from all levels of Valencian society used marriage contracts to govern the exchange of property. Domestic servants, journeyman artisans and even former slaves ensured that the assets transferred between them were properly recorded and notarized in dotal instruments. These contracts were essential because they clearly laid out the economic foundation of the marriage, indicating who contributed what to whom. In case there was ever any dispute about whether or not the marriage had actually taken place, the existence of the contract was fundamental as testimony to the union. Marriage contracts also helped to ensure that assets were returned to the correct donors, or their heirs, when the conjugal union was dissolved, either by death or any other means.

Valencia was somewhat different from other regions in the Iberian peninsula at the time the *Furs* were redacted in the thirteenth century, as this law code implemented a marital property system based on the separation of goods. According to the *Furs*, a dowry of some kind was donated to the groom by his bride and/or another donor. In return, provided she was a *donzella* (virgin woman), the bride received a counter-gift, called the *creix*, valued at half the dowry. Although these two gifts were administered by the husband, they were viewed as distinct and separate from any other property owned by the couple. Valencia utilized this system of marital assigns because it was influenced by Roman law, particularly the *Corpus Iuris Civilis* of Justinian. Elsewhere in the Iberian peninsula, most notably parts of Castile, the Roman system of dowry was much slower to penetrate. For example, the customary *fueros* of Cuenca and Teruel (redacted in 1190 and 1176) based their marital property regimes on the Visigothic practices laid out in the *Liber Judiciorum*. According to this system, the groom provided the central donation, called the *arras* to his bride, who was not required to formally give any assets in exchange; however, brides usually brought property called *ajuar* consisting of household goods, which made up their trousseaus.[61]

It is interesting to note that at approximately the same time that he promulgated the romanized *Furs* in Valencia, Jaume I also had a compilation of general laws and customs drawn up for another of his domains, the kingdom of Aragon (1247). But the *Fueros de Aragon* followed the Visigothic system of marital assigns, rather than the Roman dotal regime mandated by the *Furs*.[62] While Jaume had more or less a free hand in determining the legal system to be adopted in Valencia, in the kingdom of Aragon, he had to comply with the wishes of powerful noble families who had no desire to see their king institute a legal code that would increase his authority in any way.

In Castile, Jaume I's son-in-law, Alfonso X 'El Sabio', also had a romanized legal code written in the mid-thirteenth century, known as the *Siete Partidas*. Alfonso was actively involved in the completion of this text, as he hoped it would bring legal uniformity to his kingdom, much in the same way that the *Furs* had for Valencia, as Castile had a great number of overlapping local and regional laws.[63] As Joseph O'Callaghan has remarked, both Jaume and Alfonso wanted to put forth 'new concepts of monarchy, influenced by Roman law, tending towards uniformity and centralization, subordinating to the Crown all persons, no matter their social status'.[64] In its system of marital property, the *Siete Partidas* mandated the Roman dotal system; however, its imposition was resisted by Alfonso X's subjects and the code was not officially promulgated until 1348, under his grandson. Even at this point, Alfonso XI, aware that his subjects would not accept the *Siete Partidas* as the sole legal authority in Castile, made it subordinate to the myriad of customary *fueros* that already existed.[65]

By the fifteenth century, most regions in the Iberian peninsula had adopted the Roman system of dowry, although this regime sometimes existed in conjunction with customary practices. Couples of every social status throughout the Crown of Aragon used dowry contracts to regulate the exchange of property at marriage. Even Castilians, initially so resistant to the romanized aspects of the *Siete Partidas*, had dowry contracts drawn up; however, these were used in concert with other customary contracts which combined any assets the couple acquired after marriage. By the late medieval period, therefore, the dowry system predominated throughout the Iberian peninsula.

The dotal marriage contracts used by Valencians in the fifteenth century followed a fairly formulaic style that was common throughout southern Europe. For labouring-status couples, these notarial instruments were fairly short and simply indicated their background, the consent of their family and friends (and sometimes employers) to the union, the amount and type of property to be donated as dowry and the value of the *creix*. For example:

> I Johana, daughter of the deceased swordsmith Ferdinand de Sant Marti of Valencia, with the consent of my *curator* the carpenter Pere Stropinya of Valencia, and of my family and friends, join myself in marriage with you Jacob Bernat, tailor of the said city. And I give and hand over to you as my dowry, 35 pounds of Valencian money in this form: namely, 24 pounds in cash and the rest in household goods. And moreover, I the said Jacob Bernat accept you Johana as my future wife ... And I recognize [to have received] from you the said dowry... And according to the laws of Valencia, for your virginity, I owe you an *augmentum*. Therefore I give to you Johana, present, an *augmentum* or donation on account of marriage of 17 pounds, 10 sous of the said [Valencian] money. Thus in dowry and *augmentum* there is 52 pounds, 10 sous which I promise to restore to you for any reason or event. And I obligate all my goods to you.[66]

While the most common form of dotal contract had the bride's father providing the dowry, labouring-status women also received these assets from their mothers, siblings, extended family members, friends and through their own labour. Women whose fathers were deceased such as Johana de Sant Marti or who were immigrants to the city, and who were over the age of 20 (the age of majority in Valencia at which time a person could legally enter a contract on their own), often concluded their own contracts in the absence of family members.

The naming of donors in marriage contracts was important so that dowries could be properly restored if a woman died without heirs or intestate. The *Furs* mandated that if a childless daughter preceded her father in death, the dowry was to be returned to him, provided that he was the original donor. The reason given is 'so that he does not have two injuries, that he lose both his daughter and the dowry he has given'.[67] In conjunction with naming the donors, indicating the monetary value of dowries was essential so that it could be restored in full, either to wives or to the original donors. Although dotal contracts usually designate the type of property being given as dowries, husbands or their heirs were only obliged to return the original amount, but not necessarily in the form it was given. The description of what kind of property had been donated as a dowry was important in terms of the actual reception of the goods, moveable goods, cash or immoveable property that had been promised, as it allowed the husband to indicate clearly what property had yet to be handed over as dowry, in cases of dispute.

While the inclusion in dotal contracts of familial consent to a marriage followed the laws laid out by the *Furs*, it is interesting to note the added agreement of a woman's friends to the union. Paulino Iradiel asserts that for artisan families living in the city of Valencia, the influence of colleagues in marital decisions was as important, if not more so, than that of their kin group.[68] In a city characterized by a great deal of social mobility, fluidity and immigration, the ties that bound people together were not always of blood. Instead, associations were based on common economic functions and proximity, linking those that practised the same trade and lived in the same neighbourhood. This was true for young women who immigrated to the city of Valencia on their own as servants, who consulted their friends, neighbours and even employers in making spousal choices, either in the absence of blood kin or in conjunction with them.

In return for receiving a dowry from his bride, according to the *Furs*, a groom was obliged to provide a *creix*, as long as he was marrying a virgin.[69] Historians of marriage and the family have debated extensively the reason for this counter-gift. Diane Owen Hughes asserts that the gift from the husband to the wife developed out of the Germanic custom of the *morgengabe*. This term refers to a gift given to the bride by her new husband the morning after the consummation of their marriage in exchange for her virginity. Hughes contrasts the *morgengabe* with the Germanic brideprice which was the amount initially paid by the groom to the bride's family, or to the woman herself, to purchase the right to control her. She sees the medieval *creix* as having developed out of the custom of *morgengabe* rather than brideprice. Hughes came to her conclusion after examining marriage charters from Visigothic Spain in which men repeatedly specified that the marriage gifts they were giving to their brides were in acknowledgement of their virginity.[70]

Jack Goody concurs with Hughes's assertion and adds that the indirect dowry, as he calls it, may also have been influenced by the Roman *donatio propter nuptias* which was given to the bride prior to the wedding and was considered a counterpart to the dowry donated by her.[71] Spanish historian, Maria del Carmen Carlé, disagrees with Hughes and Goody's theories that the *creix* developed out of the *morgengabe*. She makes the point that as this gift was given before the consummation of the marriage, it is therefore different in intent from the gift in exchange for the bride's virginity. Instead Carlé views the *creix* as simply part of the husband's patrimony given to the bride as a guarantee of marriage.[72]

Marriage contracts from fifteenth-century Valencia are very clear as to the intent of the *creix*. First, it is referred to in these Latin contracts as '*donatio propter nuptias*' or '*augmentum*', thus linking them with the Roman gift given to brides on account of marriage. Second, marriage contracts also state that the *creix* was given to the bride 'on account of your virginity and dowry' (*secundum forem Valentie propter virginitatem et dotem*) or 'the dowry must be made with an *augmentum* to girls, namely virgins' (*Et secundum forem Valentie dos debeat cum augmentum puellis videlicet virginibus*). Added to this, the *Furs* states that if a husband died without consummating his marriage, his wife was not entitled to a counter-gift.[73] The role of the *creix*, therefore, is clearly to pay the bride for sexual rights, making it difficult not to see it as descended from the *morgengabe*. This explains the reasoning behind the denial of a *creix* for widows, as they no longer have their virginity to give to their new husbands.

Like other kinds of notarial instruments, dotal contracts were regulated by the *Furs* to ensure both parties fulfilled their obligations. If the contract was breached in any way, the party who did so was penalized. For example, if a husband did not receive a dowry for his new wife, he was not obligated to give her a *creix*. But, if the dowry was paid in part, he had to provide a *creix*. A husband had five years to seek full payment of his wife's dowry and if he did not receive it in the allotted time, he still had to produce a *creix*.[74] In some cases, dowries were paid out over time, with donors providing assets as they earned them. The length of time between the conclusion of a marriage contract and the payment of a dowry varied widely. In an examination of sixty-one dowry contracts and *apochas* (receipt contracts), about half of the dowries were at least partially paid on the same day that the dotal agreement was drawn up by the notary. In another one-quarter, partial or full dotal payments were made within one month of concluding the marriage contract. For example, on 6 October 1438, approximately one month after the conclusion of their marriage contract, Romia, the daughter of the deceased Bernat Alcodor of Paterna handed over twelve pounds out of her thirty-three-pound dowry owing to her groom, the *llaurador* Pere Colomines of Vilamarxant. This property had been paid to Romia by her former master Guillem Castrella of Valencia for fulfilment of her domestic service contract.[75] In the remaining contracts, the dowry was paid out several months to years after the initial conclusion of the agreement.

Dowries could also consist of property to be received after the death of the donor, in which case a husband might have to wait several years before receiving it. Such was the case when Ramoneta, the widow of a weaver, provided the shieldmaker Pere Garces with a sixty-pound dowry for her daughter Johana. The dowry consisted of a house, the rights to which Ramoneta retained until her death.[76] The *llaurador* Arnau Simon of Morvedre promised to contribute fifteen pounds to his daughter Simona's forty-pound dowry for her marriage to the swordsmith Miquel Mater of Valencia in 1433. The donation contract stipulated that the fifteen pounds was to be paid out to Simona at the time of her father's death. Dowry donations such as these allowed labouring-status parents to contribute to their daughters' dowries even if they did not have or could not spare the promised assets at the time of marriage.

Whether a husband received his wife's dowry at marriage, or had to wait several years, the *Furs* gave him administrative control of these assets, along with the *creix*, for the duration of the union.[77] He also retained any profits made on this property as well as any income that his wife earned. The reason for this, according to the *Furs*, was the husband sustained the 'burden of marriage' (*carregà matrimoni*), by providing food, clothing and shelter and therefore needed these funds to do so. Once again, we see the idea of reciprocity built into the marital union. However, if the husband did not fulfil his obligations to support his wife, she had the right to sue him for control of her dowry.[78] Numerous women who came before the court of the civil justice in Valencia cited their husbands' refusal to provide the necessities of life as the reason for their suits of dowry restitution. They were successful in their cases because of the agreement made between spouses at marriage.

All marriage contracts in fifteenth-century Valencia contained a clause in which husbands obligated all of their possessions as surety for their wives' dowries. Roman law refers to this obligation as a hypothec, but this term does not appear in the *Furs*. Maria Belda Soler states that it was not used in Spanish legal codes until the early sixteenth century.[79] Instead of hypothec, the *Furs* discusses a *callada obligació*, or silent obligation and an *expresa obligació*, expressed or stated obligation. In terms of the dowry and *creix*, Valencian law stipulates that all husbandly property is obligated as surety for his wife's marital assets, whether or not this is stated in their marriage contracts. This is the *callada obligació*. The *expresa obligació* refers to two situations. The first is when the husband names specific immoveable assets as surety for his wife's dowry and *creix*. According to the *Furs*, this *expresa obligació* then excepts the rest of his property from that obligation.[80] In the second instance, the *expresa obligació* refers to the husband's obligation of '*omnia bona mea*', all his goods, in exchange for his wife's dowry, stated in their marriage contract. Both the *callada obligació* and the *expresa obligació* were only in effect on dotal goods that the husband actually received and they applied to both partial and full dowry payments.[81] This is the reason why documents such as dowry *apochas* were so essential in the Valencian dowry regime.

If a husband did not own enough property to obligate for his wife's dowry, other people could use their property as surety in his stead. For example, on 27 May 1435 the carpenter Bertomeu Andreu concluded a contract of marriage with Bertomeu Carbonell for his daughter Andrea. At the end of the contract, Carbonell's widowed mother Ursola obligated '*omnia bona mea*' for Andrea's fifty-pound dowry and twenty-five-pound *creix*.[82] The possession of enough assets to act as surety for a wife's dowry and *creix* was a necessary requirement of the Valencia dowry regime and thus men like Carbonell could turn to their family members for help if needed; however, I found very few marriage contracts such as this one in the Valencian archives. Either all labouring-status men waited to marry until they possessed sufficient assets to obligate for their future wives' dowries or clauses such as '*obligo omnia bona mea*' were simply formulaic and actual possession of the necessary amount of property by grooms was not investigated by the bride or her family at the time of marriage. In reality, the obligation of all his goods as surety for his wife's dowry and *creix* made by the groom only became important when the union was dissolved (usually at death) or if the wife sued her husband for restitution of her dowry in civil court.

The husband was not the only one who had to meet certain requirements in order to fulfil the terms of a marriage contract. His wife also faced penalties if she did not do so and could lose both her dowry and *creix*. In 1418, Alfons el Magnànim added a clause to the *Furs* which stripped a wife of her dowry where she had committed adultery. In such cases, the husband was to retain control of these assets until the couple's children came of age (20 years old). If they had no offspring, the dowry was to be returned to the original donor at the husband's death. The clause preceding this one in the *Furs* mandated that an adulterous wife should also lose her *creix*.[83] Evidence from the Justicía Civil indicates that husbands did pursue control of their wives' marital property for this reason. On 4 March 1421, Lopiç Martí filed a petition against his wife Ursola, seeking control of her forty-pound dowry and twenty-pound *creix* in trust for their son Martínez. His suit stated that Ursola had committed adultery and abandoned him and their son to live with her lover. The justice ruled that Lopiç was to retain these assets until his son reached the age of majority.[84] Both husbands and wives, therefore, faced censure if they did not live up to the obligations created by their dotal contract, and evidence from the Justicía Civil demonstrates that spouses were more than willing to sue one another if they did not fulfil these promises.

While the *Furs* mandated that the dotal regime was to be utilized by couples to regulate their marital property, some chose to follow a very different system. This was *germanía*, by which a couple combined all of their assets at marriage into a conjugal fund, the fruits of which they both enjoyed for the duration of their union. When one member of the couple died, the survivor received half of their communal assets. The term '*germanía*' derives from the Catalan word '*germa*', meaning brother, and is defined as an 'affectionate relationship between brothers; a quality of brotherhood'.[85] José María Font Rius states that this form of marriage contract was based on the ideal of artificial brotherhood where couples 'unite in marriage and use their present and future goods in common, working and labouring in common, in whatever form of exploitation or industry, in order later to divide these goods in equal parts'.[86] He stresses the equal nature of these contracts as recognizing the contribution that both husbands and wives make to the household.

Germanía contracts were therefore based on quite different principles of marital property holding than dotal ones. Unfortunately, their origin is difficult to determine. María Belda Soler asserts that they were used by Mozarabic Christians living in Valencia under Muslim rule, but other historians state that there is no conclusive evidence to support such claims.[87] Given the small numbers of Christians that remained in Valencia at the time of its conquest by Jaume I, it is unlikely that this was the origin of *germanía* marriage contracts. Rather, the use of this form of marital assigns by Valencians appears to have been influenced by customary practices in parts of Catalonia and Aragon. The *Costum de Tortosa*, a codification of existing customs redacted in 1272, contains clauses which refer to '*mig per mig*', or half by half, marriage contracts where couples held all of their goods in common, much the same way that the *germanía* marital property regime functioned.[88] Notarial evidence demonstrates that similar kinds of instruments were utilized in Zaragoza and Perpignan.[89]

It is difficult to trace customary practices, particularly so when they are not codified, as was the case in Valencia. The initial versions of the *Furs* from 1240 and 1261 do not mention *germanía* at all. It is not until 1428 that *germanía* appears in the code in reference to clauses dealing with adulterous wives and inheritance practices.[90] It seems that Catalan and Aragonese immigrants to Valencia brought their own customary marriage practices to the kingdom which, in part, influenced the development of the *germanía* system. But while a significant minority of Valencians did choose to utilize this marital property regime (see Chapter 4 for a complete analysis of what sorts of people used *germanía* contracts), the majority followed the dowry system that was mandated and supported by the *Furs*.

Marriage in community opinion

Although canon and civil law created a set of rules regulating marriage in late medieval Valencia, this does not necessarily mean that society viewed this institution in the same way. While it is often difficult to determine how medieval communities, particularly at the lower levels, viewed institutions such as marriage, witness testimony from dowry restitution cases brought before Valencia's *Justicía Civil* can provide some information. As these disputes were over who had the right to control a woman's dowry and often her *creix*, both secular legal markers of a legitimate marriage, the first question asked of each witness was 'How did you know that so and so were married?'.[91] The answers given by witnesses, while often formulaic, detail the various criteria used by labouring-status society to determine a valid marital union.

Many of the markers cited by witnesses indicate the influence that the Catholic Church and the *Furs* had on society's views of marriage. Witnesses claimed that they knew a couple had solemnized their union '*in faç esglesia*' and sometimes provided the court with the name of the parish church where the wedding took place. For example, testifying in the case of Francesca Romira against her husband Joan Romira, the *llaurador* Francesc Dantença stated that the couple had been married thirty years previously in the parish church of St Esteve in Valencia.[92] Others stated that they were present at the creation of the marriage contract. They provided information such as the amount of the dowry, the name of the notary who had drawn up the contract and the place where it was witnessed. The carpenter Francesc Colomer testified that he had seen the marriage contract concluded between Johana and Joan Perez in which Johana promised Joan a dowry of sixty pounds. Colomer also indicated that an *apocha* had been drawn up by the notary Pere Pasqual between Johana and her husband for receipt of the entire sixty-pound dowry.[93] But it is other criteria noted by witnesses that are interesting from a socio-historical view, as they indicate the aspects of marriage that were determined socially, rather than by religious or legal doctrine. Overall, witnesses testified to six markers which demonstrated to them that a couple was indeed married: having a wedding feast; cohabitation; appearance together publicly; being or acting as husband and wife; calling one another husband and wife; and public knowledge (*publica fama*) that they were married.

Testifying in the suit of Isabel Gomiç against her husband Garçia, the wooldresser Bernat Gari stated that after the nuptial mass, 'he ate at the wedding celebration … held in the port of the city of Valencia'.[94] Two other witnesses in Isabel's suit also indicated that they had eaten at the couple's wedding feast. While some witnesses in dowry restitution cases, such as those that appear in Isabel's suit, stated that they were simply guests of the couple, others actually hosted the celebration. This was the case for Maria Oviet, who held the wedding feast with her husband Francesc for their former servant as described in the introduction of this book.[95]

María García-Herrero has stated that the three pillars of any medieval Spanish wedding were eating, drinking and dancing.[96] For couples of all backgrounds, wedding feasts were important as celebrations since they helped to bring together communally the family and friends of the bride and groom. The act of eating together held both social and religious resonance in the late medieval period. Monarchs often held sumptuous banquets in honour of new alliances they had concluded. Monks and nuns ate together daily, in part to demonstrate the cohesiveness of their communities. For artisan guilds, eating was seen as a form of fraternity that gave 'tangible expression to the companionship of the guild'.[97] These societies, built on the idea of fraternity, frequently held banquets that were designed to promote 'love and charity among members'.[98]

Feasting therefore had great symbolic value, as it ritually represented connections between those at the table. By breaking bread together, the couple and their kin groups physically demonstrated the new alliances created by the marital union. Noble and patrician families also used wedding feasts to demonstrate their wealth and power to the rest of society. Municipal councils throughout Spain frequently passed sumptuary laws to limit the length and size of such celebrations as some lasted as long as eight days with hundreds of guests in attendance.[99] As witness testimony from dowry restitution cases demonstrate, even families of labouring-status held such festivities, although they were not as long or opulent. Instead of lavish dishes, artisan and *llaurador* wedding feasts featured food such as bread, rice, fruits, vegetables, olives and meat, if they could afford it. Valencians even had a special bread called *pa de noçes* that was eaten by all members of the wedding party to demonstrate the new union.[100] Such celebrations showed acceptance by a couple's family and friends of their marriage.

The second marker of marriage that most witnesses in dowry restitution cases attested to was a couple's cohabitation. For example, after stating that he had eaten at Isabel and Garcia Gomiç's wedding feast, Bernat Gari continued, 'And in the said port after the wedding, [the couple] slept in one house and one room.'[101] Other witnesses indicated that a couple 'lived together as husband and wife' (*habitare ensemps com a marit et muller*).[102] As with Bernat Gari's testimony above, in some cases, witnesses even provided details as to where the couple lived, giving the name of their parish or street. Emphasis was placed in this testimony on the fact that the couple lived together on a daily basis in the same location, and that they slept there, sharing a bed. Witnesses do not cite the couple's sexual relationship as a marker of their union, although this can be implied by stating that they slept together. As evidence from church courts in other European cities indicates, premarital sex was somewhat common among those of labouring-status; however, it was the acts of cohabitation on a daily basis that demonstrated that a couple was indeed married.[103]

Witnesses were able to attest to a couple's cohabitation because many of them were, in fact, their neighbours. This proximity allowed them to view the couple regularly, and their testimony stressed specific actions that defined conjugality. For example, simply appearing in the neighbourhood together indicated for some witnesses that a couple was indeed husband and wife. The tanner Ramon Bort testified that he had seen Caterina and Pere Saragoça together in the tannery area of Valencia.[104] Similarly, in another case, Joan Gregori stated that Pere Çoll and his wife Johana appeared in the streets of the city together 'as husband and wife'.[105] Connected to the idea that publicly appearing together in the neighbourhood marked a couple as man and wife, witnesses almost always cited two other actions. The first was that a couple had called one another husband and wife (*la dita aquell marit et lo dit aquella muller appellant*); the second they had acted, behaved or been as a husband and wife (*star com a marit et muller*).[106] In fact these two criteria were cited by witnesses as signs of a couple's conjugality more than anything else in dowry restitution cases.

While it is quite clear what witnesses meant by stating a couple had called one another husband and wife, it is more difficult to determine their definition of being or acting in such a manner. Didactic conduct manuals such as the Franciscan Francesc Eiximenis's *Lo llibre de les dones* (1388) provide indications of how ecclesiastical authorities wanted married couples to behave. For example, Eiximenis states that a wife 'ought to … govern her house wisely and guard her person from all reprehensible behaviour'.[107] She should speak to her husband honourably and feed him with abundant and appetizing food and drink.[108] Overall, a good wife should love, honour and obey her husband who, in return, should treat her with courtesy and honour. Even if his wife needs correction, Eiximenis counsels that a husband should not do so with sour words or in front of others.[109]

Ecclesiastical authorities not only wrote about how husbands and wives should behave, they also preached sermons on this topic in an effort to instruct a much broader audience. Vicent Ferrer expounded upon the subject of married behaviour in numerous sermons given in Valencia between 1412 and 1418. To Ferrer, marriage was one of the seven columns upon which the church was founded and should be based on mutual loyalty and the nourishment of children through doctrine and wisdom.[110] In a sermon on the Feast of St John, Ferrer warned husbands to 'treat your wife honourably, and not as a beast' and counselled both members of the couple to serve each other and not mix with other people of the opposite sex.[111] But while sources such as Eiximenis's *Lo llibre de les dones* and Ferrer's sermons provide excellent prescriptive evidence, they tell us very little about what 'acting as husband and wife' consisted of for those of labouring-status. The church may have desired couples to behave in the manner set out by Eiximenis and Ferrer, but this does not necessarily mean that they did so. Nor does it indicate that these prescriptive actions were what dowry restitution witnesses meant when they stated that a couple had 'acted as husband and wife'. Unfortunately, this testimony never reveals what such behaviour entailed but it clearly demonstrated to the neighbourhood that the couple was married.

Within a neighbourhood, conjugality was determined not just by a couple's actions but also through their reputation. Numerous witnesses testified that it was '*publica fama*', well known, that a couple was married. For example, providing evidence in Johana Dabella's suit against her husband Nartis, the wooldresser Joan Pereç stated that the couple 'lived and appeared together as husband and wife. And this was well known in Valencia, as well as other places.'[112] Other witnesses stressed the reputation as husband and wife that a couple had in the neighbourhood. The ropemaker Miquel Bou stated 'he had seen them act and live together as husband and wife in the said city and, Tomàs Dauder and Teresa had a reputation [as] husband and wife in the said city among their friends.'[113] This kind of testimony added legal and social weight to proof of a couple's conjugality as it demonstrated the public nature of their relationship. *Publica fama* was 'what everyone knew, so it was socially accepted as reliable.'[114] This public reputation as husband and wife was likely created through neighbourhood observations of their wedding feast, cohabitation, public appearance, behaviour and actions; all of the criteria that witnesses in dowry restitution cases cited as proof that a couple were actually married.

For those of labouring-status who lived in the city of Valencia, marital relationships were therefore subject to a number of norms that determined their validity. Canon law set out regulations that governed the sacramentally correct manner for a couple to be joined in holy matrimony. Although simple consent followed by consummation was all that was needed for a legal union, increasingly over the course of the Middle Ages, the church stressed that marriages should be blessed by parish priests. Synodal legislation from Valencia ensured that parish priests followed a canonically valid method of blessing these unions, and made certain that they took place during the correct time of year. The success of their drive to have marriages celebrated within the church is demonstrated by dowry restitution petitions which always state that a couple's marriage had been solemnized '*in faç esglesia*'.

Although the Catholic Church emphasized the sacral aspect of marriage as centrally important, to most Valencians, it was the exchange of property that indicated a marriage had been truly contracted. The vast number of articles contained in the *Furs* that regulated the transfer, and subsequent administration, of marital assets, helped to ensure that this aspect of marriage was performed in accordance with Valencian civil law. The dowry system was the legally approved marital property regime in fifteenth-century Valencia, and most couples chose to utilize this regime to regulate their assets. Emphasis was placed on the reciprocal nature of these contracts, with both husbands and wives facing censure if they failed to live up to their end of the bargain. But a minority of labouring-status Valencians chose to use the *germanía* system, based on the idea of artificial brotherhood, where a couple shared a conjugal fund. It is unknown how the use of this type of marriage contract evolved in Valencia, although Catalan and Aragonese influence appears likely.

Finally, while those of labouring-status were greatly influenced by canon and secular legal precepts about marriage, they also had their own criteria as to what made a valid union. Testimony from dowry restitution cases stressed the public nature of a marital relationship, citing the key importance of a couple's reputation as husband and wife. That reputation was gained through a number of public acts including feasting and cohabitation as well as conjugal behaviour and appearance. All of these markers were based on how a couple was viewed by their neighbours, demonstrating clear community opinions regarding marriage. Overall, labouring-status Valencians drew on a myriad of ideas that influenced how they thought about marriage. A central aspect of any marital union was the choice of spouse, a decision that was determined by the couple and/or their friends and families. This momentous event was influenced by a number of factors, which the following chapter will consider.

Notes

1 Manuel Sanchis Guarner, *La ciutat de València: síntesi d'història i de geografia urbana* (Valencia: Ajuntament de València, 1972), p. 169.
2 The term *horta* refers to the rich, alluvial field surrounding the city. Most of this territory was directly under the control of the city of Valencia and the people who lived within it were considered townsmen. The *horta* had a number of small villages and towns and people within this area moved back and forth from the city. See Thomas Glick, *Irrigation and Society in Medieval Valencia* (Cambridge, MA: Harvard University Press, 1970), pp. 11–12.
3 Furió, *Història del País Valencià*, p. 44.
4 Mark D. Meyerson, *Jews in an Iberian Frontier Kingdom: Society, Economy and Politics in Morvedre, 1248–1391* (Leiden: Brill, 2004), p. 272.
5 See Alan Ryder, *The Wreck of Catalonia: Civil War in the Fifteenth Century* (Oxford: Oxford University Press, 2007).
6 Furió, *Història del País Valencià*, p. 160.
7 Antoni Furió, 'La Baixa Edat Mitjana (segles XIV i XV)', in Milagro Gil-Mascarell, Thomas F. Glick, Antoni Furió *et al.* (eds), *Història del País Valencià* (Valencia: 3i4 Papers Bàsics, 1992), p. 99.
8 Furió, *Història del País Valencià*, p. 125.
9 Furió, 'La Baixa Edat Mitjana', p. 101.
10 Furió, *Història del País Valencià*, p. 188.
11 Sanchis Guarner, *La ciutat de València*, p. 169. See also Agustín Rubio Vela, *Peste Negra. Crisis y comportamientos socials en la España del siglo XIV: La ciudad de Valencia (1348–1401)* (Granada: University of Granada, 1979).
12 Paulino Iradiel, 'L'evolució econòmica', in Ernest Belenguer (ed.), *Història del País Valencià Volum II: De la conquesta a la Federació Hispànica* (Barcelona: Edicions 62, 1989), p. 268.
13 *Jurats* held the highest political positions in the city of Valencia during the medieval period. By the fifteenth century, six *jurats* from noble and patrician background (usually two nobles and four patricians) led the municipal council in its governance of the city. See Rafael Narbona Vizcaíno, *Valencia, municipio medieval. Poder politico y luchas ciudadanas, 1239–1418* (Valencia: Ajuntament de Valencia, 1995), pp. 26–37.
14 Francisco Roca Traver, 'La inmigración a la Valencia medieval', *Boletín Sociedad Castellonense de Cultura*, 52 (abril-junio 1976), p. 171.
15 *Ibid.*, pp. 73–75.
16 *Ibid.*
17 The term *llaurador* refers to someone who works the land (i.e. a farmer). The socio-economic status of *llauradors* varied in Valencia, as some produced crops at a subsistence level (the wives and daughters of whom are the basis of this book), whereas others owned large manor homes and controlled vast amounts of land.
18 Furió, *Història del País Valencià*, p. 207.
19 Rafael Narbona Vizcaíno, *Valencia, municipo medieval. Poder politico y luchas ciudadanas, 1239–1418* (Valencia: Ajuntament de Valencia, 1995), p. 155.
20 *Blanquer*, *assaonador* and *aluder* are all trades associated with tanning. The difference lies in the type of skins they treated and the practices used to do so. See Luis Tramoyeres Blasco, *Instituciones gremiales: su origen y organización en Valencia* (Valencia: Domenech, 1889), p. 76.

21 Germán Navarro, 'L'Artisanat de la soie à Valence à la fin due moyen âge', *Razo: Cahiers du Centre d'études médiévales de Nice* 14 (1993), p. 169; Tramoyeres Blasco, *Instituciones gremiales*, p. 361.
22 Furió, *Història del País Valencià*, p. 207.
23 José Hinojosa Montalvo, *Diccionario de historia medieval del Reino de Valencia* (Valencia: Biblioteca Valenciana, 2002), vol. II, p. 392.
24 Paulino Iradiel, 'Corporaciones de oficio, acción política y sociedad civil en Valencia', in *Cofradías, gremios y solidaridades en la Europa medieval* (Pamplona: Gobierno Navarra, Departimento de Educación y Cultura, 1993), p. 264.
25 *Ibid.*, pp. 270–272.
26 See Paulino Iradiel, 'Familia y función económica de la mujer en actividades no agrarias', in Yves-René Fonquerne and Alfonso Estaban (eds), *Condición de la mujer en la edad media* (Madrid: Casa de Velázquez/Universidad Complutense, 1986), pp. 232–235 and 257–258; Germán Navarro, 'L'Artisanat de la soie à Valence à la fin du moyen âge', in F.A. Roca (ed.), *El tono de vida en la Valencia medieval* (Castellón de la Plana: Sociedad Castelleonense de Cultura, 1983), pp. 169–170; Tramoyeres Blasco, *Instituciones gremiales*, pp. 360–362.
27 For example, Eleanor Bertran was apprenticed to the shieldmaker Ramón Canyelles in April of 1422. Unlike male apprentices, however, who only received bed and board in their apprenticeship, the contract stated that Eleanor was to receive twenty pounds at the end of her apprenticeship (plus bed and board during it). The inclusion of a monetary payment makes Eleanor's apprenticeship contract more like domestic service contracts and raises the question of whether or not it was expected she would work as an independent journeyman shieldmaker after its completion. The amount of payment is similar in size to that received by domestic servants (ARV 417 Juan de Campos (Sr), s.f. (27 April 1422)).
28 Narbona Vizcaíno, *Valencia, municipo medieval*, p. 69.
29 Women predominantly directed workshops in the tailor, mercer and weaver trades in Barcelona. See Pierre Bonnassie, *La organización del trabajo en Barcelona a fines del siglo XV* (Barcelona: Consejo Superior de Investigaciones Científicas, 1975), p. 106.
30 *Ibid.*, p. 107.
31 See Ricardo Cordoba de la Llave, 'La femme dans l'artisanat de la péninsule ibérique', *Razo* 14 (1993), pp. 103–114; Cristina Segura Graíño, 'La sociedad urbana', in Pilar Folguera Crespo, Margarita Ortega López, Cristina Segura Graíño et al. (eds), *Historia de las mujeres en España* (Madrid: Editorial Síntesis), pp. 185–218.
32 See Steven A. Epstein, *Wage Labor and Guilds in Medieval Europe* (Chapel Hill, NC: University of North Carolina Press, 1991), pp. 115 and 122–123; David Herlihy, *Opera Muliebria: Women and Work in Medieval Europe* (New York: McGraw-Hill, 1990), p. 162; Maryanne Kowaleski and Judith M. Bennett, 'Crafts, Gilds and Women in the Middle Ages: Fifty Years after Marian K. Dale', *Signs: Journal of Women in Culture and Society*, 14(2) (1989), pp. 474–488; Martha Howell, *Women, Production and Patriarchy in Late Medieval Cities* (Chicago: University of Chicago Press, 1986); James R. Farr, *Artisans in Europe, 1300–1914* (Cambridge: Cambridge University Press, 2000), pp. 37–38.
33 Furió, *Història del País Valencià*, p. 197.
34 *Ibid.*, p. 201.
35 Iradiel, 'L'evolució econòmica', p. 276; Francisco Roca Traver, 'La inmigración a la

Valencia Medieval', *Boletín Sociedad Castellonense de Cultura* 53 (abril–junio 1977), p. 221.
36 'Corporaciones de oficio, acción política y sociedad civil en Valencia', p. 269.
37 José Damián González Arce, 'La corporaciones laborales agrarias como formes de identidad, cohesión y representación en la Castilla medieval', *Congreso de Historia Agraria* (Córdoba, 2008), 1.
38 Narbona Vizcaíno, *Valencia, municipio medieval*, p. 87.
39 Iradiel, 'L'Evolució Economica', p. 284.
40 Furió, *Història del País Valencià*, p. 94.
41 Ferran Garcia Oliver, *Terra de Feudals: el Pais Valencia en la tardor de l'Edat Mitjana* (Valencia: Edicions Alfons el Magnànim, 1991), pp. 64 and 95.
42 See Chapter 2 of this book for more information on the percentage of young girls who moved from outside Valencia to take up positions as domestic servants in the city. For apprentices, see R. Sixto, 'La contraction laboral en la Valencia medieval: aprendizaje y servicio domestico (1458–1462)' (Tesis de Licenciatura, Valencia, 1993).
43 Archivo de Protocolos del Patriarca de Valencia (hereafter APPV) Prot. 23409, Joan Peres, non-paginated (26 February 1433).
44 ARV Prot. 793, Martí Doto, non-paginated (19 January 1437).
45 James Brundage, *Law, Sex and Christian Society in Medieval Europe* (Chicago: University of Chicago Press, 1987), p. 235.
46 Ibid., 236; see also Federico R. Aznar Gil, *La institución matrimonial en la Hispania cristiana bajo-medieval (1215–1563)* (Salamanca: Publicaciones de la Universidad Pontifica de Salamanca, 1989), p. 15.
47 For parental consent: *Furs de Valencià, Volum V* (Barcelona: Editorial Barcino, 1990), VI-IX-II, p. 238; for consent of the woman herself: *ibid.*, V-I-XIII, p. 13.
48 *Furs de Valencià*, Volum V, VI-IX-II, p. 238.
49 Heath Dillard, *Daughters of the Reconquest: Women in Castilian Town Society, 1100–1300* (Cambridge: Cambridge University Press, 1984), p. 41.
50 *Furs de Valencià*, Volum V, fn. 3, p. 6.
51 Ignacio Pérez de Heredia, 'Sinodos medievales de Valencia: edición bilingüe', *Anthologica Annua*, 40 (1993), pp. 559–560.
52 *Ibid.*, pp. 558–560.
53 *Ibid.*, p. 561.
54 *Ibid.*, p. 562.
55 Ferrer, *Sermons: volum cinquè*, p. 8.
56 *Ibid.*
57 García-Herrero, *Las mujeres en Zaragoza en el siglo XV*, p. 181.
58 ARV Prot. 2426, Vicente Zaera, non-paginated (11 September 1429).
59 ARV Prot. 789, Martin Doto, non-paginated (23 November 1421).
60 ARV Justícia Civil Peticiones 3717, m. 1, f. 14r. (21 January 1428).
61 Dillard, *Daughters of the Reconquest*, pp. 48–54. See also *Fueros de Teruel*, ed. and trans. José Castañé Llinas (Teruel: Ajuntamiento de Teruel, 1994), pp. 303–304; *Fueros de Cuenca*, ed. Rafael Ureña y Smenjaud (Madrid: Tipografia de Archivos, 1935), pp. 189–190.
62 *Fueros de Aragon: según el ms. del Archivo Municipal de Miravete de la Sierra* (Zaragoza: Anubar, 1992), pp. 235–238.
63 E.N. Van Kleffens, *Hispanic Law until the End of the Middle Ages* (Edinburgh:

Edinburgh University Press, 1968), p. 148.
64 Joseph F. O'Callaghan, 'Kings and Lords in Conflict in Late Thirteenth-Century Castile and Aragon', in P.E. Chevedden, D.J. Kagay and P.G. Padrilla (eds), *Iberia and the Mediterranean World in the Middle Ages: Essays in honor of Robert I. Burns, S.J.* (New York: E.J. Brill, 1996), p. 134.
65 Van Kleffens, *Hispanic Law*, p. 183. See also *Las Siete Partidas*, ed. Samuel Parsons Scott (Chicago: Commerce Clearing House, 1981), part IV.
66 APPV Prot. 23414, Joan Peres, non-paginated (23 July 1435).
67 *Furs de Valencià*, V-V-IV, p. 41.
68 Paulino Iradiel, 'Familia y función económica de la mujer en actividades no agrarias', in Yves-René Fonquerne and Alfonso Estaban (eds), *Condición de la mujer en la edad media* (Madrid: Casa de Veláquez/Universidad Complutense, 1986), p. 232.
69 *Furs de Valencià*, V-I-II, p. 6.
70 Owen Hughes, 'Brideprice to Dowry', p. 27.
71 Jack Goody, *The Development of the Family and Marriage in Europe* (Cambridge: Cambridge University Press, 1983), p. 252.
72 María del Carmen Carlé, 'Apuntes sobre el matrimonio en la Edad Media Española', *Cuadernos de historia de España* 63-64 (1980), pp. 157-158.
73 *Furs de Valencià*, V-I-XVI, p. 16.
74 *Ibid.*, V-V-XIV, p. 50.
75 APPV Prot. 22098, Joan Peres, non-paginated (6 October 1438).
76 ARV Prot. 1094, Juan Garcia, non-paginated (20 June 1428).
77 *Furs de Valencià*, V-I-XVII, p. 17.
78 *Ibid.*, V-V-XVI, 52; V-V-XIX, p. 54.
79 María Belda Soler, *El regimen matrimonial en los 'Furs de Valencià'* (Valencia: Editorial Cosmos Valencia, 1965), p. 88. Occasionally, the term *hypotheca* appears in dowry contracts from the mid-fifteenth century in Valencia in reference to the husband's obligation of all his property as surety for his wife's dowry and *creix*. For an example, see APPV Prot. 11431, Bertomeu Batalla, non-paginated (3 January 1459).
80 *Furs de Valencià*, V-I-VI, p. 9.
81 Belda Soler, *El regimen matrimonial de bienes en los 'Furs de Valencià'*, p. 91.
82 ARV Prot. 1331, Pere Llorens, non-paginated (27 May 1435).
83 *Furs de Valencià*, V-II-II, 20; V-II-III, p. 20.
84 ARV Justícia Civil Peticiones 3711, m.3, f. 37r. y v. (4 March 1421).
85 Mn. Antoni Ma. Alcover, *Diccionari Català-Valencià-Balear, Tom VI*, ed. Francesc De B. Moll (Palma de Mallorca, 1953), p. 274.
86 José Maria Font Rius, *La ordenación pacciónada del regimen matrimonial de bienes en el derecho medieval hispanico* (Madrid, 1950), p. 29.
87 Belda Soler, *El regimen matrimonial de bienes en los 'Furs de Valencià'*, p. 110; Miguel Gual Camarena, 'El regimen matrimonial de bienes en los Fueros de Valencia', *Anuario de historia del derecho español*, 37 (1967), p. 560.
88 *Consuetudines Dertosae* (Tarragona: Institucio de Estudios Tarraconenses Ramon Berenguer IV, 1972).
89 García-Herrero, *Las mujeres en Zaragoza en el siglo XV*, p. 266; Rebecca Winer, 'Silent partners? women, commerce and the family' (Ph.D. dissertation, University of California at Los Angeles, 1996), p. 72.
90 *Furs de Valencià*, V-II-IV, 21; VI-VI-X, p. 221.

91 While we do not have extant the actual questions that witnesses in dowry restitution cases were asked, it is clear that each section of their testimony was related to an aspect of the wife's petition. The first part of any dowry restitution petition provided details as when and where the couple was married, as well as information regarding their marriage contract. Witnesses were therefore commenting, and expanding upon, their knowledge of this information.
92 ARV Justícia Civil Peticiones 3733, m. 22 f. 47r. a 48v. (16 November 1439).
93 ARV Justícia Civil Peticiones 3731, m. 5. F. 25r a 25v. (7 March 1438).
94 ARV Justícia Civil Peticiones 3714, m. 6, f. 34r. (29 May 1423).
95 ARV Justícia Civil Peticiones 3723, m. 14 f. 35v. (30 September 1434).
96 García-Herrero, *Las mujeres en Zaragoza en el siglo XV*, p. 237.
97 Gervase Rosser, 'Going to the Fraternity Feast: Commensality and Social Relations in Late Medieval England', *Journal of British Studies*, 33(4) (October 1994), p. 431.
98 *Ibid*.
99 Vinyoles, *Les barcelonines a les darreries de l'Edat Mitjana*, p. 100.
100 Mn. Antoni Ma. Alcover, *Diccionari Català-Valencià-Balear, Tom VII*, ed. Francesc De B. Moll (Palma de Mallorca, 1956), p. 768; Tramoyeres Blasco, *Institutciones gremiales*, p. 384; Llorenç Millo Casas, *Gastronomia Valenciana* (Valencia: Generalitat Valenciana, 1997), p. 15; Manuel M. Martínez Llopis, *Historia de la gastronomía española* (Madrid: Alianza Editorial, 1989), pp. 147–151.
101 ARV Justícia Civil Peticiones 3714, m. 6, f. 34r. (29 May 1423).
102 For example see ARV Justícia Civil Peticiones 3717, m. 5 f. 21v. (26 February 1428).
103 For example see Guido Ruggiero's study on sex crimes in Venice, *Boundaries of Eros: Sex Crime and Sexuality in Renaissance Venice* (Oxford: Oxford University Press, 1985); Judith Bennett, 'Writing Fornication: Medieval Leyrwite and Its Historians', *Transactions of the Royal Historical Society*, 6(13) (2003), pp. 131–162; A.J. Finch, 'Sexual Relations and Marriage in Later Medieval Normandy', *Journal of Ecclesiastical History*, 47(2) (April 1996), pp. 236–256.
104 ARV Justícia Civil Peticiones 3711, m. 6 f. 42r. (20 May 1421).
105 *Ibid*., m.1, f. 21r. (21 January 1421).
106 ARV Justícia Civil Peticiones 3723, m. 14, f. 36v. (30 September 1434).
107 Eiximenis, *Lo llibre de les dones: Vol. I*, p. 118.
108 *Ibid*., p. 120.
109 *Ibid*., p. 129.
110 Ferrer, *Sermons: volum segon*, p. 28.
111 *Ibid*., p. 18.
112 ARV Justícia Civil Peticiones 3711, m. 4 f. 40v. (6 March 1421).
113 ARV Justícia Civil Peticiones 3723, m. 14 f. 36r. (30 September 1434).
114 Chris Wickham, '*Fama* and the Law in Twelfth-Century Tuscany', in Thelma Fenster and Daniel Lord Smail (eds), *Fama: The Politics of Talk and Reputation in Medieval Europe* (Ithaca, NY: Cornell University Press, 2004), p. 16.

2

Marital alliances and the choice of spouse

In late medieval Europe, marriage choice was influenced by a number of different factors. Many scholars have argued that family members, particularly fathers, often had a great deal of say in their daughters' choice of husband, as advantageous marriage alliances could greatly advance the family fortunes. These historians, whose work focuses on noble and patrician women, have discussed in detail the importance of marriage in cementing political and economic ties.[1] For high-status families, marriage between a daughter and a son could work to create powerful alliances and new political dynasties. In Valencia, the constant competition for power that characterized the municipal *consell* (largely a result of the yearly election of offices) meant that for many patrician families, marital alliances were crucial for consolidating and maintaining power.[2] Elite families, therefore, had a considerable investment, and great influence, in the marital choices of their children. At the lower levels of society, the choice of spouse was equally important but historians have argued that women of this status had more freedom in their options for marital partners.[3] They stress that, as there was less at stake, labouring-status families were likely to give their daughters greater leeway in this matter.

This chapter seeks to examine the marital choices of artisan and *llaurador* women in late medieval Valencia. I argue that because of their socio-economic and immigrant background, labouring-status women exercised agency in the first 'project of marriage': choosing a spouse. Some of these women were influenced by family members in their marital decisions. For others, the lack of familial presence in Valencia, and the fact that many of their fathers were deceased, had an impact on the ability of labouring-status women to make their own spousal choices. At the same time, these women were influenced by friends, neighbours and employers. While families looked for marriage alliances that could augment their economic resources and cement social ties within neighbourhood and guild structures, these factors were also considerations for women themselves as they sought husbands with whom they could create economically and socially viable households. While high politics were not a concern in the marriage choices of artisans and *llauradors*, nevertheless economic and social factors were influential. Women, their blood and social kin, therefore, often worked together to establish marriage alliances that would be beneficial for everyone.

'Cum consilio parentum et amicorum'

Most marriage contracts in late medieval Valencia, whether dotal or *germanía* contained the phrase '*cum consilio parentum et amicorum*' which translates as 'with the advice of family and friends'. Although formulaic, the inclusion of this phrase suggests the legal importance of familial and peer consent for the formation of marital unions among the Valencian populace. As discussed in the previous chapter, canon law stipulated that the consent of the couple themselves was all that was needed to create a religiously valid union; however, the *Furs* made the consent of the bride's family crucial to the secular legal aspect of marriage, in particular, the exchange of property. How did canonical and secular legal principles regarding marital consent and the choice of spouse play out in practice? Evidence from 455 marriage contracts from the 1420s and 1430s, demonstrates that labouring-status women in Valencia did have some influence over their spousal choices.

Table 2.1 Central actors in labouring-status marriage contracts, 1420–39

	Widows	Donzellas	Total
Woman alone	109	201	310
Father	2	87	89
Mother	1	18	19
Mother and father	0	4	4
Other kin	2	14	16
Woman and kin	1	9	10
Tutors	0	1	1
Master	0	1	1
Unknown male	1	4	5
Total	116	339	455

As Table 2.1 indicates, more than two-thirds of labouring-status women concluded their own marriage contracts. This percentage increases to 94 if we look only at widows; yet, for *donzellas*, almost 60 per cent concluded their only contracts, while 33 per cent were concluded by family members (approximately 26 per cent by fathers). If we compare these statistics to the marriage contracts of elite women, the percentage remains the same for widows, but is drastically different for *donzellas* whose marital agreements were overwhelmingly concluded between fathers and grooms. For example, on 18 April 1433 the master butcher Francesc Lobet concluded a contract of marriage with the master butcher Laurent Comes. Lobet provided a two hundred-pound dowry for his daughter Ursola, who was absent.[4] Part of the reason for this vast difference lies in the types of marriage contracts used by elite and labouring-status women. All elite women followed the dotal regime which allowed for persons other than the bride to act as the central contractor. Labouring-status women had two options in terms of their marriage contracts. Most chose to conclude dowry contracts like elite women, but approximately 20 per cent preferred to conclude a *germanía* agreement. *Germanía* contracts involved only the bride and groom and the structure of this alternative marital property regime is one reason why more labouring-status women concluded their own marriage contracts in comparison to elite women.

Excluding *germanía* contracts and looking only at dotal agreements, three other factors influenced labouring-status women's involvement as the central actors in their marriage contracts: widowhood, deceased fathers and immigration. Just over 25 per cent of the women marrying in our sample were widows. Ninety out of ninety-seven widows concluded their own dowry contracts. Legally and economically independent, as they controlled the dowry and *creix* from their first marriage as well as any other property they may have inherited, widows had a great deal of freedom in choosing their second husbands. This was the case regardless of social class, although scholars of elite women suggest that young widows likely had less control over their spousal choices than older women. As Christiane Klapisch-Zuber has remarked 'young widows were in fact the target of a whole set of forces struggling fiercely for control of their bodies and their fortunes'.[5] This may have been the case for higher-status young widows, but for those of labouring-status, their socio-economic background freed them from many of the familial battles fought among the marital and natal kin of elite women as many of them did not have family living in Valencia. But labouring-status widows faced other pressures in choosing spouses, most commonly economic necessity, as some of them were unable to survive on their own.

For *donzellas*, deceased fathers and immigration greatly influenced their presence as the central actors in marriage agreements. Of the 132 women who concluded their own dowry contracts, 94 either had a deceased father, or had immigrated to Valencia. Just under half of these women had fathers who were deceased at the time of their marriages. This is not surprising given that many labouring-status men did not live past the age of 50 in this period. Antoni Furió's work on *llauradors* has demonstrated that 50 per cent of these men did not reach the age of 40 and 75 per cent did not reach 50. For urban areas, Furió found the mortality rates were slightly lower, but not significantly.[6] As labouring-status women tended to marry between the ages of 17 to 20, and labouring-status men around age 25, many of them would have concluded their marriage contracts after the deaths of their fathers. For example, Romia, the daughter of the deceased Bernat Alcodor of Paterna concluded a dotal contract with the *llaurador* Pere Colomines of Vilamarxant on 7 September 1439. Romia brought a thirty-three-pound dowry, twelve pounds of which she earned as a domestic servant in the household of Guillem Castrella.[7]

Not only was Romia's father deceased at the time of her marriage, but she herself was an immigrant to Valencia, having moved there as a young girl to work for Castrella. Just over one-quarter of the women who concluded their own dowry contracts were immigrants to Valencia. Many of them were like Romia Alcodor, and had come to the city between the ages of 4 and 17 (most commonly in their early teens) to work as domestic servants in urban households. Their fathers therefore lived outside of Valencia, either in one of the numerous villages in the surrounding *horta* region, from elsewhere in the kingdom of Valencia or even from towns in Aragon and Castile. Johana, the daughter of the deceased fisherman Juan Martinez of Castile concluded a contract of marriage with the *llaurador* Pastasius Martí of Cilla in the *horta* on 28 May 1435. As dowry, Johana brought fifteen pounds in cash, all of which she had earned as a servant to the merchant Gabriel Font of Valencia.[8]

Clearly domestic service worked to bring immigrant women out of their natal families' sphere. Moving to the city on their own meant that the families of these women came to play less of a role in their daily lives. The fact that they had come to the city by themselves brought these women into contact with a much wider variety of men that they would have met in their natal regions. Coupled with the fact that many labouring-status women had deceased fathers at the time of their marriages, these factors gave them greater agency than elite women in contracting their marriages, as their families simply were not present. When Teresa Dalarit of Sogorbe concluded her dotal contract with the barber Tomas Dauder, she stated she was doing so with the consent of her father, but it was Teresa who was the central actor in the creation of her marriage agreement. She had moved to Valencia at the age of 12 to work as a servant in the house of Maria and Francesc Oviet.[9]

P.J.P. Goldberg has argued that there is a clear link between women who had greater economic autonomy and their ability to influence matters relating to marriage. In particular, Goldberg states that servants who had immigrated to the city had great freedom in their spousal choices, especially in comparison to girls from rural areas who chose to marry men from their natal regions.[10] Evidence from Valencia supports Goldberg's assertions. *Llaurador* women who did not work as servants, who lived in the countryside, and who married men from outside the city of Valencia, were much less likely to conclude their own marriage contracts. Only one-third of these *donzellas* were the central actors in their dowry contracts, in comparison to 50 per cent of labouring-status *donzellas* who followed the dotal regime overall. Indeed, among these rural women, factors such as a deceased father did not have as much of an impact on their ability to conclude their own marriage agreements. About half of the women in this cohort had deceased fathers at the time of their marriages, and rather than using this situation as a means for influencing their spousal choices themselves, these women tended to turn to other family members to act in the paternal role. For example, on 13 March 1430 Sancius Squenda of Torrent concluded a contract of marriage with the *llaurador* Joan Martí alias Goncalbo of Museros for his niece Francisca, the daughter of his deceased brother. Squenda also provided Francisca with a forty-pound dowry for her marriage.[11] If we consider the women in this group whose fathers were alive, only three out of eighteen women concluded their own dotal agreements.

But there are some caveats that we need to keep in mind. First, just because a woman's father did not conclude her marriage contract, does not mean he was not involved, or that he was not present. Many of the women who concluded their own dowry contracts state they were doing so with the consent of their fathers or other family members. Second, dowry contracts indicate who the central actors were in these agreements, as well as some of the witnesses present, but they do not indicate all of the people who were there. So it is possible that family members were there at the time the agreement was made; however, in the cases of domestic servants who were from far-flung villages in the kingdom, it is also highly unlikely that their families were in attendance, given the distance between the city and their natal regions.

Despite the lack of familial involvement in the marriage agreements of labouring-status women, it is important to note that the factors guiding the spousal choices of labouring-status women were not necessarily all that different from those that their families would have considered. These women wanted to form unions that would be economically viable and stable, and they therefore sought husbands with whom such households could be created. For example, on 12 June 1424, Francesca, the daughter of the deceased *llaurador* Joan Galiana of Valencia concluded an agreement of marriage with the fisherman Tristan Gueralt. Francesca provided Tristan with a dowry of forty pounds, but Tristan himself brought a boat and all the tools necessary to set himself up as a fisherman. This property had been donated to Tristan by his father, Jacob Gueralt on account of his marriage to Francesca.[12] Assets such as these made Tristan Gueralt an attractive marriage partner for Francesca Galiana and their combined property created a firm foundation for their new union.

Francesca Galiana's father Joan likely would have approved of his daughter's marriage to Tristan Gueralt, given Gueralt's perceived economic assets. Francesca's union with Tristan was not only important for her own survival, it also brought essential alliances with the Gueralt family. Many labouring-status families used the marriages of their daughters to create alliances that could be advantageous for the whole kin group. These alliances were used for a variety of socio-economic reasons and their importance led some lower-status fathers, as well as other relatives, to play central roles in the marriage contracts of their daughters and female relatives. While it was rare for widows' family members to be involved in their marriage contracts (only five out of ninety-seven widows had their dotal agreements concluded by kin), this practice was far more common for *donzellas*. Just under half of *donzellas* who followed the dowry regime had contracts that were concluded by family members, with fathers, more than any other family member, the central actors in these documents. As the legal guardians of their daughters (if the girls were minors), fathers retained an interest in whom they married and worked to use marital alliances to help their families. For example, on 7 January 1430, the weaver Joan Martí of Valencia concluded a contract of marriage with the wooldresser Joan Aznar. Martí provided a dowry of 100 pounds in cash, household goods and jewellery for his daughter Violant, who was absent.[13]

Valencian dowry contracts always noted whether or not the bride was present at their conclusion and absent brides such as Violant were somewhat unusual for those of labouring-status. Just over 10 per cent of lower-status dowry contracts indicate the bride was absent. Most of these brides had dowries that were well above the twenty- to forty-pound average for labouring-status women. In fact, 50 per cent of them had dowries that were more than four times this amount. The greater involvement of fathers in the marital choices of these women is similar to the roles that elite fathers played in arranging the marriages of their daughters. With much more property at stake, along with crucial social, economic and political alliances, these fathers ensured they had complete control over every aspect of their daughters' projects of marriage, starting with their choice of spouse.

Other family members were equally aware of the importance that such unions played for their fortunes and so occasionally stepped in and performed the paternal role of guardian, concluding the contract of marriage and handing over the dowry. Mothers most commonly fulfilled this role as the *Furs* named them guardians of their children once their husbands were deceased.[14] The practice of appointing mothers as guardians of children was widespread in the Iberian peninsula, and across social statuses, during the medieval and early modern periods. As Grace Coolidge has discussed, female guardians played important roles in negotiating complex arrangements for marriage among the Castilian nobility; choosing spouses for their children, handing over dowry and other assets upon marriage and ensuring such alliances were to the political, economic and social benefit of the family.[15] It was not only elite women that played such roles in late medieval Europe. While labouring-status widows were not negotiating marriage arrangements at the same level as the elite women studied by Coolidge, they still performed many of the same functions as guardians of their minor daughters. For example, Agnes, the widow of the deceased tailor Jaume Dezpi of Valencia concluded a contract of marriage with the tailor Ieorgio de Blanes, for her daughter Gracia, as well as providing the forty-five pounds for Gracia's dowry.[16] Although mothers were the most common family member to act on behalf of labouring-status women in marriage contracts, brothers, aunts, uncles and even grandparents also appeared as central actors in these dotal agreements.

Both labouring-status women and their families looked for spouses with whom they could form financially stable households and create advantageous alliances. Overall, artisan women tended to marry artisan men and women from *llaurador* families married *llaurador* men; however, some of these women did form exogamous unions with men from other socio-economic backgrounds. To explore fully the spousal choices made by artisan and *llaurador* women (and their families), the rest of this chapter will look at each of these groups separately and consider the varying factors that influenced their decisions in choosing a husband.

Table 2.2 Artisan marriage alliances, 1420–39

	Women	Men
Artisan	130	133
Llaurador	19	47
Higher status	12	19
Total	161	199

Artisan marriage alliances

On 4 September 1421, Johana, the daughter of the deceased mason Joan Vilar of Valencia, together with her mother Francesca, concluded a contract of marriage with the barber Joan Nouvell, also of Valencia. Johana brought a dowry of forty pounds in cash that had been donated by her mother.[17] In choosing Joan as a husband, Johana followed the typical marriage pattern for artisan women in fifteenth-century Valencia. Eighty-one per cent of artisan daughters married endogamously, in comparison to the 12 per cent who married *llauradors* and 7 per cent who concluded marriage contracts with men of higher status (merchants, notaries and apothecaries; see Table 2.2). For artisan men, 68 per cent married women of artisan background, 24 per cent married *llaurador* women and 8 per cent married daughters of merchants, notaries or apothecaries. This type of marriage pattern continued in the city of Valencia into the early modern period and was also common in many other late medieval European cities.[18]

While artisan women were far more likely to marry men of a similar status to themselves, they were unlikely to marry within their fathers' specific trade. In fact, artisan families frequently married their children to people who practised a trade distinct from their own.[19] In fifteenth-century Valencia, only 12 per cent of artisan marriages were endogamous within specific trades, mirroring evidence from other regions of medieval and early modern Europe.[20] Some trades were much more likely to practise endogamy than others. This was certainly true for those involved in the textile industry. Since its conquest in the thirteenth century, the city of Valencia had developed as an important manufacturer of cloth.[21] Textile production was one of the city's three central industries alongside leatherwork and ironwork.[22] The guild of the *peraires*, or wooldressers, was the most important in the city and there were large numbers of men who practised this trade, particularly at the journeyman level.[23] Wooldresser families often intermarried: for example, Caterina, the daughter of Berenguer Xuquer, a wooldresser of Valencia married Bernat Martí who practised the same trade.[24] Overall, textile artisans married within the trade itself with 38 per cent of daughters marrying endogamously and 34 per cent of men.

Marital endogamy was especially important for textile artisans due to the nature of cloth production. The preparation and production of cloth, particularly wool, was labour intensive and involved a number of stages, each performed by a different type of textile artisan. From the carders, combers and spinners (frequently women),[25] who began the whole process, to the weavers, fullers and wooldressers, who took the woollen thread and formed it into the standard broadcloth product, cloth production demanded cooperative labour practices. Marrying the daughter of another textile artisan, therefore, allowed these men to pool their economic and labour resources in this high-demand and competitive industry. Preparers of cloth such as wooldressers and weavers also frequently intermarried with members of the garment industry who used the finished product to create various types of woollen clothing. Tailors such as Bartolomé Banada married women like Isabel, the daughter of a wooldresser, Guillem Martí.[26] Similar to the endogamous practices of cloth preparers, marriages between tailors and wooldressers, for example, worked to diversify the family interests while maintaining a hold within the wider industry of textile production.

As Simona Cerutti has noted, marriage alliances between artisans of different crafts and economic interests helped to create a network of 'business connections, sources of credit and destinations for children as apprentices or spouses'.[27] Allying one's family with that of a different trade allowed for the family fortunes to be expanded, diversifying interests and providing greater economic stability. For master artisans, marriage cemented political and economic alliances both within and between guilds. Close relations with guild members allowed master artisans to rise in importance within their own corporations. Allies from other guilds were also essential for consolidating political power as four representatives from each guild were chosen to sit on Valencia's municipal *consell*. Among the three groups represented (citizens, nobles and guild members), there was a constant struggle for power.[28] Alliances by marriage were therefore used to make key connections between diverse trades.

For artisan families of lower status, whose men worked as journeymen and apprentices, marital strategies could be equally as important. Marriage alliances were used to foster economic opportunities, creating networks with a wider pool of possible employers. These connections also created social ties which were essential in the constantly shifting population of the lower classes in the city. Feuds often developed and allies were needed in the fight for social status in the neighbourhood. By marrying the daughter, sister or niece of a fellow artisan, a ready-made pool of support was generated for these social battles. If disputes turned violent, compatriots could be found from within the newly expanded marital family.[29] This could be especially important for new arrivals to the city who were a familiar sight as the population was in a perpetual state of flux. New immigrants sought to create social networks within their neighbourhoods. Marriage to the daughter of a fellow journeyman could help to replace the familial ties which would have been present in a smaller and more static society.

James Farr asserts that in general, journeymen's daughters were much more likely to marry journeymen than master artisans or their sons.[30] But there were some journeymen who married the daughters of master artisans and therefore created the opportunity of social mobility for themselves. Guilds in Valencia, such as that of the shoemakers, provided monetary bonuses to journeymen who concluded marriages with the daughters of master shoemakers.[31] In some cases, the journeyman who married a widow or daughter of a master was offered significant financial incentives by the guild for doing so. For example, some guilds paid for the couple's wedding celebration and provided them with financial support to start up their own workshop.[32] Others paid the examination fees which would allow the husband to attain master status within the guild. In fact, the best chance for a journeyman to become a master within his specific trade was to marry a master's daughter or widow.[33] While this sounds like an excellent way to promote social mobility within the Valencian guild system, in fact these kinds of opportunities were few and far between, especially as the fifteenth century progressed and membership within guilds became more and more restrictive.[34] Only a select few journeymen were able to take advantage of these clauses, using marriage to vault themselves into a higher social class.

Overall, the daughters of master artisans married master artisans or their sons and the daughters of journeymen married journeymen or their sons. Endogamous marital strategies were therefore mostly used laterally to create and cement ties within one's own social group. For those of journeyman status, they worked to provide a more coherent social identity and culture which was likely different from that of master artisans. Journeymen in Valencia had their own separate confraternities and brotherhoods which worked in similar ways to guilds but were more social in nature, although this was changed as the fifteenth century progressed as these journeymen institutions were absorbed into the master guilds.[35] Marriage alliances reinforced the professional and social bonds that journeymen developed in the workplace and in confraternities.

Although artisans, especially artisan women, were much more likely to marry within their own social group, occasionally they looked outside of it for marital partners. Twelve per cent of artisan women chose to marry *llaurador* men. These men lived in the city and travelled to farm-rented or owned plots of land in the surrounding *horta* region or resided in one of the numerous small villages surrounding and under the political power of the city. For example, Bàrbera the daughter of Bernat Gerp, a wooldresser of Valencia, concluded a contract of marriage with Joan Pereç, a *llaurador* from Valencia.[36] While lower artisans and *llauradors* were often of the same social status, the set of skills acquired by artisan women either as servants, apprentices or as helpers in family workshops would have discouraged the creation of marriage alliances between these two groups. These women desired to marry men with whom they could set up a household where their skills would be essential to maintaining its economic viability. Connected to this practical reason was the fact that parishes in Valencia, like in most medieval cities, were organized by trade bringing artisans into contact with other artisans. For example, the parish of Sant Lorenç was associated with the shoemakers, that of Sant Joan with the carpenters, of Sant Miquel with the wooldressers and of Sant Catalina with the silversmiths.[37] Artisan women, therefore, had less contact with men of *llaurador* status, making them less likely to be considered as marital partners.

Another form of exogamy practised by both artisan men and women, was to marry a spouse of higher status, in our sample from notarial, merchant or apothecary families. Seven per cent of artisan women and 8 per cent of artisan men contracted a marriage with someone of a higher status. For example, Pere Roig, a tailor, concluded a dotal contract with Bonjorna, the daughter of the merchant Bonanat del Belpuig on Christmas Day in 1429.[38] Roig's father was also a tailor and his marriage to Bonjorna was a step up for his family. Isabel Amparo asserts that in seventeenth-century Valencia, it was not uncommon for the daughters of merchants to marry artisans, especially in the textile trade.[39] In the fifteenth century, both merchants themselves and their daughters contracted marriages with textile artisans, especially tailors. Amparo suggests that this fact is not surprising given that many merchants initially came from artisan families.[40] Given the pre-eminence of the cloth trade in Valencia, those merchants of artisan background were very likely from textile families.

Linked to this was the relationship of mutual dependence that merchants and artisans had as producers and sellers of artisanal goods.[41] By marrying their children to one another, these two groups in society were fostering already present alliances.

In their evaluation of evidence from the Tuscan Catasto of 1427, David Herlihy and Christiane Klapisch-Zuber suggested that while marriage was a form of social advancement for men, women generally suffered a loss in social status.[42] Evidence from Valencia supports this assertion, although in a very limited way. Nineteen artisans married women of a higher status in comparison to twelve artisan women who married men of notarial, apothecary or merchant background. Nevertheless, some women were actually able to use their first marriages as jumping off point for higher social ambitions. Such was the case of Ursola, the daughter of Bernat Davies, a silversmith, who initially married Pere Guier, a merchant. In her second marriage, Ursola was able to move from merchant to patrician status, concluding a dotal contract with the *honrat* Francesc Scola, a notary of the city.[43] As Ursola's father was a silversmith and practised a high-status trade, her first marriage to the merchant Guier is not surprising. Her coup in terms of social mobility came with her marriage to Scola, not merely a notary but a man of patrician status. At the time of Ursola's second marriage to Scola, her father was still alive and her family likely reaped the benefits of her increase in status. In fact, although Ursola signed the contract of marriage herself, her dowry, a princely 750 pounds, was donated by her father and brother, Francesc Davies, also a silversmith. The alliance with a member of the *honrat* class was worth a great deal in terms of the honour and prestige that the match would have brought the Davies family, not to mention the business rewards from an opening into the class that was the greatest consumers of the goods produced by the two men.

Llaurador marriage alliances

On 21 August 1431 the *llaurador* Michael Pujol of Valencia concluded a dotal contract with the *llaurador* Joan Gil of Valencia for his daughter Isabel. Pujol also donated a dowry of forty pounds in cash and household goods.[44] Like members of the artisan class, *llauradors* and their families typically followed a pattern of endogamy. Sixty per cent of *llauradors'* daughters married men of a similar status compared to 40 per cent who married artisans. Endogamous marital choices increased with *llauradors* themselves with 78 per cent marrying women of the same status versus only 22 per cent who married women of artisan background. As with artisan marriages, this pattern of endogamy remained the same in Valencia into the early modern period.[45]

The structure of peasant farming is one of the central reasons for *llaurador* endogamy. As Antoní Furió has discussed, agricultural work in late medieval Valencia was organized around the home and was based on the labour of family members.[46] Production was largely at the subsistence level and a viable farm needed the involvement of all, both men and women. Farmers' daughters had valuable skills which could be used to keep the family afloat. In her examination of peasant marriages in the Vallès Oriental region of late medieval Catalonia, Mercè Aventín has argued that marital alliances were equally as important for peasants as for patricians and nobles but should be thought about in different ways. She places less emphasis on the word 'alliance' and suggests we think about these relationships in terms of solidarity and mutual help.[47] In contrast to the patrician and noble use of marriage as a way to create long-lasting political and economic ties, Aventín argues that for peasants, agricultural collaboration was short-lived and used only in moments of necessity.[48] She relates this to the structure of the peasant family – a nuclear unit that used its production to feed itself, pay rent and sold the little it had left at the market. Peasants, Aventín purports, had a limited economic relationship with the outside world which worked to foster marital endogamy.[49] Most peasants, in this area, married the daughters of their next door neighbours and rarely looked further away than 10 kilometres for a bride.[50]

Aventín's arguments work well to demonstrate some of the reasons behind the high rate of endogamy for Valencian *llaurador* families. It is important to recognize that farming families had a somewhat different cultural background from artisans and likely viewed marital alliances in divergent ways. Antoní Furió supports this difference stating that the rural family unit was essentially self-sufficient economically whereas the artisan family was enmeshed in a system of interdependence.[51] Help was likely needed and welcomed during the ploughing or harvesting season, but, overall, agricultural production was based on the single family unit. Although some farmers travelled to the market in the city to sell their products, this form of commercial activity was limited as the majority of family holdings in Valencia produced only enough crops for subsistence.[52] Simply by virtue of living and/or working in the *horta* and the city itself, Valencian *llauradors* likely came into contact with a greater variety of people than Aventín's Catalan peasants; however, they still preferred to marry those of the same cultural and economic background.

While the majority of farmers tended to marry women of the same class, this was not necessarily true for their daughters. Forty per cent of *llaurador* women married exogamously, choosing husbands of artisan background. Some were like Maria, the daughter of Alfons Garcia, a *llaurador* from Valencia, who married Joan Cressi, a carpenter of the same city.[53] Maria signed her *germanía* marriage contract with Garcia of her own accord. Other women of *llaurador* status had marriages with artisan men contracted for them by family members who lived in the city and were of the artisan class themselves. Such was the case of Margarita, the daughter of Vicent Bertí, a *llaurador* from Alboraia, whose maternal uncle and aunt, the blacksmith Jacob Torres and his wife Margarita, concluded a dotal contract with Michael Ruiro, also a blacksmith.[54] Although Margarita's father was not present for the drawing up of the contract, his permission for her to marry was noted in the document, demonstrating the importance of paternal consent. In addition, the fact that Margarita's uncle, like her new spouse, was a blacksmith shows the influence that extended family ties could have on the choice of marital partner.

Margarita's marriage contract indicates one of the ways in which women of *llaurador* status could marry into the artisan class. That Margarita's aunt and uncle also donated her dowry shows the great influence that family members could have in choosing a spouse. But women of the farming class had another means by which to meet potential artisan spouses without direct familial influence. This was through the fulfilment of service contracts which brought them into urban households and into contact with urban men. Large numbers of *llaurador* families, particularly poorer ones, came to the city looking for domestic service positions for their daughters. For example, on 11 November 1433 the small farmer Pere Rossell from Ademuz, a village located over 100 kilometres from Valencia, concluded a domestic service contract with Caterina, the widow of a dyer. The agreement concerned Rossell's daughter Pastasia, age 13 who was to work for Caterina for six years, earning a salary of forty-three pounds. Caterina promised to provide Pastasia with food, drink, clothing, shoes, a bed and a blanket.[55] Five years later, Pastasia Rossell came before the notary Joan de Campos Sr once again, this time on her own in order to conclude her contract of marriage with Ferdinand Sanchez, an espadrille-maker from Valencia. As her dowry, Pastasia brought thirty-five pounds, thirty of which she had earned as a domestic servant to Caterina Madriz.[56]

On the same day that he contracted Pastasia as a domestic servant to Caterina Madriz, Pere Rossell also concluded a contract for his other daughter Maria, age 9 with the notary Bernat Estreller of Valencia. Maria was to work for Estreller as a servant for four years and receive a salary of twenty pounds.[57] In the late medieval period throughout Spain, it was not uncommon for *llaurador* fathers to place some, or all, of their daughters in domestic service positions. As Pierre Bonnassie and others have argued, parents used these positions to better their daughters' lives and increase their marriage prospects.[58] Designed to provide girls with money for their dowries, these contracts lasted from a few months to twelve years, usually ending when the girl was aged between 18 and 20, at which time it was assumed she would marry. Salaries fluctuated between two and fifty pounds, dependent upon the length of contract and the status of the employer. For example, on 24 January 1437, the *llaurador* Guillem Marti of Foios, a village in the *horta* concluded a domestic service contract for his daughter Caterina, age 13, with Vicent Eiximenez of Valencia. The contract was to last for five years, at the end of which Caterina would earn 19 pounds.[59] In another contract from 1432 between the tailor Martí Ferrandez and the silk weaver Pere Nelli alter Grasso, Francisca, age 6, was to earn a salary of thirty pounds after ten years of service.[60] On average, domestic service contracts in late medieval Valencia lasted seven years, with salaries of twenty-one pounds, or three pounds per year, plus clothing, shoes, food and drink for the duration of the contract.

Although both urban and rural families used service contracts as a method of providing or augmenting dowries for their daughters, the majority of girls placed in service in Valencia were from outside the city walls. In an examination of sixty-one domestic service contracts from the 1420s and 1430s, I found that 69 per cent of the girls originated from outside the city of Valencia. Twenty out of 41 were from one of the numerous villages in the *horta*. A further 13 girls were from elsewhere in the kingdom, especially the northern areas which were experiencing the greatest demographic decline during this period. This was the case for Pastasia Sanchez mentioned earlier who came from Ademuz, a village located in the north-west corner of the kingdom, close to the border with the kingdom of Aragon. Eight girls out of 41 were from outside the kingdom of Valencia, most of them from the Aragonese city of Teruel with which Valencia had a long-standing trade relationship.

Many of these young women chose to marry men from Valencia, rather than returning to their natal regions to choose a spouse. Thirty of the 367 dotal contracts examined were concluded by women identified as domestic servants. It is likely that many others involved such women as well, but this is not indicated in their marriage contracts. Of the thirty, 16 women were originally from outside Valencia and 75 per cent of them (12 out of 16) married Valencian men. Service contracts therefore worked to bring *llaurador* daughters out of the agricultural world and into the urban one, creating contacts with a wider variety of potential husbands. For example, Johana, the daughter of Joan Martí, a *llaurador* from the *horta*, contracted a marriage with Antoní Ortola, a tanner from Valencia in 1424. Thirty-five pounds out of Johana's total dowry of fifty-five pounds came from a service contract with Bartolomé Peçonda, a silk weaver. The rest of her dowry was donated by her father whose consent to the marriage Johana indicated in the contract.[61] In another example, Francesca, the daughter of the deceased Miquel del Porro, a *llaurador* of Teruel, concluded a contract of marriage with Antoní Vicent alias Riguau, a tanner of Valencia. Francesca's dowry consisted of twenty-five pounds from her service contract to Jacob Fuster, an apothecary, and ten pounds she had received from her two brothers.[62] Domestic service and immigration therefore had a great impact on the influence that *llaurador* women had over their spousal choices. In fact, for women whose fathers were alive, who were originally from outside Valencia, and married Valencian men, 100 per cent of them concluded their own marriage contracts.

Domestic service not only brought *llaurador* women into contact with a broader group of potential husbands, it also meant that some of these women were subject to influences beyond their kin group in their marital decisions. Some scholars have suggested that the employers of former servants may have had some influence over the marital choices that these women made, reflecting work alliances that they themselves were hoping to conclude.[63] Valencian marriage contracts indicate this was possible as some former servants married men who practised trades in the same industries as their masters. For example, on 29 September 1432, Johana, the daughter of a *llaurador* from Ruçafa concluded a contract of marriage with the wooldresser Bartolomé Mazaret of Valencia.[64] Thirty pounds out of Johana's seventy-pound dowry came from her work as a domestic servant for the dyer Joan Azner. Johana's groom and former master were both involved in the textile industry and Azner may have influenced Johana's decision to marry Mazaret, hoping to benefit himself from the union.

Paulino Iradiel has argued that dotal contracts can be used to consider the paternal influence of employers on the marital choices of their domestic servants because in some cases, it was the employer himself who donated the dowry directly to the husband.[65] Dennis Romano's examination of service in fifteenth- and sixteenth-century Venice supports this argument as he found that some service contracts stipulated that it was the responsibility of the master to find an appropriate husband for his servant.[66] Evidence from the 1420s and 1430s indicates that this kind of dotal donation did happen. For example, on 18 April 1430, Miquel Cardona of Valencia donated a dowry in the amount of twenty pounds to

Pere Martínez, alias Assensi, on behalf of Ramona, his servant. Cardona noted that he was doing so on account of the service contract that had now been fulfilled by Ramona.[67] Unfortunately, this contract does not indicate the social status of either Ramona's employer or her new husband, so we are unable to postulate as to the possible alliance forged between the two men.

Despite lacking numerous examples of this kind, Iradiel's assertion certainly seems plausible, especially given the structure of medieval households. David Herlihy and Christiane Klapisch-Zuber have demonstrated that both masters and mistresses played a kind of parental role for servants that lived with them.[68] In Valencia, girls could enter into service as young as 4 years old and lived in their employers' households for up to twelve years. Employers were obliged to provide their servants with food, clothing and shelter, provisions traditionally supplied by the girls' fathers. Except in the highest levels of society, Valencian households only had two to three servants. As our evidence indicates, some of these young girls were initially from the *horta* and were now living in the city, away from their natal families. On top of all this, Klapisch-Zuber asserts that servants who had signed service contracts as girls were closely watched by their employers to ensure good and honourable behaviour as this would have an impact on the honour of the household itself.[69] In Valencia, some employers even provided dotal money above and beyond that stipulated by the service contract. In her testament of 23 October 1436, Clara, the widow of the spice seller Joan Stela of Valencia left her servant, also Clara a dotal bequest of five pounds in addition to her twenty-pound salary.[70] All of these factors suggest a closer familial relationship between servants and their employers who could very well have retained a great deal of interest in whom they married.

Not only does domestic service indicate that people other than the families of these young women had influence over their marital choices, it also demonstrates that the women themselves had some agency in these decisions. Moving to the city away from their families brought these women into contact with a much wider variety of men than those they would have met in the *horta*. In addition, the fact that some of these women had moved to the city on their own meant that their families came to play less of a daily role in their lives. These two factors, coupled with the income they earned as domestic servants, gave these *llaurador* women a great of control over their spousal choices. When Francisca, the daughter of the deceased *llaurador* Guillem Bertran of Benguazar married the barber Martí Rodriguez of Valencia, thirty pounds out of her fifty-pound dowry came from her work as a domestic servant for the *honrat* Ramón

Vilalba. A further twenty pounds was donated by Francisca's mother María, but it was Francisca herself who concluded the dotal contract with Martí.[71]

The flow of young and adolescent girls from the surrounding *horta* into the city of Valencia to work as servants in urban households was clearly related to the greater pattern of marital exogamy for women of *llaurador* status. We see far fewer cases of *llaurador* men marrying artisan women, although this does not mean that the sons of farmers did not conclude labour contracts in the city. Similar to young girls of this status whose families signed service contracts for them with urban employers, the sons of *llauradors* were brought to the city by their families whose resources were insufficient to support them. They were placed in apprenticeship contracts, often with artisan families who trained them in the particular trade that they practised. For example, on 26 February 1433, the *llaurador* Joan Sanxo of Paterna apprenticed his son Joanet, age 8, to the wooldresser Joan Enyego of Valencia for a period of nine years. Enyego was to provide Joanet with food, clothing and a bed, as well as teach him the wooldresser trade.[72] Once apprenticed, these young boys lost their status as members of a farming family and instead became connected to the household in which they worked. Once their apprenticeship was completed, they identified themselves in contracts according to the trade that they now practised, not by status of their natal family. This was different from *llaurador* girls who had fulfilled service contracts for, as unmarried women, they were always identified according to the name and status of their father. We therefore are only able to track the marriage patterns of men who still identified themselves as *llauradors* as adults, limiting somewhat our ability to determine their marital choices.

As with *llaurador* sons who came to the city and were integrated into urban society, some women of farming background who married artisans in their first marriage remained in Valencia and expanded their social ties within their new communities through subsequent marital alliances. For example, in 1422, Francesca the widow of Dominic Paris, a blacksmith of Valencia, contracted a marriage with Jacob Albesa, a tanner of the same city. Francesca was the daughter of Berenguer Jordi, a *llaurador* from Pego.[73] In her marriage to Albesa, Francesca not only expanded her communal relations to those in the tanning industry, she brought her own alliances, developed from her first marriage to Paris. In another example from 1430, Elionor, the widow of Bernat Galter, a cutler of Valencia, concluded a dotal contract with Lanzer Ballester, a blacksmith. Elionor's father, Gerard Ferrar, was a *llaurador* from Museros whose consent to the marriage was noted in the document.[74] Elionor, initially married to a cutler, was marrying a blacksmith, cementing her ties to the metal-working community of the city. In this case, even after marriage to an artisan, Elionor had retained her relationship with her natal farming family, indicated by her father's consent to her marriage to Ballester. The social network of her family was expanded to include those alliances that she had now made in the city with her new marriage.

Not all women from agricultural families that came to work in the city as servants married into the urban classes. Some fulfilled their service contracts, received their dowries, and then returned to their birthplaces at the time of marriage. Such was the case of Caterina, the daughter of Bartolomé Aquilar, a *llaurador* of Albal. Caterina had worked as a servant in Valencia for the notary Gerard Despont, earning a dowry of twenty pounds. She then returned home to marry Joan Alfons, like her father, a *llaurador* of Albal. Caterina's father Bartolomé concluded the contract of marriage for his daughter with Joan Alfons and provided an additional ten pounds towards her dowry.[75] Her father retained a great deal of interest in whom she married, and we have no way of knowing if this match was one that Caterina would have chosen for herself.

Artisan and *llaurador* women faced many considerations when choosing a spouse in late medieval Valencia. These women tended to follow a pattern of endogamy, although 40 per cent of *llaurador* women chose to marry exogamously. This factor was related to their immigration to the city to work as domestic servants which brought them into contact with a wider pool of potential spouses. The families of these women had some influence over their marital decisions; however, this was not universal, as other groups, such as social kin and women themselves had an impact on spousal choices. In making this decision, artisan and *llaurador* women weighed many of the same factors as their families, focusing primarily on economic and social considerations that would create the best marriage alliance. The independence that these women were able to gain with marriage was largely determined by the dowry they brought with them into the new union and it is to an assessment of this property that we now turn.

Notes

1 For example, Stephen Bensch, *Barcelona and Its Rulers, 1096–1291* (Cambridge: Cambridge University Press, 1994); Chojnacki, 'From Trousseau to Groomgift', 'Dowries and Kinsmen' and 'Kinship Ties and Young Patricians', all in *Women and Men in Renaissance Venice*; Anthony Molho, *Marriage Alliance in Late Medieval Florence* (Cambridge, MA: Harvard University Press, 1994).

2 Rafael Narbona Vizcaíno, 'Vida pública y conflictividad en los reinos hispánicas

(siglos XIV–XV)', in Juan Ignacio Ruiz de la Peña Solar (ed.), *Las sociedades urbanas en la España medieval* (Pamplona: Gobierno de Navarra, Departamento de Educación y Cultura, 2003), pp. 541–589 and *Valencia, municipio medieval*.

3   Diane Owen Hughes, 'Domestic Ideals and Social Behaviour: Evidence from Medieval Genoa', in Charles E. Rosenberg (ed.), *The Family in History: Lectures Given in Memory of Steven Allen Kaplan* (Philadelphia: University of Pennsylvania Press, 1975), p. 136. See also Monica Chojnacka, *Working Women of Early Modern Venice* (Baltimore: Johns Hopkins University Press, 2001).

4   ARV Prot. 3093, Martí Doto, non-paginated (18 April 1433).

5   Klapisch-Zuber, '"Cruel Mother"', p. 120.

6   Furió, *Història del País Valencià*, p. 192. Furió states that his statistics for rural and urban men exclude rates of infant mortality which was around 50 per cent for children younger than 5.

7   APPV Prot. 22098, Joan Peres, non-paginated (7 September 1439).

8   ARV Prot. 2432, Vicent Çaera, non-paginated (28 May 1435).

9   ARV Justícia Civil Peticiones 2723, M. 14, f. 8r. sig. 35r. a 38v. (30 September 1434).

10 P.J.P. Goldberg, '"For Better, for Worse": Marriage and Economic Opportunity for Women in Town and Country', in P.J.P. Goldberg (ed.), *Woman Is a Worthy Wight: Women in English Society, c.1200–1500* (Alan Sutton, 1992), pp. 109–118.

11 ARV Prot. 471, Berenguer Cardona, non-paginated (13 March 1430).

12 APPV Prot. 22110, Miquel de Ripoll, non-paginated (12 June 1424).

13 ARV Prot. 2427, Vicent Çaera, non-paginated (7 January 1430).

14 *Furs de Valencià*, V-II-X, p. 25.

15 Grace E. Coolidge, *Guardianship, Gender, and the Nobility in Early Modern Spain* (Burlington, VT: Ashgate, 2011), pp. 94–111.

16 APPV Prot. 22121, Joan Peres, non-paginated (21 April 1425).

17 ARV Prot. 1266, Andres Julian, non-paginated (5 September 1421).

18 Isabel Amparo Baixauli, *Casar-se al'Antic Règime: Dona i família a la València del segle XVII* (Valencia: Universitat de Valencia, 2003), p. 92; Martha Howell, *The Marriage Exchange: Property, Social Place and Gender in Cities of the Low Countries* (Chicago: University of Chicago Press, 1998), p. 190; James Farr, *Hands of Honor: Artisans and Their World in Dijon: 1550–1650* (Ithaca, NY: Cornell University Press, 1988), p. 134.

19 Iradiel, 'Familia y función', p. 233.

20 Farr, *Artisans in Europe, 1300–1914* (Cambridge: Cambridge University Press, 2000), p. 245.

21 Jacqueline Guiral-Hadziossif, *Valence: Port méditerranéen au XVe siècle (1410–1525)* (Paris: Publications de la Sorbonne, 1986), p. 375.

22 *Ibid*.

23 El Marques de Cruilles, *Los Gremios de Valencia: Memoria sobre su origen, vicistudes y organización* (Valencia: La Casa de Beneficencia, 1883), p. 152.

24 ARV Prot. 790, Martín Doto, non-paginated (21 September 1426).

25 Guiral-Hadziossif, *Valence: Port méditerraneen au XVe siècle*, p. 373.

26 APPV Prot. 69, Bertomeu Martí, non-paginated (25 August 1421).

27 Simona Cerutti, *La ville et les métiers: naissance d'un langage corporatif (Turin, 17e–18e siècle)* (Paris: Éditions de l'École des hautes études en sciences socials, 1980), p. 145.

28 Narbona Vizcaíno, *Valencia, municipo medieval*, p. 69.

29 Mark Meyerson, 'Bloodshed and baptism: Christian, Muslim, and Jewish violence and

the transformation of Spain' (paper presented at the Friends of the Library Pontifical Institute for Medieval Studies 2003 Lecture, 24 October).
30 Farr, *Hands of Honor*, p. 135.
31 Leopoldo Piles Ros, *Estudio sobre el gremio de zapateros* (Valencia: Ayntamiento de Valencia, 1959), p. 43.
32 Tramoyeres Blasco, *Instituciones gremiales*, p. 358.
33 Farr, *Hands of Honor*, p. 135; Tramoyeres Blasco, *Instituticiones gremiales*, p. 224.
34 Iradiel, 'Corporaciones de oficio, acción política y sociedad civil en Valencia', p. 276.
35 Tramoyeres Blasco, *Instituticiones gremiales*, p. 194.
36 APPV Prot. 26371, Jaume de Sant Vicent, non-paginated (3 August 1431).
37 Tramoyeres Blasco, *Instituticiones gremiales*, p. 375.
38 ARV Prot. 2143, Juan Sarañana, non-paginated (25 December 1429).
39 Amparo Baixauli, *Casar-se al'Antic Règime*, p. 104.
40 *Ibid.*
41 Iradiel, 'L'evolució econòmica', p. 316.
42 David Herlihy and Christiane Klapisch-Zuber, *Tuscans and Their Families: A Study of the Florentine Catasto of 1427* (New Haven, CT: Yale University Press, 1985), p. 226.
43 APPV Prot. 16383, Dionis Cervera, non-paginated (7 January 1420).
44 APPV Prot. 26181, Joan Marroma, non-paginated (21 August 1431).
45 Amparo Baixauli, *Casar-se al'Antic Règime*, p. 111.
46 Antoní Furio, 'Tierra, familia y transmisión de la propriedad en el pais valenciano durante la baja edad media', in Reyna Pastor (ed.), *Relaciones de poder, de producción y parentesco en la Edad media y moderna* (Madrid: Consejo Superior de Investigaciones Científicas, 1990), p. 307.
47 Mercè Aventín i Puig, *La societat rural a Catalunya en temps feudals: Vallès Oriental, segles XIII–XVI* (Barcelona: Columna Edicions, 1996), p. 484.
48 *Ibid.*
49 *Ibid.*, p. 486.
50 *Ibid.*, p. 484.
51 Furió, *Història del País Valencià*, p. 487.
52 Furió, 'Tierra, familia y transmisión de la propriedad', p. 309.
53 ARV Prot. 11237, Desconocido, non-paginated (25 July 1424).
54 ARV Prot. 2426, Vicente Zaera, non-paginated (16 July 1429).
55 ARV Prot. 422, Joan de Campos (Sr), non-paginated (13 November 1433).
56 ARV Prot. 425, Joan de Campos (Sr), non-paginated (13 December 1438).
57 ARV Prot. 422, Joan de Campos (Sr), non-paginated (13 November 1433).
58 Pierre Bonnassie, *La organización del trabajo en Barcelona a fines del siglo XV* (Barcelona: Consejo Superior de Investigaciones Científicas, 1975), p. 104; Gloria Lora Serrano, 'El servicio doméstico en Córdoba a fines de la edad media', in Manuel González Jiménez and José Rodríguez Molina (eds), *Actas del III Coloquio de Historia Medieval Andaluza: La sociedad medieval Andaluza, Grupos no privilegiados* (Jaén: Diputación Provincial de Jaén, 1984), p. 240.
59 APPV Prot. 22098, Joan Peres, non-paginated (24 January 1437).
60 ARV Prot. 3120, Joan Jimenez, non-paginated (8 April 1432).
61 ARV Prot. 1893, Andrés Puigmicha, non-paginated (29 March 1424).
62 ARV Prot. 2422, Vicente Zaera, non-paginated (17 February 1423).
63 Iradiel, 'Familia y función', p. 241.

64 ARV Prot. 2773, Bernat Vidal, non-paginated (29 September 1432).
65 *Ibid.*
66 Romano, *Housecraft and Statecraft*, p. 155.
67 ARV Prot. 471, Berenguer Cardona, non-paginated (18 April 1430).
68 David Herlihy, *Medieval Households* (Cambridge, MA: Harvard University Press, 1985), p. 153; Klapisch-Zuber, 'Women Servants in Florence', p. 74.
69 Klapisch-Zuber, 'Women Servants in Florence', p. 72; Romano, *Housecraft and Statecraft*, p. xxi. See also Molho, *Marriage Alliance*, p. 142. Molho gives an example of a servant girl who was seduced and impregnated by the brother of her employer who went to a great deal of effort to preserve both the honour of the girl and that of his family.
70 ARV Prot. 793, Martí Doto, non-paginated (23 October 1436).
71 APPV Prot. 6582, Francesc Pelegrí, non-paginated (16 June 1433).
72 APPV Prot. 23409, Joan Peres, non-paginated (26 February 1433).
73 APPV Prot. 14403, Jaume Venrell, non-paginated (18 January 1422).
74 ARV Prot. 471, Berenguer Cardona, non-paginated (20 August 1430).
75 APPV Prot. 22842, Joan Peris, non-paginated (11 November 1423).

3

Marital property of labouring-status wives

Although the choice of spouse was centrally important, the heart of every marriage contract lay in the exchange of property. Despite the Catholic Church's attempts to sacralize it, for most people in medieval Europe marriage was based on financial considerations. The aim of this chapter is to examine the marital property exchanged in early fifteenth-century Valencian artisan and *llaurador* marriages, the dowry and the *creix*. Both were integral to the marital economy; however, the dowry far outweighed the *creix* in both amount and importance. For all women, the dowry acted as 'the sum of money that would define their adult lives'.[1] Dowries were representative of their own, and their families', honour and status. A suitable dowry allowed women regardless of their social background to marry well. As discussed in the introduction to this book, popular representations (both religious and secular) equated women's worth with the size of their dowries. For labouring-status women, the value of this property, along with their ability to work, meant that they made an important contribution to the marital economy.[2] These assets were therefore a crucial part of their ability to exercise agency in their lives.

According to Roman law, the dowry was designed to provide the economic foundation of the new marital union; however, in the Middle Ages, dowries came to be seen as daughters' shares of their family patrimonies.[3] As such, dowries had another important function: to provide for wives in widowhood. For these reasons, despite the fact that their husbands controlled them during their marriages, dowries were always viewed as the property of wives and they were able to regain them both during and at the dissolution of the marriage. Thus, Paulino Iradiel has argued that dowries were a sign of women's economic independence.[4] In order to comprehend fully the dowry system and how labouring-status women manoeuvred within it, this chapter will examine the Valencian dotal regime in the fifteenth century. In doing so, I will explore the rules that set the framework for the marital property exchange, looking at the amount and type of property artisan and *llaurador* women brought as dowries and received as *creix*, the counter-gift provided by their husbands. Despite the complex nature of this regime, labouring-status women negotiated these patriarchal structures to their advantage, gaining a measure of control over this property, right from the moment they (or others) concluded the dotal contract with their future husbands.

Dowry size: artisans

Although historians use medieval marriage contracts as sources for exploring topics such as familial networks, gender relations and social connections, in the Middle Ages, the primary function of these documents was economic. Thus, the monetary amount of dowries conferred on grooms was always indicated by the notaries redacting these agreements. For example, a contract from 23 July 1435 began:

> [I] Johana, daughter of the deceased swordsmith Ferdinand de St Marti of Valencia, with the will of my *curator* the carpenter Pere Stropinya, as well as the consent of my family and friends, join myself in marriage with you Jacob Bernat, tailor of Valencia. In and for my dowry, I give to you Jacob, thirty-five pounds of Valencian money, namely twenty-four pounds in cash and the rest in household goods.[5]

Johana de St Marti's marriage agreement then continued by discussing the amount of her *creix* as she was a virgin (seventeen pounds, ten sous) and included a promise from her groom to restore these assets in any event or case of dowry restitution as outlined in the Valencian legal code.

Table 3.1 Size of artisan dowries, 1420–39

Pounds	Donzellas	Widows	Total
>20	1	6	7
20–40	50	24	74
41–60	36	9	45
61–80	8	3	11
81–100	17	7	24
101–150	12	3	15
150+	1	2	3
Unknown	0	1	1
Total	125	55	180

Johana de St Marti's dowry of thirty-five pounds was average for artisan women in early fifteenth-century Valencia. Although lower-status dowries ranged from a low of five pounds to over 150 pounds, most fell between twenty and sixty pounds, with the largest cohort at twenty to forty pounds (see Table 3.1). Few artisan women had dowries below this amount; however, those that did were almost exclusively widows.[6]

The loss of a husband could place a woman at a serious economic disadvantage. The state of her husband's finances at his death, particularly the amount of debt that he owed, as well as the number and age of living children she had, affected a widow's ability to survive financially in the future. Difficulty in obtaining her dowry from her husband's executors could also have an impact. In some cases, women had to go to court and fight unwilling in-laws and others designated as executors to have their dowries restored to them. There is a great deal of notarial and court documentation regarding widows suing the executors of their husbands' estates in an attempt to have their dowries restored.[7]

There was no doubt in the minds of late medieval Valencian jurists that such property should be restored to widows. Heirs, on the other hand, wanted to hold on to dotal assets as long as possible in order to benefit from this property as their fathers had. As Thomas Kuehn has remarked for Italy, the return of the dowry was a 'perpetual legal headache' for widows.[8] Litigation over dowry restitution could severely limit widows' abilities to support their families. In addition, it could hinder them from easily contracting new marriages as they were unable to offer a new dowry until the one from their previous union had been restored; however, some women such as Francesca, the widow of Joan Sobirats, were able to use the promise of a dowry to come to conclude new marriages. In a notarial contract from 26 March 1424 Francesca, now married to Pasqual Perpanya, sought the return of her dowry from Joan Vernell, the executor of her first husband's estate. Sobirats had died three years earlier and Francesca's dowry had yet to be returned to her. At the time of her union with Perpanya, Francesca had indicated her dowry would come from the dotal assets of her first marriage, once they were returned to her.[9]

Yet widowhood did not necessarily mean a smaller dowry for artisan women. While one-quarter of the marriage contracts in my sample were concluded by widows, such women represented one-third of artisan women whose dowries were above sixty pounds. When Isabel, the widow of a butcher from Valencia married Antoni Marti, also a butcher, she brought as dowry 100 pounds in household goods, cash and rights to a rented house. Isabel received a dotal donation from her sister and brother-in-law for her marriage to Marti, but other women used assets they inherited from their husbands. For example, in his testament of 22 June 1428, the hosteller Joan Portagelet returned to his wife Clara the fifty-pound dowry she had given to him at the time of their marriage. He also bequeathed a house to her.[10] Occasionally artisan men named their wives as their universal heirs such as the blacksmith Pasqual Moreno who donated his entire estate to his wife Isabel in his testament from 1431.[11] In general, artisan women who received these kinds of bequests from their husbands did not have children and they were able to add these assets into their dotal fund for subsequent marriages.

Widowhood was not the only factor that contributed to some artisan women having higher than average dowries. Over half of the women whose dowries were above sixty pounds had deceased fathers or came from a more prestigious artisan backgrounds. When Angelina, the daughter of a deceased tailor married the wooldresser Pere Oller in 1437, she brought as dowry 103 pounds in cash; 100 pounds of this property was left to her in her father's testament. Although the dowry was increasingly seen as daughters' share of the family patrimony in this period, if no other children survived, some artisan women were able to inherit larger amounts of property which they could then use as dotal assets.

Women from superior trade artisan families, or who married non-artisan men of higher status, also tended to have higher than average dowries. The most important guilds in late medieval Valencia were those of the tailors, silversmiths and wooldressers. Indeed, the wooldresser guild was the most numerous, economically powerful and had the greatest social prestige.[12] While the women this book focuses on were not the wives and daughters of master artisans who controlled these guilds, nevertheless, their journeymen husbands and fathers were still members of these corporations and therefore garnered some status within their neighbourhoods. On 11 May 1421, Johana, the daughter of a wooldresser from Liria concluded a marriage contract with the silversmith Bernat Catala. As dowry she brought 100 pounds in household goods, jewellery and rented land.[13] Catala's higher status likely demanded a larger dowry from Johana. Similarly when Leonor, the daughter of a butcher from Morvedre married the merchant Nicholau Salvador in 1422, her above average dowry of seventy-seven pounds was influenced by Salvador's higher status as a merchant.[14] Overall, almost three-quarters of women whose dowries were above sixty pounds were widows, had deceased fathers or were from/marrying into a higher-status family.

Although my evidence clearly demonstrates that the average amount of artisan dowries was twenty to forty pounds, Paulino Iradiel has argued that, by the first decades of the fifteenth century, the average artisan dowry in Valencia was valued at fifty to 100 pounds, up from ten to fifteen pounds in the second half of the fourteenth century.[15] As Iradiel's spread for dowry size over this period is much smaller (ten to fifteen pounds), it appears somewhat more precise, although he does not provide documentary evidence to back up either of these claims. While it is apparent that Valencian dowries inflated during this period, Iradiel's figures suggest that dowries doubled from the second half of the fourteenth to the beginning of the fifteenth century.

It is likely that dowries would rise in accordance with general inflation. An increase in the cost of living meant that it was more expensive for husbands to support their wives, leading to the inflation of dowry size.[16] But wage and price evidence for late fourteenth and early fifteenth-century Valencia does not explain the twofold increase. Although wages did grow over this period, they did not do so by two times. In 1392, a journeyman rug-maker earned 48 pence/day for his labour. By 1420, his wages had increased to 52 pence/day. A carpenter's helper could earn 30 pence/day in 1392, a wage which increased to 36/pence a day by 1420. For journeyman masons, there was no apparent wage increase. The 42 pence/day wage that they earned in 1392 did not rise until the second half of the fifteenth-century.[17] Although information is far more sporadic for commodity prices, there does not appear to have been a huge increase in the cost of goods from the late fourteenth into the early fifteenth century. In fact, prices appear to have remained relatively stable or even fell during this period.

If the twofold increase in the size of artisan dowries cannot be explained by general inflation of the Valencian economy, what then was the cause? Dowry inflation is a topic that has been widely discussed by historians of medieval and early modern Italy, in particular, who have argued that this phenomenon was a plague on fathers desiring to marry their daughters well.[18] The reasons for the rapid inflation of Italian dowries during this period have been attributed to two central factors: age difference and social honour. As elite Italian men tended to marry women ten to twelve years their junior, the resulting surplus of women and competition for suitable grooms drove up dowry sizes.[19]

The stress on age difference and the importance of social honour impacting dowry size of elite women in late medieval and Renaissance Italy is not reflective of lower-status marriage patterns during this same period. In Valencia, artisan and *llaurador* women and men tended to be closer in age, with women marrying in their late teens to early twenties to grooms that were two to three years older.[20] Although research about the marriage age of this level of society in southern Europe is still developing, the information that is available indicates that the Valencian pattern

Table 3.2 Size of *llaurador* dowries, 1420–39

Pounds	Donzellas	Widows	Total
>20	0	4	4
20–40	36	8	44
41–60	22	2	24
61–80	5	2	7
81–100	11	1	12
101–150	5	2	7
150+	5	1	6
Total	84	20	104

was the norm. For example, Monica Chojnacka has found that urban labouring women and their grooms in Venice tended to be approximately the same age as those in Valencia.[21]

The later age of marriage for artisan and *llaurador* brides can be explained both by their need to accumulate enough money to pay for a dowry, as well as the necessary skills to attract a good husband.[22] Even if their fathers were providing the dowry, these women needed to be able to work with their husbands to keep the newly formed union afloat. Hence their ability to work would be equally as attractive as the size of their dowries. This aptitude for work by artisan women meant that grooms could marry earlier as the daily economic burdens of the household were borne by the conjugal couple together, something that was quite different from patrician marriages. For this reason, historians have often described lower-status marriages as more akin to partnerships, with each member of the couple working to support the household.[23]

The most plausible explanation for the increase in artisan dowry size from the fourteenth into the fifteenth century is the high mortality rate that existed within the city and the surrounding countryside. From the initial devastating onset in 1348, Valencia, like many other cities in medieval Europe, was hit with successive waves of plagues over the course of the late fourteenth and throughout the fifteenth century. Serious epidemics raged in the city in 1362, 1374–75, 1395, 1411, 1428 and 1439 when there were 7,200 deaths in one year alone.[24] Famine also hit Valencia, with 1435 a particularly bad year.[25] The mortality rate for children under 5 was above 50 per cent[26] with the average family having two surviving children.[27] With fewer children living until adulthood, artisan fathers had greater resources to expend on each child. Instead of dividing dotal money between three or four daughters, these men were able to provide larger dowries to fewer female children. In addition, other extended kin would have greater funds to donate to new brides as there were fewer demands on their resources.

Dowry size: *llauradors*

Like artisan women, the daughters of *llauradors* also averaged dowries that were between twenty and sixty pounds, with the largest cohort at twenty to forty pounds (see Table 3.2). For example, Caterina, the daughter of a *llaurador* from Liria, and the servant of a sailor from Valencia, brought a dowry of twenty pounds when she married the *llaurador* Antoni Eximeno of Ruçafa in 1432.[28] As with artisan women, 70 per cent of *llaurador* dowries were below sixty pounds. The similarity in dowry size between artisan and *llaurador* women is surprising, as one would expect *llaurador* dowries to be smaller, given that scholars have argued for a social devaluation of agricultural work in this period.

Over the course of the later Middle Ages, Valencian *llauradors* had been decreasing in status and wealth, in comparison to artisans. Paulino Iradiel has argued that agricultural work no longer held its previous importance in the city during this period, largely the result of the growth of guilds. *Llauradors* in Valencia did have confraternities; in fact there were four separate ones specifically for them. In fourteenth-century processions, *llauradors* had been placed close to the superior trades, but by 1459 these confraternities were grouped with the humblest artisan trades.[29] As the lines between confraternity and guild became more sharply drawn in the course of the fifteenth century, the artisan guilds grew in status, while the *llaurador* confraternities fell in comparison. Artisans had skills that allowed them to garner higher wages than *llauradors* working as day labourers. On average, journeymen made 30 to 40 per cent more than day labourers in their daily wages, indicating the greater skill necessary to perform their trades.[30] One would expect these higher wages to provide artisans with greater funds to dower their daughters and their higher social status to demand larger dowries than *llauradors* in order to marry honourably.

At the same time, however, there were some *llauradors* that were able to capitalize on the greater economic opportunities offered in Valencia during this period. Geographical proximity to the city of Valencia allowed them more opportunities to earn income which could be used to augment their daughters' dowries. As many *llauradors* lived in Valencia itself, and then farmed land in the *horta*, they were able to contract numerous day labourer jobs which would provide them with extra funds. Most *llauradors* performed a number of different economic tasks, alongside farming their family plots as these provided subsistence level production at best. Every member of the family contributed economically to the well-being of the household, which included providing daughters with dowries. Not only fathers but mothers sold their labour for a daily wage, with daughters themselves able to go into service. In this manner, a woman's entire family contributed to her dowry.

In addition, some *llaurador* families were able to avoid the pitfalls of partible inheritance by conducting land transactions among themselves in order to consolidate their holdings. Better off *llaurador* families utilized all branches of the family unit, organizing themselves to successfully work the various land parcels of the patrimony, some of which had been bequeathed to younger generations through inheritance and marriage.[31] This gave the family greater wealth which could then be used to create advantageous marriage alliances with higher-status members of Valencian society. For example, in 1420, the *llaurador* Bernat Prats provided a dowry of four hundred pounds for his daughter Mariana in her marriage to Jaume Roch, a merchant.[32] Prats held a great deal of land in the *horta*, farmed by day labourers and family members. His social ambitions ran higher than artisans and other *llauradors* for his daughter's marriage. As a wealthier farmer, Prats was able to contract a marriage of significant status for Mariana. Her four-hundred-pound dowry made her an attractive potential spouse and her father identified with those of higher status in the city, indicating that not all *llauradors* were scratching out a meagre existence.

Mariana Prats was clearly not a woman of labouring-status as her dowry was equivalent in size to the dotal assets of many elite Valencian women. But some lower-status *llaurador* women were able to provide dowries above sixty pounds. Similar to artisan women, widowhood, deceased fathers and marrying men of higher status all had a positive impact on the dowry size of *llauradors*. When Tomasa, the widow of a deceased *llaurador* married the *llaurador* Pere Exarch, her dotal assets were valued at 110 pounds.[33] Guillomena, the daughter of a deceased *llaurador* from Alboraya brought an equally large dowry of 100 pounds in cash, household goods and jewellery when she married the *llaurador* Bartolome Serra of Buralesa. The entirety of Guillomena's dowry came from a paternal inheritance handed over to Serra by her brother.[34] Tomasa's dotal assets could also have been augmented through inheritance, perhaps through a testamentary bequest from her first husband.

Another factor that influenced the amount of assets *llaurador* and artisan women brought as dotal property was the involvement of their fathers in the creation of their marriage contracts. Labouring-status women with larger dowries were considerably more likely to have marriage contracts concluded by their fathers than those women with dowries that fell in the twenty to sixty pound average. For example, on 1 January 1422 the *llaurador* Bartolome Miquel of Patraix concluded a dotal agreement with the *llaurador* Nicholau Pet of Rucafa for his daughter Jacmeta. As dowry, Miquel provided 100 pounds in cash, household goods and jewellery.[35] Like elite women who garnered considerably more dotal assets than women of artisan and *llaurador* background, the central role of fathers is linked to the higher value of these assets as well as the important social, political and economic ties created through these marriages.

Only 4 per cent of *llaurador* women in my sample had dowries that fell below twenty pounds, ranging from five to fifteen pounds. All women were widows. When Jacmeta, the widow of a *llaurador* from Valencia married the *llaurador* Joan Soriano of Piquanya, she brought as dowry a mere five pounds in cash.[36] Although the reasons behind the paltry amount of Jacmeta's dowry are left unspoken in her marriage contract, Jacmeta appears to have fallen on hard times after the death of her first husband. The economic well-being of widows left behind could be seriously affected by heavily mortgaged family patrimonies that might be seized by creditors at the husband's death. Although the *Furs* guaranteed women the return of their dowries at widowhood, if these assets were squandered during the marriage, there was little property left to restore. This may have been the case for Jacmeta who, unable to support herself from the remnants of her first husband's estate or from the meagre earnings she could garner, turned to marriage as a method of increasing her own and possibly her family's economic viability. So while some widows were able to use their status as a means of providing larger dowries, perhaps due to a testamentary bequest from their previous husbands, others struggled to gain enough assets to provide a few pounds as dowry to their new husbands.

In general, artisan and *llaurador* women married within their own status and the amount of property they brought as dowry was related to that which was deemed respectable for them. The average labouring-status dowry, at twenty to forty pounds, was ten to fifty times lower than the average dowry of merchant, patrician and noblewomen. For example, on 6 July 1423, Bernarda, the daughter of the deceased *honrat* draper Bernat Dalbesa, gave one thousand pounds as her dowry to Jaume de Vallmajor, also a draper.[37] In another marriage contract from the same register, *honrada* Castellena, daughter of the deceased *honrat* Mateu Vital, provided as her dowry to *honrat* Anthoni Castellens, two thousand pounds of which fifteen hundred had been left as a testamentary bequest by her father.[38] Both of these dowries were considerably higher than those of artisan and *llaurador* women, and demonstrate the connections between social status, family honour and dowry size in late medieval Valencia.

Dotal property: moveable assets

While the size of a woman's dowry was clearly related to social status, the composition of her dotal property was not. Artisan, *llaurador* and elite women all brought dowries that consisted of moveable goods (cash, household goods, clothing and jewellery), immoveable property (land and houses) and investments. This similarity points to the influence of patriarchal values at all levels of Valencian society on strategies for the transmission of property to women. As the Middle Ages came to an end, there were increasing attempts to exclude women from control of immoveable property in order to consolidate these assets in the hands of men.[39]

Approximately 80 per cent of artisan and *llaurador* dowries consisted exclusively of moveable property, most commonly a combination of cash, household goods and jewellery (see Table 3.3). For example, in her 1429 marriage contract with the *llaurador* Antoni Tarasquo of Paterna, Mariana, the daughter of Pasqual Pasqual, also a *llaurador*, provided 20 pounds as her dowry. Ten pounds of this property was in cash and a second ten pounds consisted of household goods and jewellery.[40] This kind of property was also the norm for artisan dowries such as that of Caterina, the widow of a bricklayer who brought fifteen pounds in household goods and jewellery when she married another bricklayer, Nicholau Martí.[41] While dotal contracts almost always indicated the division between cash and household goods/jewellery, they never distinguished the specific and

Table 3.3 Type of artisan and *llaurador* dotal assets, 1420–39

	Artisan	Llaurador	Total
Moveable assets	132	68	200
Immoveable assets	5	6	11
Combination (moveable and immoveable)	15	17	32
Censals plus moveable or immoveable	3	3	6
Usufruct rights	0	1	1
Total	155	95	250

separate value of household goods or jewellery being donated but instead refer to them together as '*raubis et jocalibus*'.

The reasons behind the predominance of this kind of property for artisan and *llaurador* dowries are manifold. To begin with, it was difficult for those of labouring-status to amass immoveable property – land and houses, whether rented or owned outright. Most *llauradors*, and some artisans, did hold some form of agricultural land, usually in emphyteutic tenure. This mode of landholding gave the renter a perpetual right to cultivate the land, provided they paid a fixed rent, at a fixed time, to the owner. Under this system, the renter could sell or donate the land by testament or other means but if the person holding the land died without heirs, the land then reverted to the lord. Given the subsistence nature of Valencian farming, and the laws of partible inheritance, most families wanted to keep their land holdings as intact as possible. They therefore preferred to provide their daughters with other kinds of property for their dowries which would have less effect on the economic survival of the natal family unit. Since daughters brought wealth out of the natal family through marriage, *llaurador* families donated moveable property such as cash, household goods and jewellery as their dowries, leaving the family land holdings to be passed on to sons as a protective measure. Although it was more common for artisan families to own or rent houses in the city than to own or rent agricultural property in the *horta*, again the desire to keep the family patrimony as intact as possible likely influenced their choice of moveable dotal property.

Another reason for preferring moveable goods for dowries was the relative stability of this kind of property in comparison to land or agricultural produce.[42] Land could be devalued and produce was perishable, making the woman's dotal investment somewhat volatile. Cash, jewellery, household goods and clothing remained stable in value and were therefore easily returned at the dissolution of the marriage. The volatility of land as dotal property was dependent upon whether or not its value had been estimated at the signing of the marriage contract. Valencian law protected women against the possible devaluing of their dotal property by stipulating that if a wife gave estimated property as her dowry, her husband was obliged to return the property intact, or its estimated value.[43] Both moveable and immoveable property could be estimated; however the *Furs* mandated that all estimations of dotal property had to be made prior to the marriage as those estimations made after were not considered valid.[44] If a woman's dowry consisted of unestimated property, her husband was only obligated to return the property itself at the end of the marriage.[45]

Although estimated dotal property ensured that wives received the full value of their dowries when their marriages were dissolved, this kind of property valuation was not always to their benefit. The *Furs* stipulated that all fruits produced from estimated property, whether agricultural produce from land or rents from houses, became the property of the husband.[46] The wife was only entitled to the property or a payment equivalent to its value, removing her right to anything produced from it for the duration of the marriage. Her husband was responsible for any losses to the estimated dotal property which helped to ensure that his wife was not penalized if he administered this property badly. Indeed, the misuse (*mal usar*) and poor administration (*mal administrat*) of dotal assets was often used by wives as a reason to seek the restitution of their dowries form their still-living husbands. The *Furs* may have legislated that the wife had a right to her full estimated dowry at the end of the marriage, but some women were obviously concerned that their husbands would devalue this property to the point of no return and therefore sought its restitution earlier. In contrast, for a wife whose dotal assets were unestimated, while she received all fruits, she was equally responsible for all losses.[47] Valencian law may have contained a series of checks to ensure wives regained their dotal property, but this protection was ambiguous. On the one hand, women were afforded security against dotal loss while being denied the right to any gains. On the other hand, they had the chance of dotal increase while also being responsible for potential loss.

While most estimated property consisted of immoveable assets, notarial evidence demonstrates that this was not always the case. In her 1429 marriage contract the widow Celestina Deroda provided a 150-pound dowry to the silversmith Barthomeu Olma which included a house in the parish of St Caterina worth 100 pounds, and all of the furnishings contained within, estimated at fifty pounds.[48] This worked to Celestina's advantage since furnishings, through use, could have easily depreciated in value. Women with considerably smaller dowries than Celestina's also occasionally had their property estimated prior to marriage. For example, Caterina, the daughter of a sailor from Valencia brought a dowry of fifty pounds when she married the sailor Pere de Murneto in 1422.[49] Thirty pounds of her dowry was cash with the remaining twenty pounds in estimated household goods and jewellery.

The fact that some artisan and *llaurador* women had worked as servants prior to marrying, is another factor determining the composition of their dotal property. Like elsewhere in the Mediterranean region, Valencian girls who worked as domestic servants to raise dotal funds were paid in cash, household goods and clothing.[50] For example, on 14

November 1433 Pere Rossell concluded a service contract for his daughter Pastasia with the widow of a dyer. Pastasia's contract was for six years, at the end of which she was to be paid thirty-four pounds in cash and household goods.[51] Five years later, in 1438, Pastasia married Ferdinand Sanchez, an espadrille-maker and brought as dowry, thirty-five pounds, also in cash and household goods.[52] An *apocha* or receipt for these assets was drawn up one year later between Pastasia, her husband Ferdinand and her former mistress Caterina Madriz.[53] Numerous other marriage contracts from former servants also demonstrate that their dowries generally consisted of a combination of cash, household goods and jewellery. There were some exceptions to this rule, but even in such cases the cash part of the woman's dowry was usually the payment for her work as a domestic servant

The legal role of dowries to bear the burden of matrimony also reflects the prevalence of moveable assets in artisan and *llaurador* dowries. Roman law mandated that it was only fair that husbands should receive the fruits of their wives' dowries as it was their responsibility to provide for the family[54] and the romanized legal codes of southern Europe incorporated this concept into their clauses on marriage and dowries.[55] The use of the dowry as an economic foundation for the conjugal union varied, dependent upon a couple's social status. For master artisans, dowries were used as capital to set up workshops, or the purchase of a house which would act as both working and living space. For artisans of lower status, dotal cash bought tools necessary for the practice of their craft. In some cases, a woman's dowry actually consisted of these tools, most notably for women marrying silk weavers.[56] For *llauradors*, dotal money was used to rent land in the *horta* or to buy implements necessary for farming property already held. Cash could also be used to rent rooms, a small house or an apartment as a living space for the couple. Goods such as linens, furniture and cooking utensils that were donated as dotal property provided the couple with effects necessary to set up their new household.

The final reason for the prevalence of moveable property for the dowries of artisan and *llaurador* women was linked to the tradition of the bridal trousseau, or *aixovar*. This property customarily consisted of the clothing, jewellery, cooking utensils, linens and other household goods that brides brought to their new marriages. Historians have argued that this term *aixovar* came to be synonymous with *exovar*, the Catalan word used to indicate a woman's dowry, although there is much debate as to how this practice came to be implemented in Valencian law and society.[57] Tracing the links between dowries and trousseau is difficult, especially in an area such as Valencia which was settled by Muslims, Aragonese,

Catalans as well as other Europeans. Each of these groups brought their own ideas and practices making it difficult to determine clearly where practices followed in fifteenth-century Valencia derived. Almost all medieval Mediterranean societies, whether Muslim, Christian or Jewish, had a marital system which entailed some form of property exchange. This could be modelled on a bridewealth system (payment by the groom or his family to the bride or her family) or a dotal one. It was also customary in most medieval Mediterranean societies and cultures that women brought a 'trousseau', in some cases in addition to their dowries, at others included in them.[58]

Overall, it is evident that the Valencian *exovar* was greatly influenced by the Catalan and Aragonese customary practice of women bringing clothing, household goods and jewellery to a marriage along with their cash dowries. In the early fifteenth century, 80 per cent of artisan and *llaurador* women brought household goods and/or jewellery as part of their dowries. This practice represents a blending of Catalan custom with the romanized dowry mandated by the *Furs* and accounts for the high percentage of artisan and *llaurador* women who brought household goods and/or jewellery as part of their dotal property.

Dotal property: immoveable assets

While the majority of artisan and *llaurador* women had dowries consisting of moveable property, some women of this status were able to bring other kinds of assets. Forty-five out of 250 artisan and *llaurador* women provided immoveable property (rented land and houses) as part of their dowries. For some of these women, their entire dowries consisted of immoveable property. This was the case for Caterina, the widow of a weaver who brought a forty-five-pound dowry when she married the cobbler Jacob Castloses in 1431. These assets were divided between rights to a rented house in the city and control over two pieces of agricultural land in the *horta*.[59] For the most part, however, labouring-status women brought immoveable property as only one part of their dotal assets with the remainder of the assets in cash, household goods and jewellery.

Artisan and *llaurador* women with immoveable dotal assets had two common characteristics: the large size of their dowries and their family/marital background. In terms of monetary value, 80 per cent of artisan dowries with immoveable property and 60 per cent of *llaurador* ones were above the twenty to forty pound average. Approximately 40 per cent of these women had dowries that were over eighty pounds. This ability to generate higher amounts of dotal funds meant they were better off financially than many of their artisan and *llaurador* neighbours, allowing them to have access to immoveable property which could then be transferred to their own or their daughters' dowries.

The largest group of artisan and *llaurador* women who brought immoveable dotal property were those that could be classified as independent, either financially and/or legally; the majority of these women had deceased fathers or were widows. Given that women of this background tended to have higher than average dowries, it is therefore not surprising that this group also had the majority of dowries containing immoveable assets. Although women whose fathers were deceased at the time of their marriages could be legally under the control of a guardian, especially if they were under the age of 20, financially they had already received an inheritance from their fathers. Control of that inheritance likely fell to their guardians until they married. In most cases, those guardians were their mothers who often played important economic roles in managing such assets which could be substantial and include land or houses, as Valencia followed a system of partible inheritance.[60] The inheritance of such kinds of immoveable was most likely if no male siblings survived.

The *Furs* also stated that there was no law against women giving all of their property as dowry[61] and therefore the dowries of women with deceased fathers could potentially be larger and/or include immoveable assets and investments in comparison to those of women marrying while their fathers were still alive. Of course, such heiresses did not have to give the entirety of their inheritance as dowry. Any property that they held outside of their dotal assets, called *bens parafernals*, was administered by their husbands for the duration of the marriage; however, wives retained complete right of alienation over this property at all times.

While some *donzellas* used testamentary bequests of immovable assets as dotal property, widows also received an inheritance from their fathers which was then included in their dowries. As daughters first married between the ages of 17 and 20, and labouring-status fathers tended not to live past 50, it was unlikely their fathers would be alive for their subsequent marriages. Widows inherited immoveable property and investments from their husbands as well which were then included as part of their dotal assets in subsequent marriages. The *Furs* tried to mandate against the exchange of property by spouses while alive, and discouraged this practice in testamentary bequests. It forbade all living-will donations between spouses beyond last-breath requests and encouraged husbands and wives to bequeath their estates to their children;[62] however, testamentary evidence indicates that men did will immoveable property and investments to their wives as both co- and central heirs. For example, the *llaurador* Antoni Speralbo divided his property equally between his daughter, Caterina, who was married to a weaver, and his wife, also Caterina. His wife received several pieces of rented land in the *horta* which she was to retain even if she remarried.[63] The elder Caterina was also named executrix of her husband's estate, a common practice for those of labouring-status which was forbidden by the *Furs*.[64] In another testament from 1428, the hosteller Joan Portagelet gave his wife Vicenta the rights to his rented house in Valencia. Portagelet donated an additional forty pounds to his niece Margalita to be used for her dowry at marriage.[65] He appears not to have living children of his own, which may explain the donation of immovable property to his wife. Without offspring to bequeath such assets to, some labouring-status men chose to give their immovable property to their spouses rather than seeking other male extended family members as heirs. Widows whose previous marriages had been governed by a *germanía* contract could also receive immoveable property which could then be used as dotal assets in their subsequent marriages. These women were entitled to half of the total marital assets which would include any immoveable property the couple had controlled.

Both artisan and *llaurador* women brought rented land and houses as part of their immoveable dotal assets; however, the type and quality of such land and value of such living spaces was affected by socio-economic background and gender. In general, *llaurador* women brought slightly larger and better-quality land as dowry property than artisan women. The rented plots brought by *llaurador* women measured from 1 to 15 *fanecades* (one *fanecada* = one-twelfth hectare), although the majority were 4 to 9 *fanecades* in size.[66] The rent paid on these plots varied from 2 sous, 6 *diners* to 21 sous per year. For example, in her 1429 marriage contract to the *llaurador* Ramón Pujol, Ursola, the daughter of the *llaurador* Ferran Davilla of El Puig, brought a total dowry of 100 pounds that contained two pieces of land. One parcel was 15 *fanecades* with a yearly rent of 14 sous, the other of 10 *fanecades* with the annual rent of 10 sous.[67] The rented land brought by artisan women as part of their dowries was of modest size and value. These plots measured approximately one to 4 *fanecades* for which the tenant paid 3 to 7 sous a year in rent.

Interestingly, half of all *llaurador* women who brought rented land as dotal property had dowries of average size (twenty to forty pounds). For example, in her dowry contract of 13 August 1430, Johana, the daughter of the *llaurador* Simon Bonfill of Turis brought twenty pounds in rented land (4 *fanecadas* of vineyards with annual rent of 3 sous and 6 *fanecades* of land in Tirol with an unknown yearly rent) when she married Pere Marti.[68] Simon Bonfill donated these assets to his daughter as dotal property. In another contract from 1425, the widow Nicholana provided a dowry of thirty pounds in rented land for her marriage to the *llaurador* Andreu Casals of Massalfassar.[69] The fact that 50 per cent of *llaurador* women who brought rented land as dotal property had dowries in the twenty to forty pound range contrast sharply with the situation for artisan women. Only one out of the ten artisan women with rented land as dotal property had an average size dowry. The remaining nine had dowries above fifty pounds, with several over 100 pounds.

As the centrally important commodity for *llaurador* families, rented land as dotal assets worked to create more advantageous marriages for women with smaller dowries. For artisan women, other types of dotal assets were more attractive to grooms (such as tools, rented living spaces or cash to buy such items). Indeed, artisans tended to invest most of their labour (and economic power) in urban industry. The rented land they controlled in the *horta* did help to diversify their interests, providing an income through either rent paid by a tenant or through the sale at market of any crops produced. The size of these plots ensured that this extra revenue was likely miniscule, but it could help the family to survive any economic hardship. Artisan families were therefore perhaps reluctant to allow such assets to be brought outside of the family.

Although *llaurador* women tended to bring larger pieces of rented land as part of their immoveable dotal property than artisan women, it is clear they received smaller pieces and possibly inferior land compared to that granted to *llaurador* men by their families at the time of their marriages. Alongside many dowry contracts, the notarial records from Valencia contain large number of *donationes inter vivos*, or living-will donations, granted to grooms by their families on the occasion of their marriages. For example, on 28 April 1426, the *llaurador* Joan Pruella (Sr) donated 9 *fanecades* of agricultural land in Russafa to his son Joan Pruella (Jr), also a *llaurador*, on the occasion of his marriage to Elionora, the daughter of a tailor. The rent for this land was 63 sous a year, indicating that the land was likely of high quality and irrigated.[70] While the size of the land grant made to Joan Pruella (Jr) by his father was not necessarily larger than those made to *llaurador* women, its annual worth was much higher, which demonstrates the desire of *llaurador* families to prevent their most valuable resources from leaving the kin group.

Some *llaurador* and artisan women received rented land earmarked for their dowries as part of their paternal inheritance.[71] This was the case for the three daughters of the *llaurador* Antoni Dalresa of Matamoros who were each given eleven *fanecades* of land in the *horta* in their father's will to be handed over on the occasion of their marriages and not before (*de llur matrimoni et no abans*). The bulk of Dalresa's estate was bequeathed to his son Jaume who was still a minor.[72] But for the most part, daughters received large amounts of land as the central heirs of their fathers in the absence of sons. Often paternal testaments indicated that part of this inheritance was to be used specifically for the daughters' dowries, or as part of their marital donation. Such was the case of Ursola, the daughter of the deceased *llaurador* Bernat Cebria, who brought six pieces of leasehold land valued at 110 pounds as part of her 175-pound dowry in her marriage to the *llaurador* Jaume Ametler of Massamagrell in 1429. This property had been bequeathed to Ursola in her father's 1425 will, which also granted Ursola's elder sister Caterina sixty pounds in rented land for her marriage to the *llaurador* Antoni Carbonell in the same year. Alongside her marital donation, the elder daughter Caterina was made her father's central heir, since he had no male offspring, which may account for the smaller amount of money provided for her marriage to Carbonell.[73]

While *llaurador* women were more likely to bring leasehold land, rented houses were more prevalent for artisan women as part of their immoveable dotal property. The economic vitality and demographic expansion of Valencia during the fifteenth century presented the city with constant challenges in providing sufficient housing. While master artisans might own the house in which they worked and lived, journeymen and their families rented their living spaces. Dotal property which included rented housing was attractive to artisans trying to establish themselves in the city, particularly if they had recently immigrated. Architecturally, Valencian houses had two floors, with some even having an attic. The lower floors were used for artisan workshops and stores; the upper ones for living spaces.[74] Extra rooms and attic spaces were rented out to *llaurador* and journeymen artisan families who could not afford the cost of an entire dwelling. These spaces could even be sublet to others for a higher price providing some income for the original renter.[75] As dowry contracts demonstrate, these rented properties could be passed down by families, through inheritance or as dotal property. For example, in his testament from 1428, the carter Pasqual Alvarro left his daughter Sperança a house in Valencia to be used as part of her dotal property. The yearly rent on the property was 9 sous and it was to be held in trust by his wife Margalida as executor of his estate until the time of Sperança's marriage.[76]

Much like leasehold land, artisan and *llaurador* men were given rented houses as *donations inter vivos* at the time of their marriages. Not surprisingly, these houses had higher rents and were worth more than those given to labouring-status women as dotal assets. On 22 August 1425, the dyer Andrea Solanes donated a house in Valencia with an annual rent of 28 sous to his son Joan Solanes, also a dyer and his new bride Bonaventura.[77] While a few artisan women brought houses valued as highly as 100 pounds, the vast majority were worth less than fifty pounds. The rents for these properties tended to fall below 20 sous per annum. Solanes was one of two artisan men who received this kind of property at marriage from their families. More typically, artisan *donationes inter vivos* consisted of cash and artisanal tools; goods that were useful in setting themselves up to support a new household. The situation was different for *llaurador* men who commonly received the rights to a rented house in the *horta* alongside various pieces of rented land from their families at the time of marriage. In fact, just over half of *llaurador* men given a *donatio inter vivos* when marrying received a rented house as part of these assets.

Dotal property: *censals*

The least common type of dotal assets brought by women of *llaurador* and artisan status were *censals*, a form of investment. Only 3 per cent of *llaurador* and artisan women had dowries which contained *censals*. With *censals*, the investor lent a certain amount of money as capital to a vendor and in return he or she received an annuity plus stipulated interest. This form of investment was developed in the fourteenth century by the Valencian municipal government as a means of dealing with public debt.[78] The funds raised through the sale of *censals* were used to finance such things as royal loans, wars and city improvements.[79] Although the sale of *censals* went against the Catholic Church's pronouncements against usury, they were viewed as less morally problematic since the interest paid on *censals* was much lower than that of regular loans (7–8 per cent versus 20 per cent).[80] *Censals* were attractive because of their flexibility as their ownership could be transferred to another person through inheritance, as living-will donations or as dotal property.

Censals originated as a form of raising municipal funds; however, individuals of varied socio-economic background soon came to favour them as a form of investment. Members of the nobility and urban patriciate of Valencia participated in the city's financial market holding *censals* with the municipal government. This kind of municipal investment was present in many European cities and continued to develop into the early modern period.[81] Noble and patrician women who brought *censals* as part of their dowries had large sums invested which paid out a handsome annuity. On 6 July 1430, Guillomena, the daughter of *honrat*

Pere Vich of Xàtiva, signed a dotal contract with *honrat* Pere Lorent, a notary of Valencia. Guillomena brought a total dowry of 600 pounds which included 150 pounds in *censals* valued at 210 sous annually.[82] In the following year, Johana, the daughter of the deceased merchant Bernat Sant brought a 675-pound dowry consisting entirely of *censals*. The first *censal*, worth 350 pounds, paid 500 sous annually; the second, worth 325 pounds, paid another 500 sous per year.[83] These *censals*, held with the Valencian municipal government, would have provided both of these women and their husbands with a comfortable yearly income.

Although members of the Valencian nobility and patriciate were the primary investors in municipal *censals*, those of more modest economic means also had access to this form of investment through lower-level or private contracts. Private *censal* contracts allowed people to raise money quickly to pay for dowries, buy horses or oxen, rent land or houses or purchase any necessary tools. With private *censals*, the investor provided the capital and the debtor then repaid the principal, plus interest, in the form of an annual pension. The interest rate for private *censals* was 8.33 per cent; a little higher than the 7.14 per cent paid out for municipal *censals*.[84] The monetary amount invested and the annuities paid out on private *censals* were much lower than public ones and this is reflected in the *censals* brought by artisan and *llaurador* women as part of their dowries. In 1421, Bartolomena, the widow of the tanner Dominic Çaro, brought sixty pounds in *censals* worth ninety sous annually as part of her sixty-five-pound dowry in her marriage to the sailor Berenguer Roig. The annuities on these *censals* were paid by the tanner Pasqual Marti and his wife Margalida for a term of approximately twelve years.[85] In another example from 1431, Caterina, a widow and the daughter of a deceased *llaurador* brought eighty-six pounds in two separate *censals* as part of her dowry. A cobbler paid the 45 sous annuity of the first *censal* and a wooldresser and his wife paid the 49 sous annuity of the second one.[86] The monetary amount of and the annuities paid on these *censals* were considerably lower than the municipal bonds held by the patrician and merchant women indicated above; however the annual income they generated would have been equally as important, and attractive, as dotal property.

In general, most investors in *censals* were urban residents, although this was not always the case, as evidence from labouring-status dowry contracts indicates. Seventy per cent of lower-status women who brought *censals* as part of their dowries were widows or had deceased fathers, demonstrating once again that legal/financial independence could influence a woman's access to property beyond moveable goods. These women inherited *censals* from their husbands, fathers and mothers. For example, the *llaurador* Luis Mestre of El Puig handed over a dowry of eighty pounds to the *llaurador* Nadal Defort of Foyos for his sister Francesca. The dotal property included twenty-nine pounds, 10 sous in two *censals*; the first valued at eighteen pounds paid an annuity of 30 sous, the second at eleven pounds 10 sous paid an annuity of 18 sous. Two separate *llaurador* men paid the annuities on these investments. Mestre indicates that this property had been bequeathed to Francesca by their father Francesc in his last will and testament.[87] Women could also receive *censals* as testamentary dotal bequests from their mothers as in the case of Ursola, the daughter of a baker, whose mother Tuçenta bequeathed *censals* valued at 82 sous annually to be given to her at the time of her contract of marriage.[88] We have no way of knowing whether or not Tuçenta bought these *censals* as an investment for her young daughter's future marriage or if she herself had been given them at the time of her own marriage to Ursola's father. Unlike access to immoveable property, which was increasingly restricted for women during the late medieval period, *censals* were less problematic as female-owned assets. Given that *censals* were investments bought with cash, they could represent the amount of money designated by a woman's family for her dowry. The use of them was therefore free of the anxiety surrounding the dissolution of family patrimonies.

Censals were used as a way to invest for dowries, both for young girls and by widows. For the parents of young girls, investing in *censals* provided them with a fairly stable method of financially protecting their daughters' dowries until the time of their marriages. In this way, *censals* were similar in intent to the *Monte delle doti* of Florence. While the *Monte delle doti* guaranteed an eventual income amount, *censals* established an ongoing income stream that was quite attractive as dotal property, although it is still unknown how many Valencian patrician and noble families made use of *censals* in the same way that those of the Florentine privileged classes used the *Monte* fund. For widows, the annuity from *censals* provided a regular income which could be essential if they lost all other forms of support with their husbands' deaths. Evidence from other medieval cities demonstrates that wealthy widows often made these kinds of investments with their dotal property as a form of livelihood.[89] Whether initially purchased by their families, their husbands, or by themselves, *censals* as dotal property could be crucial to the survival of women in widowhood.

Dotal property: usufruct rights

On 7 December 1419, Caterina, the widow of Pere Enyego of Meliana and the daughter of Bernat Gil of Quart, contracted a marriage with Arnau Pujol (Jr) of Almàssera.[90] In her first marriage to Enyego, Caterina moved from her father's house in Quart, just east of Valencia city's walls, to Meliana, located 6 kilometres north and closer to the Mediterranean sea. In her second marriage to Arnau Pujol, Caterina remained in the northern part of the *horta* moving a few kilometres south to Almàssera. Her dotal contract with Pujol states:

> In the name of God, I Caterina, a widow, the daughter of Bernat Gil of Quart and once the wife of Pere Enyego of Meliana, freely with the will and consent of the same, my abovesaid father and my mother and other relatives, in contemplation of the marriage about to be concluded between myself and you, Arnal Pujol (Jr) of Almàssera confirm for you, in and for my dowry according to the laws of Valencia, fifty pounds of Valencian money which I hold and which pertain to me in *the goods of the above said man, that is my first husband, in usufruct by virtue of his testament for all of my life, both with a husband and without one.* [author's emphases][91]

Caterina's marriage contract is unusual because of the kind of property she brought as her dowry. The description of her dotal property as 'the goods of the above said man, that is my first husband [which I hold] in usufruct by virtue of his testament' goes directly against Valencian law which explicitly, in several clauses, denies widows the right to take their deceased husbands' property into any subsequent marriages.[92] Although artisan and *llaurador* women did in fact bring property belonging to previous spouses into subsequent marriages as dotal assets, Caterina is the only widow I found who explicitly described her dotal property as deriving from usufruct rights over her first husband's goods.

One key factor in Caterina's use of these rights as dotal assets in her second marriage is that she appears to have no children from her union with Pere Enyego. If Caterina and Pere did not have children, her claim to the usufruct rights of his property was stronger, especially if she was named his universal heir; however, even in such circumstances, Caterina's donation of usufruct rights to her first husband's property as dowry for her second marriage still went against the precepts espoused in the *Furs*. If they so chose, any other surviving heirs of Pere Enyego had grounds for a civil suit against Caterina to disallow her use of these assets in such a manner but there is no evidence that such a case was brought before the Valencian civil courts.

The receipt of usufruct rights over their husbands' property was common for widows throughout southern Europe in the High Middle Ages but historians such as Stephen Bensch have argued that this practice was decreasing by the end of the thirteenth century.[93] Evidence from Valencian testaments in the fifteenth century demonstrate that while this may have been the case for noble and patrician women (the group examined by Bensch for Barcelona), this was not necessarily so for those of a lower social status. Of the sixty-four testaments of artisan and *llaurador* men examined, widows were given usufruct rights over their husbands' property in just over half (thirty-five). While this does not conform to Paulino Iradiel's assertion that artisan widows, in particular, were always given usufruct rights,[94] it does demonstrate that husbands both wanted to provide for their surviving spouses and trusted their widows' administration of their estates.

Most of the testaments granting usufruct rights to widows had one condition. The widows of these men would only retain the right to administer their deceased spouses' property if they remained unmarried. These stipulations were reinforced by the *Furs* which mandated that remarrying widows must relinquish all control of their former husbands' goods to his heirs, whether or not the couple had surviving children. For example, on 17 January 1439 Caterina, the widow of *llaurador* Dominic Perez of Buralesa concluded a contract with her son Salvator, handing over control of her deceased husband's property. The document following this donation in the notary's register was Caterina's marriage contract with the *llaurador* Joan Dari, also of Buralesa and thus her transfer of Perez's property was prompted by her second marriage.[95] While remarriage was common in late medieval Europe, religious ideals held that widows should remain loyal to their husbands' memories, living a life of chastity and spending their days in prayer for their deceased spouses' souls. Mandating that wives give up usufruct rights upon remarriage helped to emphasize this ideology (as well as keep property out of the hands of another kin group), but the economic realities of life for labouring-status widows meant that some had no choice but to seek out another spouse.

Lo creix (the counter-gift)

While the dowry took precedence in the Valencian matrimonial property regime, the *creix* was an essential part of this system, at least for virgin brides. Derived from the Roman *donatio propter nuptias* (gift on account of marriage) and given in exchange for a bride's virginity, the *creix* only came under the control of a woman once she was widowed. While the

Furs stated that the *creix* was to return to the husband's family once the widow was deceased, until such time, she had full control of these assets and was not necessarily willing to follow the wishes of her late husband's kin group regarding their use.

Some widows chose to use *creix* assets as part of their dotal property in subsequent marriages. It is difficult to determine how many remarrying artisan and *llaurador* wives did so as their marriage contracts do not necessarily indicate from where their dotal assets are derived; however, extant evidence from elite marriage contracts demonstrates that some women from late medieval Valencia used *creix* property in this way. When Ursola, the widow of the deceased merchant Antoni Bo married *honrat* Joan Mayues in 1434, she brought a dowry valued at four hundred pounds. The assets that made up this property included a *censal* worth 87 sous per annum which was part of the *creix* she received from the estate of her deceased husband.[96] Although the marital families of widows likely preferred they did not use *creix* assets in such a way, as long as they ensured the original *creix* amount was bequeathed to any children from their first union, utilizing such property in this manner was licit.

The *Furs* may have banned men from giving their widow brides a *creix*, but the code did make allowances for other kinds of gifts. Six out of ninety-seven widows who concluded a dotal contract in the sample examined for this book received a donation from their grooms at marriage. The size of these gifts varied enormously. For example, the widow Caterina received twenty-five pounds, half the value of her dowry, from Arnal Pujol (Jr), a gift comparable in amount to a *creix*.[97] In contrast, the *llaurador* Joan Soriano gave his bride, Jacmeta, the widow of another *llaurador*, twenty pounds, a gift four times the value of her dowry.[98] It was entirely up to the discretion of the groom whether or not he wanted to give a donation, as well as how large this gift would be. Unlike the *creix*, these donations were optional and while some widows, such as Jacmeta, benefited greatly, most received nothing at all.

Those grooms who did provide gifts to their widow brides included provisions in their marriage contracts to ensure these donations were not considered a *creix*. For example, the dotal contract of the sailor Sanxo Ferran and the widow Elionor stated that although Sanxo was not obliged to give Elionor an *augmentum* according to the *Furs* because she was a widow, he was providing her with a ten-pound donation on account of their marriage.[99] Other grooms chose to have a *donatio inter vivos* attached to their marriage contract instead. Such was the case for Clemens Dabella, whose *donatio inter vivos* to the widow Francesca said 'in contemplation of the said marriage, He made a donation to the said

Francesca, his future wife, of twenty pounds of Valencian money, which he promised to give her after his death.[100] Through these kinds of notarial instruments, grooms were still able to provide their brides with assets to aid them in future widowhood, the function of the *creix* for *donzella* brides; however, they protected the notaries who drew them up from the possibility of losing their offices for disobeying the law.

The emphasis placed by the *Furs* on virginity as a condition for payment of the *creix* was unique to the Crown of Aragon, and appears to be distinctly Catalan.[101] In the Castilian territories of the Iberian peninsula, widows were not barred from receiving the counter-gift (known here as the *arras*) although Mariá Gámez Montalvo has demonstrated that some marriage contracts did include the justification that this gift was made 'for the honour of your person and virginity'.[102] Elsewhere in southern Europe, husbands' counter-gifts were directly related to the Roman *donatio propter nuptias* and were always given to women, regardless of their marital and sexual background.

Legally, the amount of the *creix* was set at half the value of a woman's dowry. This ratio followed other Catalan areas but was different from Castile, where, by the end of the fifteenth century, the size of the counter-gift became insignificant in comparison to the dowry.[103] In Italy, the size of women's counter-gifts was dependent on their social status and geographical location. For example, Florentine law required that all women receive a counter-gift, but Christiane Klapisch-Zuber argues that this was very small in comparison to the size of their dowries.[104] This contrasted with Genoa, where legally the *antefactum* (the Genoese term for the counter-gift) was to be no more than one-half the value of the dowry.[105] In practice, the size was entirely dependent on social status, as women of artisan background could receive *antefacti* that equalled or exceeded their dowries.[106]

Despite the great detail that some artisan and *llaurador* marriage contracts contain about dotal property, they are frustratingly silent on that which made up the *creix*. Where dotal property was, at the very least, described as 'money, household goods and jewellery', the *creix* was only mentioned in monetary form with no indication of what type of property grooms used to provide this donation to their new brides. As the *creix* was held in trust for women by their husbands, and not handed over until they became widows, the method of payment was dependent upon financial status of their spouses at death. One solitary notarial contract from Valencia provides us with some indication of the possible kinds of property that could be given as *creix* for labouring-status women, as well as the possible origin of this property. On 18 March 1425, Bonanat

Renar of Picanya made a living-will donation to Guillem Nogera, also of Picanya, who contracted marriage with Johana, the daughter of Dominic Martínez of Torrent, on the same day.[107] This property had belonged to Noguera's mother and was held in trust by Renar until the time of Guillem's marriage. A condition in this woman's will stipulated that this property was to be used by Nogera for his new wife's *creix*. Nogera received one *troceum* of agricultural land in Picanya, held under the dominion of the count of Torrent, along with 2 *fanecades* of agricultural land in the same location. The rents paid on this property were not indicated. In one of the two marriage contracts between Guillem and Johana that followed, Johana's father Dominic Martínez handed over a dowry worth thirty pounds in cash.

While the existence of a single piece of evidence detailing the type of property of which a *creix* could consist is certainly not conclusive in any way, it does allow us to make some very tentative general points about the kinds of assets which artisan and *llaurador* women may have received. The testamentary transmission of this property from Guillem's mother to her son suggests that she herself had received it as her *creix* from Guillem's father at his death. Although a woman had free use of her *creix* upon widowhood, at her own death, if the couple had living children, its ownership was to pass to them. If they did not have offspring, the *creix* property was to revert to the person who had originally donated it or his heirs.[108] These stipulations allowed women to pass on their *creix* to their children, which was the case with Guillem's mother. At her husband's death, this widow was given these plots of land in Picanya as a means of support, possibly with the understanding that they would later be passed onto her son. The transmission of immoveable property as *creix* did not permanently remove it from the family patrimony like dowries. Rather, its ownership was temporarily transferred. For this reason, land rights along with other immoveable property such as house rights or investments such as *censals*, would be attractive as counter-gift assets.

But given the prevalence of moveable goods as dotal assets, I suspect that Guillem's reception of land earmarked for the *creix* was somewhat unusual. If artisan and *llaurador* women rarely received immoveable property or investments as part of their dowries, it seems unlikely, despite the fact that it would eventually return to the family patrimony, that these kinds of assets would have been given to them for their *creix*. For while the *Furs* stipulated that the *creix* was to be passed down to a couple's heirs or returned to its original donor upon the widow's death, it also allowed women to retain control of this property if they remarried, provided they did so after the year of mourning (*any de plor*).[109] This article meant that any property which they controlled as their *creix* would be removed from their first husbands' patrimony for the duration of their subsequent marriages. At their deaths, it was eventually passed down to any children from their first marriages, but for during their remarriages it was controlled by other men. In addition, artisan and *llaurador* men and their families did not necessarily own enough immoveable goods to give away as *creix*, which made it far more likely that they would use moveable assets for this purpose. It was left to a husband's discretion what type of property the *creix* was to consist of. Unfortunately, the sources remain silent in providing us with these details.

Overwhelmingly, women of artisan and *llaurador* status followed a dotal regime of marital property, bringing a dowry and receiving a *creix* worth half its value if they were *donzellas*. A significant minority, however, signed marriage contracts of a very different nature which did not stipulate the dowry system mandated by the *Furs*. These were *germanía* contracts which were based on a community of goods regime that saw a married couple share equally in the conjugal assets. It is to these 'exceptions' which we will now turn.

Notes

1 Donald E. Queller and Thomas F. Madden, 'Father of the Bride: Fathers, Daughters and Dowries in Late Medieval and Early Renaissance Venice' *Renaissance Quarterly*, 46(4) (winter 1993), p. 698.
2 Iradiel, 'Familia y función', p. 253.
3 Chojnacki, 'Dowries and Kinsmen', p. 134; Furió, *Història del País Valencià*, p. 198.
4 Iradiel, 'Familia y función', p. 242.
5 APPV 23414, Joan Peris, non-paginated (23 July 1435).
6 One such woman was Maria, the widow of a wooldresser. On 26 November 1438 she donated ten pounds in cash and household goods to Simó Cayada, also a wooldresser as her dowry. See ARV Prot. 794, Marti Doto, non-paginated (26 November 1438).
7 For example, on 2 August 1420, Agnes, the widow of Vicent Castelló, at the time married to Bernat Lorent, sued Lorent Castelló, her son, for the restitution of her dowry in the amount of sixty pounds. The judge ordered that Agnes's dowry should be immediately returned to her (ARV Gobernació Litium 2224, m. 7, f. 20r. i v. (2 August 1420)).
8 Thomas Kuehn, 'Daughters, Mothers, Wives and Widows: Women as Legal Persons', in Anne Jacobson Schutte, Thomas Kuehn and Silvana Seidel Menchi (eds), *Time, Space and Women's Lives in Early Modern Europe* (Kirksville, MO: Truman State University Press, 2001), p. 110.
9 ARV Prot. 2866, Juan Peris, non-paginated (26 March 1424).
10 ARV Prot. 505, Guillem Cardona, non-paginated (22 June 1428).
11 ARV Prot. 2428, Vicent Zaera, non-paginated (4 April 1431).
12 Iradiel, 'Corporaciones de oficio, accion politica y sociedad civil en Valencia', p. 283.

13 ARV Prot. 2711, Bartolome Tolosa, non-paginated (11 May 1421).
14 ARV Prot. 821, Bernat Estrellers, non-paginated (1 September 1422).
15 Iradiel does not provide documentary evidence for this claim ('Familia y función', p. 236).
16 Eleanor S. Riemer, 'Women, Dowries and Capital Investment in Thirteenth-Century Siena', in Marion Kaplan (ed.), *The Marriage Bargain: Women and Dowries in European History* (London: Haworth Press, 1985), p. 66.
17 Earl J. Hamilton, *Money, Prices and Wages in Valencia, Aragon and Navarre, 1351–1500* (Cambridge, MA: Harvard University Press, 1936), pp. 273–275.
18 Chojnacki, 'Dowries and Kinsmen', p. 132, 'Gender and the Early Renaissance State', pp. 75–76; Julius Kirshner and Anthony Molho, 'The Dowry Fund and the Marriage Market in Early Quattrocentro Florence', *Journal of Modern History*, 50(3) (September 1978), pp. 403–438; Julius Kirshner, *Pursuing Honor While Avoiding Sin: The Monte delle Doti of Florence* (Milan: A. Giuffré, 1978); Molho, *Marriage Alliance in Late Medieval Florence*.
19 Herlihy and Klapisch-Zuber, *Tuscans and Their Families*, pp. 202–211; 226. David Herlihy has argued elsewhere that the delay of marriage by men was related to concerns about the increasing division of family patrimonies. Wealth in land equalled power and therefore families tried to prevent its dissolution by discouraging the continual partitioning of land. Rather than marrying while their parents were still alive, and hence dividing the patrimony, men waited until this inheritance could be passed down intact ('The Medieval Marriage Market', *Medieval and Renaissance Studies*, 6 (1976), p. 19). See also Kirshner and Molho, 'Dowry Fund and the Marriage Market', pp. 420–430.
20 Guiral-Hadziiossif, *Valence: port méditerranéen*, p. 451. Antoni Furió states that for those of *llaurador* status, women married at age 17 or 18 and men around age 25 (*Història del País València*, pp. 191–192).
21 Chojnacka, *Working Women of Early Modern Venice*, p. 5.
22 Ibid.
23 See Iradiel, 'Familia y función'; Owen Hughes, 'Domestic Ideals and Social Behaviour'; Chojnacka, *Working Women of Early Modern Venice*.
24 Guarner, *La ciutat de València*, p. 169.
25 Furió, *Història del País València*, p. 187.
26 Ibid., p. 191.
27 Ibid., p. 199.
28 ARV Prot. 473, Berenguer Cardona, non-paginated (14 October 1432).
29 Iradiel, 'Corporaciones de oficio, acción política y sociedad civil en Valencia', fn. 60, p. 283.
30 Hamilton, *Money, Prices and Wages*, p. 71. Hamilton indicates that the gap between journeymen and day labourers was increasing as the fifteenth century progressed.
31 Furió, 'Tierra, familia y transmisión de la propriedad', p. 320.
32 ARV Prot. 416, Juan de Campos (Sr), non-paginated (10 August 1420).
33 ARV Prot. 789, Marti Doto, non-paginated (5 October 1421).
34 ARV Prot. 790, Marti Doto, non-paginated (17 January 1427).
35 ARV Prot. 821, Bernat Estrellers, non-paginated (1 January 1422).
36 APPV Prot. 22842, Joan Peris, non-paginated (13 July 1423).
37 APPV Prot. 25988, Joan Ferrer, non-paginated (6 July 1423).

38 *Ibid.* (13 June 1422).
39 See Guiral-Hadziiossif, *Valence: Port méditerranéen*, p. 451; Daniel Lord Smail, 'Démanteler le patrimoine: Les femmes et les biens dans la Marseille médiévale', *Annales Histoire Sciences Sociales*, 52 (2) (mars–avril 1997), p. 356.
40 ARV Prot. 63, Juan Amalrich, non-paginated (28 October 1429).
41 APPV Prot. 23404, Joan Peris, non-paginated (30 January 1429).
42 Aventín, *La societat rural a Catalunya*, p. 482.
43 *Furs de València*, V-I-IX, p. 11.
44 *Ibid.*, V-V-XXXVIII, p. 68.
45 *Ibid.* For further explanation, see Belda Soler, *El régimen matrimonial de bienes en los 'Furs de Valencià'*, p. 54.
46 *Furs de València*, V-V-XXXI, p. 63.
47 *Ibid.*, V-V-XXXIII, p. 64.
48 ARV Prot. 421, Juan de Campos (Sr), non-paginated (13 April 1429).
49 ARV Prot. 14403, Jaume Venrell, non-paginated (13 May 1422).
50 Romano, *Housecraft and Statecraft*, p. 159; Klapisch-Zuber, 'Women Servants in Florence', p. 68; López Beltrán, 'La accesibilidad de la mujer al mundo laboral', p. 127.
51 ARV Prot. 422, Joan de Campos (Sr), non-paginated (13 November 1433).
52 ARV Prot. 425, Joan de Campos (Sr), non-paginated (13 December 1438).
53 ARV Prot. 426, Joan de Campos (Sr), non-paginated (29 December 1439).
54 'Dotis fructum ad maritum pertinere debere aequitas suggerit: cum enim ipse onera matrimonii subeat, aequum est eum etiam fructus percipere', in Paul Kreuger (ed.), *Corpus Iuris Civilis: Codex Iustinianus* (Berlin: Weidmannsche Verlagsbuchhandlung, 1963), XXIII-III-VII, p. 530.
55 'Dret e equaltat vol quels fruyts de l'exovar vinguen e pertanguen al marit, car per ço com lo marit sosté la carga del matrimoni deu haver los *fruyts de les coses dotals. Car al marit a qui pertany la carga del matrimoni deu pertànyer lo profit l'exovar*' (*Furs*, V-I-VIII, p. 17). Further elucidated by 'Tots los fruyts quel marit haurà preses de les coses que li seran donades en exovar deuen ésser seus per la càrrega del matrimoni que sofer' (*ibid.*, V-III-V, p. 30).
56 Navarro, 'L'Artisanat de la soie à Valence', p. 170.
57 Honorio García has argued both that the *aixovar* was an Aragonese tradition and that it derived from Muslim custom. See 'El exovar o exovuar y el creix', *Boletín de la Sociedad Castellonense de Cultura*, 3 (1922), pp. 237–238 and 'Possibilidad de un elemento consuetudinario en el Código de Jamie I', *Boletín de la Sociedad Castellonense de Cultura*, 23 (1947), pp. 428–450. For a discussion of marital property regimes in medieval Muslim Spain and North African, see Amalia Zomeño, *Dote y matrimonio en Al-Andalus y el Norte de Africa: Estudio sobre la jurisprudencia islámica medieval* (Madrid: Consejo Superior de Investigaciones científicas, 2000), pp. 20, 107; Maya Shatzmiller, 'Women and Property Rights in al-Andalus and the Maghrib: Social Patterns and Legal Discourse', *Islamic Law and Society*, 2 (1995), pp. 219–261 and *Her Day in Court: Women's Property Rights in Fifteenth-Century Granada* (Cambridge, MA: Harvard University Press, 2007); Mark D. Meyerson, *The Muslims of Valencia in the Age of Fernando and Isabel: Between Coexistence and Crusade* (Berkeley: University of California Press, 1991), p. 233. See also Míkel de Epalza and Enrique Llobregot, 'Hubo mozárabes en tierras valencianas? Proceso de islamizacion del Levante de Peninsula (Sharq al-Andalus)', *Revista del Instituto de Estudios Alicantinos*, 36 (1982), pp. 7–31.

Other scholars, such as María Belda Soler, support a pre-Muslim conquest origin for the *aixovar*, seeing it as the continuation of a 'hispano-vulgar-visigothic-roman tradition' (*El régimen matrimonial de bienes*, p. 50). See also Lluís To Figueras, *Família i hereu a la Catalunya Nord–Oriental (segles X–XII)* (Barcelona: Publicaciones de l'Abadia de Montserrat), pp. 153 and 256. It seems probable that the custom of *aixovar* came to Valencia via Catalan and Aragonese immigrants who moved to the region after its conquest in the thirteenth century. Both groups brought marital traditions, including the exchange of property and the concept of a trousseau making up part of a woman's dowry. See Vinyoles, *Les barcelonines a les darreries de l'Edat Mitjana*, p. 85; García-Herrero, *Las mujeres en Zaragoza en el siglo XV*, p. 256. She states that it was customary for women of all classes to bring bedclothes, table linens and all other household goods.

58 See Howell, *Marriage Exchange*; Anne-Marie Landès-Mallet, *La famille en Rouergue au moyen âge, 1239–1345: Étude de la practique notariale* (Rouen: Université de Rouen, 1985); Chojnacki, 'From Trousseau to Groomgift', pp. 76–94; Judith M. Bennett, *Women in the Medieval English Countryside: Gender and Household in Brigstock before the Plague* (Oxford: Oxford University Press, 1987); Dillard, *Daughters of the Reconquest*.
59 ARV Prot. 3091, Antoni Jover, non-paginated (14 January 1431).
60 For a discussion of the important economic roles that female guardians played in late medieval and early modern Spain, see Coolidge, *Guardianship*, pp. 4–8.
61 *Furs de València*, V-III-II, p. 28.
62 *Ibid*., V-IV-II, pp. 33–34.
63 ARV Prot. 821, Bernardo Esteller, non-paginated (8 July 1422).
64 *Furs*, VI-IV-XXI, p. 160. This clause forbade all women from acting as testamentary executors and mandated that if a woman was named, it should considered as if an executor had not been appointed. Despite this prohibition, in their testaments approximately 50 per cent of *llaurador* and artisan men named their wives as one of or their only executor.
65 ARV Prot. 505, Guillem Cardona, non-paginated (22 June 1428).
66 This land was described as *terre campe* (mainly wheat producing), *terre vine* (vineyards), or *terre olive* (olive producing).
67 ARV Prot. 1329, Pere Llorens, non-paginated (30 March 1429).
68 APPV Prot. 23585, Felip Lleopart, non-paginated (13 August 1430).
69 ARV Prot. 419, Joan de Campos (Sr), non-paginated (15 January 1425).
70 APPV Prot. 14472, Joan Eximeno, non-paginated (28 April 1426).
71 For a more in-depth discussion of testamentary dotal bequests, see Chapter 5 of this book.
72 ARV Prot. 789, Martin Doto, non-paginated (31 May 1421).
73 ARV Prot. 421, Juan de Campos (Sr), non-paginated (7 February 1429); ARV Notal 2525, Juan de Campos (Sr), non-paginated (18 February 1425).
74 Tramoyeres Blasco, *Instituciones gremiales*, p. 377.
75 *Ibid*., p. 379.
76 ARV Prot. 505, Guillem Cardona, non-paginated (16 September 1428).
77 ARV 2142, Joan Sarañana, non-paginated (22 August 1425).
78 Iradiel, 'L'evolució econòmica', p. 294.
79 Hinojosa Montalvo, *Diccionario de historia medieval del Reino de Valencia*, vol. I: A–C, p. 515.

80 Furió, *Història del País Valencià*, p. 202. See also Antoni Furió, 'Crédito y endeudamiento: el censal en la sociedad rural valenciana (siglos XIV–XV)', in Esteban Sarasa Sánchez and Eliseo Serrano Martín (eds), *Señorío y feudalismo en la Peninsula Iberica (ss. XII–XIX)* (Zaragoza: Institucion Fernando el Católico, 1994), vol. I, pp. 501–534.

81 For the medieval period, see William C. Jordan, 'Communal Administration in France, 1257–1270: Problems Discovered and Solutions Imposed', *Revue belge de philologie et d'histoire*, 59 (1981); Josef Rosen, 'Two Municipal Accounts: Frankfurt and Basel in 1428', *Journal of European Economic History*, 16(3) (1987), pp. 63–88; Hans-Peter Baum, 'Annuities in Late Medieval Hanse Towns', *Business History Review*, 59 (1985), pp. 24–48. For the early modern period, see James Collins, 'The Economic Role of Women in Seventeenth-Century France', *French Historical Studies*, 16 (1989), pp. 436–470; Kirshner, *Pursing Honor*.

82 APPV Prot. 26181, Joan Marromà, non-paginated (6 July 1430).

83 APPV Prot. 16181, Joan Marromà, non-paginated (day and month unknown, 1431).

84 Furió, *Història del País Valencià*, p. 202.

85 APPV Prot. 23268, Joan de Pina, non-paginated (18 October 1421).

86 ARV Prot. 791, Martin Doto, non-paginated (28 November 1431).

87 ARV Prot. 469, Berenguer Cardona, non-paginated (13 February 1427).

88 ARV Prot. 2426, Vicente Zaera, non-paginated (8 August 1429).

89 For an overview, see William Chester Jordan, *Women and Credit in Pre-Industrial and Developing Societies* (Philadelphia: University of Pennsylvania Press, 1993), pp. 72–76.

90 ARV Prot. 416, Juan de Campos (Sr), non-paginated (7 December 1419).

91 'In dei nomine, Caterina vidua filia Bernardi Gil loci de Quart uxorque fui Petri Onyego, vicini Meliana. Gratis de voluntate et consensus dicti patris mei ibidem presenti et Jacmete matris mei et aliorum parentum ibidem existentum contemplatione matrimoni fiendi inter me et vos Arnaldum Pujol minorem dierum vicinum loci Almaçera constituo vobis in et pro dote mea secundum forum Valentie 50 libros monete regalium Valentie quas habeo michi que pertinent in bonis dicti mei primi viri usufructo virtute illius testamenti de tota mei vita tam cum viro que sine viro.'

92 *Furs de Valencià*, IV-IV-VII, p. 24, 'Los béns de la mare que pendrà altre marit és entès que són obligats als fils primer matrimoni, jasia ço que nomenadament no serà dit que sien obligats e la mare que restituescha a ells totes aqueles coses que hac del primer marit'; V-II-I, p. 18 'Si el marit quant se morrà lexarà l'usufruyt de les sues coses a la muller, e aquela pendrà altre marit, perde l'usufruyt quel primer marit li havia lexat e aquel usufruyt restituesque als fils del primer marit, d'aquel dia enant que haurà pres altre marit'; V-II-XI, p. 23 'Can alcú morrà e lexarà muller e fills comuns d'ell e d'ella, si aquela muller aprés I an volrrà altre marit pendre, reta tots los béns del pare als fils damunt dits e no tinga aquels en son poder'.

93 Bensch, *Barcelona and Its Rulers*, pp. 264–270.

94 Iradiel, 'Familia y función', p. 234.

95 ARV Prot. 426, Joan de Campos (Sr), non-paginated (17 January 1439).

96 ARV Prot. 792, Martí Doto, non-paginated (9 June 1434).

97 ARV Prot. 416, Juan de Campos (Sr), non-paginated (7 December 1419).

98 APPV Prot. 22842, Joan Peris, non-paginated (13 July 1423).

99 ARV Prot. 4159, Juan Domingo, non-paginated (2 April 1426).

100 'Et dictus Clems Dabella in contemplationem dicti matrimonii fecit donationem dicte Francisce uxore sue future 20 libris monete regnalium Valentie. Quas sibi dare promissit post obitum suum' (ARV, Prot. 421, Juan de Campos (Sr), non-paginated (23 October 1428)).
101 Winer, 'Silent Partners?', p. 69; Codina, *Contractes de matrimoni al Delta del Llobregat*, p. 205; Vinyoles, *Les barcelonines a les darreries de l'Edat Mitjana*, p. 88.
102 'per honra de buestra persona e virginidad'. Montalvo's examples all come from the sixteenth century indicating that this stipulation may have become more prevalent in Castilian marriage contracts at the end of the Middle Ages and into the early modern period (*Régimen jurídico de la mujer en la familia castellana medieval*, p. 138).
103 *Ibid.*, pp. 118, 132.
104 Christiane Klapisch-Zuber, 'The Griselda Complex', in *Women, Family and Ritual in Renaissance Italy*, p. 216.
105 Owen Hughes, 'Domestic Ideals and Social Behaviour', p. 130.
106 *Ibid.*; Steven Epstein, *Wills and Wealth in Medieval Genoa* (Cambridge, MA: Harvard University Press, 1984), p. 104.
107 APPV Prot. 22852, Joan Peris, non-paginated (18 March 1425).
108 *Furs de València*, V-II-IX, pp. 23–4.
109 *Ibid.*

4

Germanía contracts: the exception to the rule

While the majority of Valencians utilized the dotal regime of marital property which mandated the separation of a couple's assets, a large minority followed an alternative system. Approximately 20 per cent of marriage contracts examined for this book (88 out of 455) were germanía contracts characterized by the combining of the couple's assets. Unlike the dowry system, the germanía regime was based on the community of goods in which all the assets owned by the husband and wife were pooled into one jointly held fund. Grounded in customary tradition, the germanía system held that both husband and wife should benefit equally from any gains made on their assets during the marriage. When one spouse died, the surviving spouse received half of the communal property, with the other half designated for the deceased's heirs. If there were no heirs, the survivor could receive all of the assets. This system of marital assigns was decidedly different from the dotal regime as it was concerned more with conjugal rather than lineage rights. Historians have argued that the society of acquisitions was more beneficial for women. They cite the fact that contracts such as these recognized the equal contribution of wives to the household by allowing them to benefit from the economic partnership created at marriage. In this chapter, I challenge the idea that 'equality' was generated by germanía contracts. The reality was ambiguous, because, on the one hand, this system of marital assigns did theoretically give women equal access to conjugal assets; on the other hand, in practice, this regime did not always function in a truly egalitarian manner.

This chapter will explore the *germanía* marital property system in Valencia during the early fifteenth century. It will focus on why particular groups of women chose to utilize the *germanía* system of marital assigns rather than the more common dowry regime, as well as whether or not these marriage contracts can be considered egalitarian as some historians have argued. Although the *germanía* system was very different from the dotal regime, the couples who used these contracts still lived in a patriarchal society that mandated particular gender roles and norms which mitigated some of the more 'equal' aspects of the regime.

The *germanía* system in Valencia

Before exploring what factors were influential in a couple's choice to use the *germanía* system of marital assigns, let us examine what such contracts were like and how they differed from more common dotal ones. On Thursday 26 June 1427, the notary Tomas Argent drew up a *germanía* contract between the *llaurador* Pere Ramon and Caterina Vilana.

> In the name of the Lord amen. Let it be announced to all that we Pere Ramon, son of the deceased farmer Guillem Ramon of Benifaraig in the *horta* of Valencia, and Caterina, daughter of the farmer Guillem Vilana of Alfara, also located in the *horta*, each with the express consent and will of our family and friends, we make and we concede between us fraternity and *germanía* concerning and upon every good and right which we now hold and concerning the rest which we may hold, by whatever form, title, cause or reasons. Thus the one of us who first leaves this world, let the other hold half of all the said goods and rights, the same with children as without out ... and thus we swear by the Lord God.[1]

Similar to dotal contracts, Pere and Caterina indicate that they are marrying with the consent of their family and friends. But beyond this commonality, the differences between this *germanía* marriage contract and dowry ones from the same time period are striking. The most obvious contrast is that Pere and Caterina's contract does not mention the specific goods being brought into the union. Instead the contract refers generally to 'all and every good and right which we now hold and concerning the rest which we may hold (presumably in the future)'. Dowry contracts always explicitly laid out the amount and type of property brought as dotal assets by the bride, so that upon the dissolution of the marriage, or, in a case of restitution, the specific goods or their value could be restored. Indeed, dowry contracts revolved around the exchange of specific property, making them very different from *germanía* agreements.

Despite the lack of explicit facts in *germanía* contracts regarding the couple's assets, extant evidence from notarial records can provide some information about this property. Of the eighty-eight *germanía* marriage contracts examined, thirty couples also concluded a *donatio inter vivos*, or living-will donation contract, on the same day. These contracts acted to provide couples with a pre-mortem inheritance from their families (or other donors) for the occasion of their marriages and they included donations of both moveable and immoveable assets. For example, on the same day that he concluded a *germanía* contract with Ursola, the daughter of the *llaurador* Jaume Splugues of Foios, Pere Peres of Quart received a *donatio inter vivos* from his mother Marí and her second husband Alvares Peres that included a rented house in Quart, 2 *cafissades* (a *cafissada* comes from *cafís de gra*, meaning a measurement of wheat) of wheat-producing land and 4.5 *fanecadas* of vineyards held in emphyteutic tenure. Pere's bride Ursola received a sixty-pound donation from her father Jaume which consisted of thirty pounds in cash and thirty pounds in household goods.[2]

The *germanía* contract indicates that the couple's assets were to be combined, creating a conjugal fund from which both were to benefit. In fact, some *germanía* contracts clearly stipulated that this property was to be used jointly, 'thus concerning the goods which we hold at present, and it is fitting, which we are about to hold, let us use them in common'.[3] This communal system of marital assigns was quite different from the dotal regime regulated by the *Furs de Valencià* which, while it gave the husband the right to control and administer his wife's property throughout their marriage, mandated that the dowry was to be held separately from his own property. In addition, under the dotal regime, a wife did not have access to any accretions on her dowry nor did she have control of any income she earned throughout her marriage.[4]

Dotal contracts were largely concerned with property being donated at the time of marriage, *germanía* contracts stipulate how the conjugal assets were to be divided when the union was dissolved by the death of a spouse. All *germanía* contracts contained a clause directing that the surviving spouse was to receive half the couple's assets. Some also indicated that the survivor was to receive complete right of alienation for his or her share of the conjugal fund. Dotal contracts, while they mentioned that the husband must return the dowry and *creix* to the wife whenever she wished, did not contain clauses regarding the devolution of marital property at the death of a spouse, at least not for couples of labouring-status. Elite marriage contracts were far more detailed and often had clauses that stipulated how a woman's marital property was to be conveyed after her death.[5] Labouring-status couples were content to rely on the numerous articles contained in the *Furs* to ensure that the dowry and *creix* were properly returned upon the dissolution of marriage by death or any other means; however, the kin groups of elite couples were concerned about keeping the family patrimony within the lineage and wanted to make certain that assets they had donated as marital property devolved to the correct heirs.

The inclusion of such clauses demonstrates that, in some ways, this system was not just about marriage but also inheritance. This is supported by evidence from the contracts themselves which sometimes have stipulations that each member of the couple include in their testaments the terms of property devolution established by their *germanía* contract. For example, in their contract of 29 January 1419, the *llaurador* Joan Fanos of Rafalell and Johana, the daughter of the *llaurador* Dominic Rielo of Valencia, promised to include the proviso granting the surviving spouse half of the conjugal assets in their testaments.[6] As this property was jointly owned, and not regulated by the legal code, it was important for the couple to determine the rules of inheritance both in their marriage contract and individual wills. On the one hand, it ensured that the surviving spouse had assets with which to support himself or herself, an essential factor for the wife who had no dowry. On the other hand, the inclusion of these clauses provided for the heirs of the deceased spouse by protecting their rights to a share of the family patrimony (which could be especially important if the survivor remarried).

Overall, while *germanía* and dotal contracts did share some similarities, especially regarding the consent of family and friends to the newly formed marital unions, in essence these documents were fundamentally different. Dowry contracts were focused primarily on regulating property held at the time of marriage whereas *germanía* contracts were more concerned with assets to be gained in the future. Both the dotal and *germanía* regimes functioned to ensure the smooth transmission of property from generation to generation, yet they did so in very different ways. Unlike labouring-status dotal contracts, *germanía* ones included provisions for inheritance alongside clauses regulating the management of conjugal assets throughout the marriage. These stipulations helped to ensure that the conjugal fund was devolved, in the absence of legal statutes, according to the wishes of the couple.

Germanía contracts: who used them and why?

While dotal contracts were employed by every socio-economic group in the early fifteenth century, from female servants to noblewomen, *germanía* marriage contracts were largely used by couples of agricultural background. In two-thirds of couples with a *germanía* contract, one spouse or both were of *llaurador* background; the remainder of couples were of artisan or slave status. Geographically, the vast majority of spouses were from villages in the Valencian *horta*, the agricultural region surrounding the city over which it held jurisdiction.

The use of *germanía* contracts by *llaurador* couples can be largely attributed to the need to create a 'threshold of property which assures the survival of the couple'[7] and their household. A key factor of these contracts was that they allowed couples to pool any financial resources they held which gave them greater economic stability. As agricultural production for *llauradors* of modest means was largely subsistence level, they had to perform a number of different tasks to support the conjugal household. It must be stressed that due to the partible inheritance laws mandated by the *Furs*, land division was a growing problem in rural Valencia. The fifteenth century saw a great increase in the percentage of land plots of fewer that 20 *fanecades*. For example, in Castellón, land parcels of 0–5 *fanecades* grew from 22.8 per cent of the total land to 39 per cent; those of 6–10 *fanecades* grew from 32 per cent to 43.9 per cent.[8] Overall, the average plot size dropped by more than half of that granted to the original settlers in the thirteenth century, leaving modest *llauradors* with often miniscule plots of land on which to scratch out a living.

In order to deal with this problematic situation, Antoni Furió, in his work on Sueca, found that a number of *llauradors* began to farm their small plots collectively. In effect, these *llauradors* made contracts with family members or friends in which they agreed to live together in one house and worked together to exploit their individual holdings. At harvest time, each paid their rent and the remaining profits were divided equally among all the participants.[9] This form of land exploitation made small properties more sustainable than if they were farmed individually, as the risks and benefits were shared. Notarial evidence indicates that this kind of land exploitation was referred to as *per germanía*.[10] It becomes apparent that *llaurador* couples, aware of the economic benefits of this system, adopted and used it to govern their conjugal property. The combination of their assets gave *llaurador* couples a firmer financial base on which to found their new household and recognized that both members of the couple shared equally in the burden of supporting the family.

The mirroring of the *germanía* form of land exploitation by married couples in the Valencian *horta* is very similar to what took place in France during the same time period. Peasants in various French regions began to use marriage contracts known as *frèreche*, or *agermanament* in the fourteenth century. Originally used by families to create multigenerational obligations for commonly held property, such community of goods contracts were then expanded and began to be employed by people with no blood ties to one another.[11] In both Valencia and France, these contracts emphasized the notion of brotherhood as indicated by their name: *frèreche* from *frère* in France and *germanía* from the Catalan *germà* in Valencia. Eventually, as in Valencia, *frèreche* contracts were adapted for use by married couples, pooling their assets to create a threshold of property to ensure their survival.

Similar systems of marital assigns which mandated a community of conjugal goods were also in use elsewhere in the Iberian peninsula and Europe. Examples of such contracts exist from Barcelona, Perpignan and Zaragoza.[12] Indeed, Teresa Vinyoles found that community of goods marriage contracts were the most common among foreigners from France who had immigrated to Barcelona. Vinyoles also argues that many couples used both community of goods and dotal contracts to regulate their assets.[13] This was the case in Castile where marriage contracts based on jointly held assets predominated until the fourteenth century, when the romanized dotal regime of the *Siete Partidas* was imposed by the Crown with greater force. By the fifteenth century, many couples in Castile followed the dotal regime and held in common any assets acquired after marriage.[14] Like the *germanía* regime in Valencia, the commonly held property was divided equally at the dissolution of the marriage, usually by death when the surviving spouse received half, with the other half going to the deceased's heirs.

Outside of the Iberian peninsula, marriage property regimes based on the community of goods were common. This was especially true in areas that did not have a notarial culture, leaving marital property arrangements unwritten. Late medieval Douai is one such city where customary law mandating the creation of a conjugal fund at marriage prevailed. In Douai, the husband held administrative and ownership rights over the conjugal fund while alive, transferring these to his wife if she survived him. Douaisien custom stated that the surviving spouse was to receive half of the marital assets but could be made heir of the entire fund by contract.[15] Other cities in northern Europe such as Cambrai, Lille and Artois had similar customs regarding marital property.[16] In all of these areas, the community of goods regime was predominant until the late fourteenth/early fifteenth century when marital property arrangements began to shift towards a system based on the separation of goods. In part, this change can be attributed to the increasing use of marriage contracts which clearly laid out the goods that each member of the couple had brought to the union.[17]

Historians who study society of acquisitions contracts elsewhere in the Iberian peninsula have argued that these contracts were used primarily by those of modest means.[18] But these authors have also found that couples with some assets were using the society of acquisitions regime to regulate their marital property.[19] Evidence from Valencia indicates that couples that used *germanía* contracts were not always of low status and in fact sometimes brought marital assets worth more than the average artisan or *llaurador* dowry. For example, on the same day that their *germanía* contract was drawn up, Francesca, the daughter of the *llaurador* Bernat Nadal of Torrent, and the *llaurador* Anthoní Milla, also of Torrent, each received a *donatio inter vivos* from their fathers. Francesca received a pre-mortem donation of seventy pounds (twenty pounds in cash and fifty in household goods) and Anthoní a rented house and six pieces of land in Torrent held by emphyteutic tenure.[20] This couple was not wealthy but the seventy-pound donation given to Francesca by her father was higher than the average dowry of a *llaurador* woman of twenty to forty pounds.

Although it is difficult to determine conclusively the economic status of those using *germanía* contracts, particularly since *llaurador* could refer to those of great wealth or complete poverty, nevertheless, extant *donationes inter vivos* indicate that these couples were not of higher status. Almost all donations made to women fall below sixty pounds and those to men largely consist of several small plots of land. The communal nature of *germanía* contracts would not have functioned well for couples of higher status given the great investment that their families made in the marriage alliances that were being created. This was especially true for women whose families donated large dowries with the understanding that this property, while under the administrative control of a husband during the marriage, would then devolve to the heirs of his wife at her death. At no time would these assets be considered his and therefore a woman's natal family would be able to protect this property from his mismanagement. This was certainly not the case with *germanía* contracts where a woman's property would be divided at her death between her husband and their heirs, giving him full ownership over it. It is not surprising, therefore, that elite families did not utilize the *germanía* system, as it worked against their desire to maintain an interest in all aspects of the family patrimony.

Although I did not find numerous examples, it does appear that some couples in late medieval Valencia attempted to use both the *germanía* and dowry systems to govern their marital assigns. In a series of documents dated 18 March 1425, Guillem Noguera received a dowry of thirty pounds in household goods and jewellery from Dominic Martinez of Torrent, the father of his bride Johana. At the same time, Guillem received a donation from the executor of his mother's estates for some pieces of land held in emphyteutic tenure, located in the *horta*. The final document in this series is a *germanía* contract concluded between Guillem and Johana.[21]

The only other example I found of a couple utilizing both the *germanía* and dowry systems comes from 1434. Unlike the series of contracts laying out the wishes of Guillem Noguera and Johana Martínez, only a single marriage contract was used in this second example. The document begins as a typical dowry contract, stating that the silversmith Gabriel Garbeller of Valencia is providing a dowry of thirty pounds in cash to the tailor Arnald Dezmur of Elche for his daughter Brigida. She received a *creix* of fifteen pounds in return. The contract then uses language associated with the *germanía* regime stating that the couple wish to 'make and concede between us fraternity and *germanía*', concerning the rest of the property they hold now and what they may hold in the future.[22]

As in Castile, the goal of these couples was to use the dotal contract to govern any dowry assets, and the *germanía* one for any other property held by them at the time of marriage, as well as any assets gained during the unions. The dotal contract gave Johana and Brigida legal protection for their dowries, ensuring these assets remained intact to provide for them in widowhood. Conversely, the *germanía* regime recognized their equal contribution to the financial sustenance of the household. Overall, the use of the two systems allowed Johana and Brigida to enjoy the economic gains of marriage but protected them in case the conjugal assets were diminished through debts incurred or by any other means. This dual use of the dowry and *germanía* system does not appear to have been common in late medieval Valencia as these two documents were the only examples I found for the 1419–39 period.

While the earliest *germanía* contracts in Valencia are dated to the early 1280s, the majority of those extant are from the fourteenth and fifteenth centuries.[23] This proliferation reflects the socio-economic crises of this time period as couples could pool their assets, whether they be cash, household goods or rented plots of land, for greater sustainability. The work of scholars such as Jean Gaudemet, Jean Yver and Jean Hilaire on rural France also denotes the increase in such types of marriage contracts during the latter half of the medieval period. It was not only married couples who increasingly chose a community of goods approach to govern their assets. Evidence from these regions suggests that such types of property holding agreements rose among people not related through marital or blood ties.[24]

By the time the plague arrived in the kingdom of Valencia in May of 1348, the territory had been in Christian hands for just over one hundred years. As elsewhere in Europe, the second half of the fourteenth century was extremely difficult for Valencia, in both the rural and urban areas of the kingdom. Repeated waves of plague decimated the population, as did endemic warfare. For example, Valencia experienced civil strife in 1348 when King Pere the Ceremonious faced, and eventually defeated, a union of rebels seeking to limit his authority in the kingdom. The harsh economic situation of the fourteenth century led to a reorganization of the kingdom economically and socially.[25] Over the first half of the fifteenth century, there were great shifts in population throughout Valencia as the poor, journeyman artisans and indebted peasants migrated in search of work.[26] The majority of them moved to the city of Valencia whose population exploded during this period, while rural areas experienced severe demographic decline. The increasing division of land led to smaller and smaller plot sizes and was largely to blame for the massive immigration of *llauradors* to urban centres in order to survive. Given these problematic socio-economic circumstances, it is not surprising that married couples and others in Valencia utilized whatever means possible to ensure the financial survival of their households.

In this period of crisis, poor rural economic conditions also influenced household structure and property devolution in many parts of southern Europe, connecting the use of community of goods marriage contracts to familial strategies for survival. For example, in the fourteenth and fifteenth centuries, we see a return to the multi-family household for economic security. Emmanuel Le Roy Ladurie argues that, for Languedoc, from 1420 to 1450, the successful exploitation of land by a single couple was impossible and thus it was not unusual for a newly married couple to live in the household of the groom's family; and in some cases, even the bride's family.[27] Evidence from Valencia indicates that the situation for *llaurador* families was similar. In rural areas surrounding the city, there was an increasing number of multi-family households, most commonly consisting of two generations of a kin group. Antoni Furió argues this shift in household structure was because, much like the situation in Languedoc, the nuclear family could not provide enough labour to exploit the land sufficiently.[28]

The use of the community of goods marital property regimes reflects these changes in household structure as well as the development of property devolution strategies aimed at maintaining the economic viability of the family. For example, notarial evidence from Montpellier shows fictive donations by parents to their children at the time of marriage. Such donations indicated that the parents (usually the fathers, unless they were deceased in which case the mothers acted as heads of household) retained usufruct rights to this property until their deaths. These gifts could consist of all or only part of the family patrimony.[29] Furió's study of Sueca in the Valencian *horta* during the same time period shows similar practices. Notarial evidence demonstrates that sometimes couples who married under the *germanía* system received donations from their parents at the time of marriage. For brides, these donations are referred to as *donationes proper nuptias* (donations on account of marriage), dowries or *donationes inter vivos* (living-will donations). In 1436, the *llaurador* Dominic Ferrando of Quart concluded a donation contract with his daughter Maria for one piece of agricultural land in Quart and thirty pounds in household goods. Twenty pounds of that donation came from Maria's salary as a domestic servant. The notarial contract indicates that this property was given to Maria by her family as a dowry or donation on account of marriage.[30] For grooms, these gifts were always termed *donationes inter vivos*. Such legal instruments allowed donors to retain control over the donated assets until their deaths, effectively creating a community of goods or *germanía* between fathers and sons.[31] The *germanía* concluded between the couple was therefore part of the much larger community of goods which existed within the household. Furió argues that actions such as multi-family households and the use of *donationes inter vivos* by parents helped to alleviate the economic stress caused by small and fragmented land holdings common to the late medieval period. In addition, most of the property given to couples at the time of marriage was insufficient for their economic survival, at least for those *llauradors* of labouring-status. Therefore, these couples were forced to rely on aid from parents, most commonly those of the groom.[32]

In Valencia, it is precisely during the time that *germanía* contracts are at their peak – the early fifteenth century – that they make their first and only appearance in the *Furs*. In 1428, regulations regarding *germanía* contracts were added to two clauses. The first of these augments the existing law which stripped an adulterous wife of her dowry, and mandates that women with *germanía* contracts who committed adultery lose their share of the conjugal fund.[33] The second clause expands statutes written by Jaume I (1261), Pere II (1363) and Marti I (1403) regarding the devolution of property inherited by sons and daughters that was then used as marital assets. In the initial clause, and three subsequent additions, the *Furs* states that any assets given as dowry or counter-gift which had been inherited by sons or daughters from their parents were to be returned to the originally designated second heir if there were no offspring from the marriage. Alfons IV in 1428 extended this law to include children who marry under the *germanía* regime, and allowed second heirs to demand the return of specific goods initially inherited, or their estimated value.[34]

The reasons for inserting these clauses at this point in Valencian history are difficult to determine. It is possible that, as law in this period was reactive, they were added because issues regarding *germanía* marriage contracts had been raised in court; however, given the fact that notarial evidence demonstrates these contracts had been used from the late 1280s, questions regarding them must have arisen in court prior to 1428. Another possibility is that the clauses added by Alfons IV reflected concerns of elite families in Valencia. Earlier monarchs had amended previous laws to protect familial inheritance rights of the elite on numerous occasions. But, as we have seen, *germanía* contracts were not used by those of patrician and noble status in Valencia and it seems unlikely that they would place pressure on the king for these reasons.

The most plausible answer at this point is merely that Alfons IV was reacting to the growth in use of these contracts over the course of the fourteenth and fifteenth centuries. We may not have concrete evidence that questions regarding the impact that *germanía* marriage contracts had on related issues, including inheritance, were brought before the courts, but this does not necessarily mean that they did not arise outside of the legal system. It is interesting that neither of the legal clauses to which *germanía* was amended worked to protect the rights of the wife over her share of the conjugal property. Rather, they were concerned with heirs and ensuring the smooth transition of assets from one generation to the next.

Benefit to women?

The omission of protection within the *Furs* for wives who married with *germanía* contracts raises the question of whether or not a marital property regime based on the community of goods truly benefited women. Historians have argued that the society of acquisitions, which *germanía* contracts were based upon, put forth 'an idea of equality that ought to exist between husband and wife'.[35] As evidence they cite that, under this system, a wife was equally entitled to any gains and increments made on the couple's common property as well as the fact that, if she was the surviving spouse, she automatically received half of the marital property. According to this argument, the society of acquisitions created de facto equality between husband and wife which erased the hierarchy of marriage created by the dotal system.

The language of *germanía* marriage contracts certainly inspires the concept of equality as couples pledged '*fraternitatem et germaníam*', fraternity and brotherhood. These words imply that an equal relationship was to exist between husband and wife, at least in terms of their marital assets. This concept, therefore, suggests that not only did each member of the couple have equal access to the profits accrued but they also had equal rights in administering this property. Yet it is unknown whether or not couples who married under a *germanía* system shared this task in Valencia. María Belda Soler argues that, as the couple together had the right of alienation, their conjugal assets were governed by agreement.[36] Honorio García disagrees and asserts that, like the dotal regime, the husband administered the couple's property for the duration of the marriage.[37] In Castile, it was the husband who managed the conjugal property. He was able to dispose freely of any moveable goods but had to have his wife's consent to alienate any immoveable property.[38] Similarly, in Aragon, the husband had the role of administrator of these assets; however, he was not allowed to alienate any goods without his wife's express permission.[39]

In both of these areas, laws regulated the administration of the community of acquisitions, providing clear mandates regarding the control of these assets throughout marriage. In Valencia, as the *germanía* regime was not legally recognized by the *Furs*, it is difficult to determine who acted in this capacity. *Germanía* contracts do state that both the husband and wife were to use the goods in common, but this does not necessarily translate into equal administrative rights, as the evidence from Castile and Aragon demonstrates. Only one contract examined for this book clearly stipulated who was to act as administrator, giving this role to the husband, as in the dotal regime.[40] Beyond this, one can speculate that administrative duties varied by couple, in some cases they controlled their assets jointly, in others the husband retained administrative rights.

The *germanía* system was beneficial to women as it clearly recognized the wife's economic contribution to the household. It gave her the right to benefit financially from the couple's combined production and also from her own separately earned income. Both of these advantages were denied to women under the dotal regime which gave all gains and income earned by wives to their husbands for sustaining the burdens of marriage. In this way, the *germanía* system can be seen as mitigating the dotal regime, which may be the reason why some couples utilized both forms of marriage contracts. Despite these positive aspects, however, there is one fundamental problem that makes the benefits of the *germanía* system for wives ambiguous: it was not recognized legally. The two clauses in the *Furs* that mention *germanía* protect the rights of the husband in the case of an adulterous wife, or the rights of heirs in regard to inheritance disputes. Neither indicates protection for the wife which was a fundamental part of the dotal regime. By Valencian law, a wife could sue her husband for mismanaging her dowry but a woman who married under the *germanía* system had no means to protect her share of the conjugal property. If her husband incurred debts, or gambled away their assets, his wife had no legal recourse to ensure she retained a measure of their jointly owned property.[41] It can be argued that *germanía* contracts were beneficial to women, provided they were able to maintain some agency in controlling the communal assets. If they had a voice in financial decisions, if their assets prospered, if they were the surviving spouse, women who married under the *germanía* regime had distinct advantages over those using the dotal system. If not, they were at a serious disadvantage and could do little to ensure the financial integrity of their jointly owned property.

Overall, historians have largely focused their attention on analysing the benefits of the society of acquisitions regime for wives, with little concern about how this system affected their husbands. In part, this is because it is assumed that, in a patriarchal society, men always had the advantage in legal matters such as marital property arrangements. Indeed, in many ways, marital property regimes such as the *germanía* were more beneficial for husbands than the dotal system because they gave them greater rights over the assets brought by their wives to the conjugal union. In the dotal system, the husband had the right to administer his wife's dowry, as well as to enjoy any profits made on this property; however, he was obligated to maintain its financial integrity in order to return it in full at the dissolution of the marriage. With the *germanía* regime, the husband became part owner of his wife's assets and enjoyed full rights over them, something that was denied him with the dotal system. Although the diminution of this property would affect his own financial status, as it was jointly owned, he was not responsible for returning its value to his wife at the end of their marriage. The central difference for husbands lay in the fact that, no matter which marital property regime was used, they always had the right of administration, something that was usually denied to their wives.

Almost two hundred years after the *Furs* mandated that Valencians use a dotal system to govern their marital property, customary practices persisted. The eighty-eight *germanía* marriage contracts examined for this book demonstrate that a significant minority of couples chose to use a community of goods regime to manage their conjugal assets for a variety of reasons. These couples were largely of *llaurador* background and lived in the villages of the *horta*, indicating that the dotal system may not have penetrated all sectors of Valencian society. In addition, this evidence demonstrates that some couples chose to use the system of marital assigns that best suited their situation. Those of limited economic means could use the *germanía* system in the hope of achieving future economic prosperity. Conversely, those couples with some assets could use it in conjunction with the dotal regime to protect wives in widowhood as well as to recognize their equal economic contribution to the household. Whether or not the *germanía* system was advantageous to women is still to be decided. Chapter 6 of this book demonstrates that it did have strong disadvantages for women in terms of protecting their assets from debt-ridden husbands. As they were not legally recognized by the *Furs*, women who concluded *germanía* contracts at marriage could not avail themselves of the same laws that allowed for dowry restitution. Many of the couples who had *germanía* contracts drawn up received living-will donations from relatives and others on the occasion of their marriages. These donations were, in many cases, not so different from the goods given to women for their dowries. The following chapter will examine marital donation under both the dotal and *germanía* regimes.

Notes

1. APPV Prot. 26371, Tomàs Argent, non-paginated (26 June 1427).
2. ARV Prot. 789, Martí Doto, non-paginated (24 August 1421).
3. See ARV Prot. 420, Joan de Campos (Sr), non-paginated (12 February 1427).
4. *Furs de Valencià*, V-I-XVII.
5. For example see APPV Prot. 16383, Dionis Çevera, non-paginated (9 September 1420).
6. ARV Prot. 416, Joan de Campos (Sr), non-paginated (29 January 1419).
7. Guiral-Hadziossif, *Valence*, p. 451.
8. Garcia Oliver, *Terra de Feudals*, p. 97. See also Furió, 'Tierra, familia y transmisión de la propriedad', p. 311.
9. Antoni Furió, *Camperols del País Valencià: Sueca, una communitat rural a la tardor de l'Edat Mitjana* (Valencia: Edicions Alfons el Magnànim, 1982), pp. 69–70.
10. *Ibid.*
11. See Jean Yver, *Égalité entre héritiers et exclusions de enfants dotés* (Paris: Sirey, 1966), pp. 41, 52–54.; Jean Gaudemet, *Les Communautés familiales* (Paris: M. Rivière et Cie, 1963); Emmanuel Le Roy Ladurie, *Les Paysans de Languedoc* (Paris: Mouton, 1966), pp. 162–167; Jean Hilaire, *Le régime des biens entre époux dans la région de Montpellier du début du XIIIe siècle à la fin du XVIe siècle* (Montpellier: Causse, Graille & Castelnau, 1957), pp. 217–367.
12. Vinyoles, *Les barcelonines a les darreries de l'Edat Mitjana*, p. 90; Winer, 'Silent Partners?', p. 72; García-Herrero, *Las mujeres en Zaragoza en el siglo XV*, p. 266.
13. Vinyoles, *Les barcelonines a les darreries de l'Edat Mitjana*, p. 90.
14. Gámez Montalvo, *Régimen jurídico de la mujer en la familia castellana medieval*, p. 88.
15. Howell, *Marriage Exchange*, p. 32.
16. Robert Jacob, *Les époux, le seigneur et la cité: Coutume et pratiques matrimoniales des bourgeois et paysans de France du Nord au moyen âge* (Brussels: Publications de Facultés Université St Louis, 1990), pp. 251–255; 281–290; 297–312.
17. Howell, *Marriage Exchange*, p. 32.

18 Winer, 'Silent Partners?', p. 73; Belda Soler, *El regimen matrimonial de bienes*, p. 110; Codina, *Contractes de matrimoni al Delta del Llobregat*, p. 56.
19 *Ibid.*
20 APPV Prot. 25474, Tomàs Argent, non-paginated (25 April 1439).
21 APPV Prot. 22852, Joan Péris, non-paginated (18 March 1425).
22 ARV Prot. 3159, Pablo Agustí, non-paginated (23 June 1434).
23 Rafael Gibert, *Historia general del derecho español* (Madrid: M. Huerta, 1981), p. 128.
24 Yver, *Égalité entre héritiers et exclusions de enfants dotés*, p. 52; Gaudemet, *Les Communautés familiales*, p. 179; Hilaire, *Le régime des biens entre époux*, p. 250.
25 Iradiel, 'L'evolució econòmica', p. 268.
26 Garcia Oliver, *Terra de Feudals*, p. 64.
27 Le Roy Ladurie, *Les Paysans de Languedoc*, p. 163.
28 Furió, *Camperols del País Valencià*, p. 60.
29 Le Roy Ladurie, *Les Paysans de Languedoc*, p. 163.
30 APPV Prot. 22097, Joan Peres, non-paginated (16 November 1436).
31 Furió, 'Tierra, familia y transmisión de la propriedad', p. 320.
32 *Ibid.*, pp. 321–324.
33 *Furs de Valencià*, V-II-IV.
34 *Ibid.*, VI-VI-X.
35 Castañeda, 'Organización familiar en el derecho valenciano', *Revista de Archivos, Bibliotecas y Museos* (1908), p. 271. Also see Honorio García García, 'La Germanía', *Boletín de la Sociedad Castellonense de Cultura*, 9 (1928), p. 171; María Belda Soler, *El régimen matrimonial de bienes*, p. 111; García-Herrero, *Las mujeres en Zaragoza*, p. 267; Philippe Godding, *Le droit privé dans les Pays-Bas meridionaux due 12e aux 18e siècle* (Brussels: Académie royale de Belgique, 1987), p. 295.
36 Belda Soler, *El regimen matrimonial de bienes*, p. 111.
37 García García, 'La germanía', p. 171.
38 Gámez Montalvo, *Régimen jurídico de la mujer*, p. 88.
39 García-Herrero, *Las mujeres en Zaragoza*, p. 267.
40 ARV Notal 2525, Juan de Campos (Sr), non-paginated (18 February 1425).
41 Heath Dillard and Martha Howell also assert that the society of acquisitions marital property regime was not always positive for women. Dillard found that in Castile, indebtedness and fines could erode conjugal wealth (*Daughters of the Reconquest*, p. 75). Similarly, Howell argues that describing the society of acquisitions as egalitarian in comparison to the dotal system is too simplistic and states that one needs to examine this marital property regime in conjunction with the social and gender implications of property law to fully understand how it functioned (*Marriage Exchange*, p. 10).

5

Earning the dowry: domestic service and donations

Whether artisan and *llaurador* women in fifteenth-century Valencia married under the dotal or *germania* system, they brought property with them which was acquired from a number of different sources. Some earned these assets as servants, apprentices and through other forms of work. Other women received donations from parents, siblings or extended kin. Work and familial donations were not the only forms of gathering marital property for labouring-status women. Neighbours and friends, that is, social kin, also provided assets to women at this important juncture in their lives. Artisan and *llaurador* women who were unable to gain enough property for a respectable dowry could receive charitable donations from a number of public and private sources. Men who married under the dotal and *germania* regimes received marital donations as well. The types and sources of these gifts reflected, rather than challenged, gendered notions of property as they supported inheritance trends prevalent in late medieval Valencia.

This chapter focuses on the methods by which labouring-status women fulfilled this second 'project of marriage': gathering sufficient marital assets. It begins by exploring the types of evidence historians have for considering this question, including notarial instruments such as *apochas* (receipts), testaments and *donation inter vivos* (living-will donations). We then turn to consider the various means artisan and *llaurador* women used to gain marital property including work (largely domestic service) and donation from family members, employers, neighbours, friends and charity. For comparison, this chapter also looks at marital donations to labouring-status men and explores how gender affected not only who women received donations from but also the type of property they were given.

As will become clear, the socio-economic and immigrant background of labouring-status women affected their ability to fulfil this project of marriage. Evidence from notarial contracts indicates that equally as many women donated their own dowries as their fathers. For those brides marrying under the *germanía* system, almost three-quarters did not receive a donation at the time of marriage. One can assume that if these women did bring assets to their new unions, they must have provided them on their own. The constantly shifting population of Valencia in the early fifteenth century meant that few labouring-status families had large networks of blood kin present. This was especially true for women with *germanía* contracts as one-third of them had immigrated to Valencia, some from as far away as Castile. While on the one hand, this could provide women with agency to marry according to their own wishes, on the other hand, the lack of familial presence may explain why some artisan and *llaurador* women did not marry under the dotal system, as they were not able to gain enough assets for suitable dowries. In the absence of family, immigrant women manoeuvred within the marital economy, responsible for providing their own marital property which often consisted of donations from a number of different sources.

Evidence: testaments, *donationes inter vivos* and *apochas*

In determining the methods by which labouring-status women gathered marital property, historians make great use of notarial documents. Dowry contracts provide some clues as they are drawn up to transfer a woman's dowry to her new husband, and therefore often indicate who is donating this property; however, labouring-status marriage contracts are often brief, formulaic and lacking in detailed information and thus do not necessarily give the entire picture of where artisan and *llaurador* women got the assets for their dowries. Three other types of notarial evidence – testaments, *donationes inter vivos* and *apochas* – can be used in conjunction with marriage contracts to help us to explore in more detail the myriad of methods that labouring-status women used in gathering dotal property, including work and donations from both familial and non-familial sources. Testaments and *donationes inter vivos* are also useful for exploring the types of donations artisan and *llaurador* men received on the occasion of their marriages.

The *Furs* had detailed laws regulating the transfer of property in late medieval Valencia, focusing in particular on the use of testaments and *donationes inter vivos*. Wills could be made in three forms: 'nuncupativo' or oral testament which a person dictated to a public notary in the presence of three or four witnesses which was then read publicly on the third day following the testator's death;[1] 'sacramental' which allowed a testator to explain to three or four men how he or she wanted his or her property disposed of;[2] finally, a testator which wished to keep his or her wishes entirely secret until death could write his/her own testament, have it sealed and signed by three to four male witnesses.[3] Unlike living-will donations, which were irrevocable once given, testators had the option to change their wills (whichever form they chose), or make entirely new ones. They were able to alter their wishes freely right up until the last day of their lives.[4]

Although most people were able to make testaments, there were some limitations laid out by the *Furs*. The testator must be older than 15 (this was younger than the age of majority to administer property which was 20); madmen, the deaf and the mute were not allowed to make testaments because of their mental and physical impediments;[5] and it was suggested (although not mandated) that married women who did not have children make their wills in the presence of their parents, provided they lived in the city of Valencia.[6] This last stipulation indicates that Valencian jurists were concerned that a woman's dowry, and other property, be returned to her family who had possibly provided her with it. They may also have been wary of the influence that her husband had over her testamentary choices.

It is interesting to note that while women were legally entitled to make testaments themselves, provided they were over the age of 15, they were not seen as fit for serving as executors.[7] Testators were able to choose freely their executors but, theoretically, the latter could not be women. In practice, this law was frequently ignored. Fifty per cent of labouring-status men named their wives as one of their executors. These men also nominated their mothers, sisters, mothers-in-law, aunts and female cousins to this position. In most cases, but not always, women were named alongside male executors. In comparison, married women rarely made other women the executors of their estates. Instead they named their husbands (75 per cent of testaments) or other family members (sons, nephews or brothers). This preference demonstrates that artisan and *llaurador* couples relied on their spouses to fulfil their last wishes regarding the division of their property.

In many ways, *donationes inter vivos* were like testamentary bequests; in fact, historians refer to these donations as pre-mortem inheritances with the bequests becoming effective during the lifetime of the donor, rather than at his or her death. Like testaments, the *Furs* allowed these donations to be concluded in verbal and written form.[8] Some donations were made conditionally and while *donationes inter vivos* were considered irrevocable, there were legal protections to ensure such provisions were met. As long as the stipulations attached to the gift were just and honest, the donation could be revoked if they were not met by the recipient.[9] Under all other circumstances, once given, these donations were final.

The *Furs* did have specific regulations regarding who was allowed to give donations by means of a *donatio inter vivos*, and to whom. Unlike testaments, in this area of property devolution the *Furs* followed the age of majority for making contracts, only allowing those over the age of 20 to use these notarial instruments. Although not forbidden to those with physical impediments as testamentary practice was, only those of sound mind could conclude a *donatio inter vivos*.[10] Beyond these stipulations, anyone could provide a donation to whomever they wished, with one caveat. In a clause that was clearly based on Roman legal principles, the *Furs* forbade all donations between husbands and wives. This proscription included both written and verbal agreements but did make allowance for last-breath requests.[11] This kind of exchange was forbidden in Roman law to ensure that marriage was based on affection, rather than gift or purchase. For Valencian jurists, greater emphasis was placed on protecting the interests of the spouses' families who wanted to prevent the loss of their patrimony to those outside of the lineage. In this manner, the proscription against donations between husbands and wives appears to have been largely concerned with immoveable property, the ownership of which had to be transferred by legal instrument. It seems unlikely that the inclusion of this statute in the *Furs* was to prevent spouses entirely from giving one another presents, especially if these gifts were brought for affectionate reasons.

Testaments and *donationes inter vivos* are useful in determining the kinds of assets labouring-status men and women brought to marriage, as well as from whom they received this property. Many of these documents stipulate whether or not the bequest was to be used for marriage. In her 1422 testament, Caterina Fortea, the wife of a *llaurador* from Valencia stated that she was donating 3 *fanecadas* of land each to her niece and her daughter, property which the girls were to use for their dowries at the time of their marriages.[12] In 1438, Jacmeta Steffani, the widow of a *llaurador* from Torrent donated several pieces of rented land and a rented house to her son, Pere Steffani, on the occasion of his marriage to the daughter of a *llaurador*.[13] The advantage of *donationes inter vivos* is that they were usually (although not always) drawn up in conjunction with a marriage contract and thus we know that the property donated was indeed used for its designated purpose. With testaments, although the testator may have stipulated the bequest was to be used as dotal assets, unless we also have the marriage contract, confirming that the wishes of the testator were carried out can be difficult.

Apochas, or receipts are the most useful documents for fully understanding the type of property, and from whence it came, that labouring-status women had at the time of their marriages. *Apochas* were drawn up between two parties, the donor and recipient, and it was not uncommon for women to have a series of these documents related to the transference of their marital assets. For example, on 6 January 1430, Sanrina, the daughter of a deceased man from Castelló concluded a dowry contract with the baker Joan Granada of Valencia. Sanrina promised to hand over a dowry of thirty pounds. Two *apochas*, one from 10 March 1430 and another from 18 May of the same year indicate that this property was indeed transferred by Sanrina in full.[14] Another series of *apochas* from October of 1433 indicate that Constança, the daughter of a deceased *llaurador* from Valencia earned half of her forty-pound dowry as a servant to the apothecary Francesc Barcelo of Valencia. The other half she received as a donation from her mother Guillamona. Constança herself handed over this property to her new husband, the *llaurador* Pere Lazer of Campanar.[15]

Documents such as these allow us to consider in more detail the source and type of property artisan and *llaurador* women brought as dowries, even if their marriage contracts do not provide a lot of information. Of course, *apochas* yield the greatest evidence when they are paired with a marriage contract. On 15 January 1422, Caterina, the daughter of a deceased *llaurador* from Alfosa concluded a dowry contract with the wooldresser Andreas Martini of Valencia. Caterina's dowry was much larger than most *llaurador* women at 150 pounds in cash, household goods and jewellery. Given the large size of her dowry, and the fact that her mother Margarita donated most of it, one would not expect that Caterina had actually worked as a servant to earn a portion of these assets; however, an *apocha* dated the same day as her marriage contract, indicates that Caterina received a payment of fifty pounds from her mistress, Maria Guitart, the widow of a wooldresser from Valencia. This detail is not included in Caterina's marriage contract and thus without the *apocha* we would have no way of knowing that she had worked as a servant prior to marriage.[16]

Earning marital assets through work

Notarial instruments of various kinds are thus crucial for understanding not only the value and type of property labouring-status women brought to marriage, but also where they got it from. Unlike elite women, whose dowries were exclusively donated by family members,[17] many labouring-

EARNING THE DOWRY: DOMESTIC SERVICE AND DONATIONS

status women earned at least a portion of their marital assets through work. The most common form of employment for young artisan and *llaurador* women in southern Europe was domestic service. These types of positions aided many young women, both those born in Valencia and those who immigrated to the city, in gathering much needed funds to marry. On average, domestic servants in early fifteenth-century Valencia worked for seven years, earning a salary of twenty-one pounds plus clothing, food, shelter and drink.

According to the terms of their contracts, domestic servants were to receive payment once their contract was fulfilled, which usually happened when they reached the age of 18 to 20 and were presumably ready to marry. On 19 January 1436, Benedicta, the daughter of a deceased *llaurador* of Teruel concluded a contract of marriage with the cobbler Simó de Romanos of Valencia. An *apocha* dated for the same day indicates that Benedicta's master, the merchant Guillem Catala handed over her salary of twenty-five pounds to Benedicta and her bridegroom.[18] This amount served as the totality of her dotal assets. Evidence from the Valencian archives indicates that this pattern of marriage (completion of a domestic service contract, followed closely by the conclusion of a marriage contract) was the most common for women who worked as servants in the early fifteenth century; however, in some cases, domestic servants fulfilled their contracts with their mistresses/masters and then waited to marry. For example, on 29 May 1434, the *llaurador* Dominic Navarro and his wife Angelina handed over property worth twenty-two pounds to the *llaurador* Dominic Suriano of Rubiol. Suriana was acting as tutor for Mariete Suriana, the daughter of a deceased *llaurador* (likely his brother). Mariete earned these assets, which consisted of cash and a dress, through her work as a domestic servant in the Navarros' household. An addendum to the *apocha* indicates that this property was then handed over to her bridegroom, the *llaurador* Joan Carbonell on 15 October 1436.[19]

In 1434, Mariete was clearly not old enough to administer property on her own and thus her salary was handed over to her tutor, a man likely appointed by her father at the time of his death or by the court if Mariete's father had not made sufficient arrangements. While Valencian law stated that adulthood was achieved at 20, anyone over 15 could administer their own assets. Orphaned children from birth to age 15 required a tutor to take care of these goods and to act legally on their behalf.[20] Unfortunately, we do not know at what age Mariete married Joan Carbonell as the addendum does not provide this information, nor was I able to find a marriage contract for the couple; however, clearly the salary she earned as a domestic servant was earmarked for marriage and likely remained under the control of her tutor until her union with Joan Carbonell was arranged.

Although the age of 15 was given by the *Furs* as the moment when a person could legally administer his or her own property, it is clear that both the law and the courts recognized that many young men and women were not capable of doing so at this age. Built into the legal code was the office of *curator*, a representative appointed by the court (or one's parents) to administer the assets and protect the rights and obligations of someone deemed unable to do so for whatever reason. Such incapacities included age (for example, unborn children of pregnant women or minor children of a remarrying mother) and the poor management of property.

Numerous young men and women aged 15 to 20 also had *curators* appointed to administer their assets and legally protect their rights and obligations. In some cases, their fathers were deceased or not present in the city of Valencia. Domestic servants who immigrated to Valencia on their own were good candidates to have *curators* appointed to take care of their salaries, especially if they did not marry immediately after fulfilling the terms of their service contracts. For example, an *apocha* from 4 June 1422 indicates that the *llaurador* Joan Coller of Ruçafa handed over twenty-five pounds to Caterina, the wife of the *llaurador* Laurent Çafont, also of Ruçafa. The contract indicates that these assets were Caterina's domestic service salary (known as *soldata*).[21] A subsequent *apocha* from the same day has Caterina then transferring this property to her husband as dowry. Joan Coller was not Caterina's father but her *curator*, and thus was charged with taking care of her *soldata* until she married or reached the age of 20.

Although Caterina's father was deceased and therefore not able to aid in taking care of her assets himself, it was not unusual for children whose fathers were still alive to have *curators* appointed. For example, the Valencian notarial records contain evidence of fathers who had *curators* appointed to property that their children inherited from their mothers.[22] It was equally possible for a *curator* to be named to the goods of a young woman whose father was not present in Valencia. *Curators* were chosen either by fathers or appointed by the court. While the court preferred to appoint *curators* from a pool of blood kin, there was nothing to bar them from choosing someone unrelated. There are examples from late medieval Valencia of courts naming neighbours to the position of *curator* in the absence of family.[23] The fact that the court approved of this practice emphasizes the centrality of social kin who could fill the void and act as natal family members would in their absence. Of course, the office of *curator* was not designed specifically to aid young women without familial presence in protecting their property, but it did fill an important need in a city such as Valencia which had large numbers of young female immigrants without family present.

Why did Mariete and Caterina need *curators* in the first place? Why did they not marry right away, and thus have their husbands administer their goods on their behalf? Domestic service contracts were usually designed to end around the age that a young labouring-status woman was expected to marry and so contracts for girls aged 11–12 were normally for terms of six to seven years. Such was the case for Caterina whose father, the *llaurador* Pastasius Malonda of Valencia concluded a service contract for her with the wooldresser Joan Mingot for six years. The contract indicates that Caterina was 11 and so could be expected to marry upon its fulfilment when she was age 17.[24] While the vast majority of domestic service contracts were like Caterina's and thus ended when the servant was 17–19, not all worked this way and there are examples for shorter terms, ending far before the young girl was of typical marriageable age for an artisan or *llaurador*. On 19 October 1426, Dolça Cerda, the widow of a *llaurador* from Castellón concluded a domestic service contract with Caterina Verdù, the wife of a cobbler from Valencia. The contract stipulated that Dolça's daughter Yolant, age 7, was to work as a domestic servant in Caterina's home for six years, earning a salary of ten pounds.

It was extremely unusual for labouring-status girls to marry at the age of 13, partially because they could not have gathered sufficient assets for an honourable dowry. Yolant's salary of ten pounds from her six-year term as a domestic servant in the Verdù household was less than half of what most labouring-status women brought as dotal assets to marriage; however, there was no legal reason why Yolant's mother Dolça could not place her in another domestic service position for three to five more years, thus increasing the size of her dowry. A series of *apochas* from 14 February 1439 indicate that some young girls did fill multiple domestic service positions.[25] In the first contract, the notary Jacob Berbegal of Valencia handed over seventeen pounds of *soldata* to his servant Benedicta, her father the *llaurador* Michael de Mahiques of Teruel and her groom the *llaurador* Garcias Penes of Valencia. A second *apocha* for another seventeen pounds shows the tanner Bernat Caraguo of Valencia paying the same recipients Benedicta's salary for her tenure as a domestic servant in Caraguo's household. Unfortunately, neither *apocha* indicates the length of each domestic service position, nor do they indicate Benedicta's age, either when she first became a domestic servant or when the *apochas* were dated. Benedicta, or her family, perhaps knew that marriage after her first domestic service contract was not possible and so looked for another position to increase her earnings and allow for more time to find a suitable groom. The fulfilment of several domestic service positions prior to marrying was quite common in areas of northern Europe such as England as servants there signed yearly contracts and thus moved from job to job on a frequent basis.[26] But this kind of mobility for domestic servants in Valencia was unusual and all but two of the sixty-one service contracts examined for this book ended when the girl was between 16 and 20.[27]

While obtaining multiple domestic service positions was not common for young women in late medieval Valencia, there are numerous other reasons why women might not marry soon after completing their contracts and thus would need a *curator* to administer any earnings. Late medieval society considered marriage the ultimate goal for all women, regardless of status; however, this social norm does not mean that all women wished to or even could marry. Demographic evidence for the percentage of unmarried women in late medieval Europe is somewhat scattered, and fluctuates considerably depending upon whether or not 'unmarried woman' refers to someone who never married or someone who had not yet married.[28] Despite these difficulties, historians argue that under 10 per cent of women in late medieval southern Europe never married.[29] Their reasons for not marrying include economic problems (an inability to raise sufficient funds to marry) and social problems (difficulty finding a spouse or the need to take care of ill/elderly family members). It is likely that some of the female servants in late medieval Valencia chose not to or were not able to marry when their contracts ended, thus explaining their need for a *curator* to administer their assets. This situation is especially true if they were under the age of 20 and did not have any family members present in the city to assist them.

Whether or not domestic servants married at the completion of their contracts, the intended use of the salaries they earned was for dowry assets. It was not common, however, for the dowries of artisan and *llaurador* women to come from domestic service alone. Eighty per cent of marriage contracts for women clearly identified as domestic servants in our sample indicate that the *soldata* was only one part of the dowry. Thus while domestic service was often a crucial means of gathering marital assets for labouring-status women, it was not the only one. Added to the *soldata* were donations from parents, siblings, extended family members, charitable institutions, neighbours and employers. The rest of this chapter will explore marital property donation from these varied sources, how it aided artisan and *llaurador* women in achieving marital unions and what kinds of assets they, and their new husbands, received upon marriage.

EARNING THE DOWRY: DOMESTIC SERVICE AND DONATIONS

Marital donation: *type of property*

Before considering who provided labouring-status women and men with marital property donations, let us first revisit the issue of what kinds of assets women and men received. In Chapter 3 of this book, the size and type of property that artisan and *llaurador* women brought for their dowries was discussed in detail. To reiterate the central points: the average monetary value of these dowries was twenty to forty pounds and they consisted largely of moveable assets such as cash, household goods and jewellery; although 20 per cent of women brought immoveable assets (rented land and houses) and *censal* investments. Testamentary bequests are reflective of the tendency to provide women with moveable dotal assets. In the eighty-nine donations for marriage made in eighty wills examined for this book, 85 per cent were monetary bequests. While women less frequently received living-will donations of property intended for their dowries (donors tended to give this directly to the husband by dowry contract instead), in the nine examples examined for this book, women received moveable assets in six. Given the system of partible inheritance followed in Valencia, the donation of moveable assets to women for their dowries reflects the desire of labouring families to keep any immoveable property they held intact to pass on to their sons.

Women who married under the *germanía* regime also largely received moveable property as marital donations. While just over half of these women were given a combination of cash, household goods and jewellery, a further one-third of donations were composed of moveable and immoveable property with only three woman receiving *donatio inter vivos* entirely of immoveable assets. All three of these women had deceased fathers and were of *llaurador* background, supporting claims made in Chapter 3 of this book regarding the important effects that such conditions had in disseminating immoveable assets to women in the late medieval period. Evidence from *germanía* contracts therefore supports the premise that a gendered division of property was practised in late medieval Valencia.

In many ways, the assets that women who used the *germanía* system received from donors can be viewed in the same manner as dowries. They were gifts of property that they received for marriage; however, this property was different in two central ways. First, wives benefited from any increases made on the marital assets that they contributed to the conjugal fund as they jointly owned it with their husbands. Conversely, they suffered any losses. This was different from the dotal regime where any gains or losses were accredited to husbands as administrators of this property, and supporters of the burdens of marriage, provided the assets were estimated. Second, when marriages dissolved, wives received half of the assets owned by the couple which diverged from dotal practice where they only recovered their dowry and *creix*.

The marital assets women received from their families were considered their share of the family patrimony,[30] whether they married under the dotal or *germanía* regime. This was also often the case for men who received a donation from their families at the time of marriage. This donation could be either part or the entirety of the patrimony they were entitled to.[31] Some families did give an equal amount of property to female and male children as marital donations, demonstrating that they desired to assist all of their children in setting up economically viable households.[32] Whereas the marital property that daughters received was often donated directly to their new husbands, sons were given these assets through *donatio inter vivos*, living-will donations. Just over 10 per cent of grooms (37 out of 367) received a living-will donation from a variety of donors on the same day that their dotal marriage contracts were drawn up. In comparison, approximately 25 per cent of grooms (21 out of 88) marrying under the *germanía* regime received a donation, largely from their families.

Paulino Iradiel has argued that *donationes inter vivos* to the groom from his family first appeared alongside marriage contracts in the fifteenth century.[33] While he does not explain why these documents developed at this specific time, one can speculate that the upheaval created in the late fourteenth century due to the plague influenced families in the early transmission of property to their male offspring. Not only does Iradiel argue that this kind of pre-mortem property devolution developed at the beginning of the fifteenth century, he also states that it was a decidedly artisan practice; however, evidence from the 1420s and 1430s indicates that *llaurador* families were as much, if not more, likely to devolve assets on their male offspring at the time of their marriages. One-third of *llaurador* grooms marrying under both the dotal and *germanía* regimes received marital donations from their families in comparison to only nine per cent of artisans under the dotal system. No artisan who concluded a *germanía* contract received a *donatio inter vivos* at the time of marriage. While it was possible for grooms to receive donations for marriage on other days, the evidence analysed for this book still suggests that, contrary to Iradiel's assertion, *llaurador* grooms were granted them more commonly than their artisan counterparts.

While both sons and daughters received marital donations, the type of property that they were given was determined by gender. Female

EARNING THE DOWRY: DOMESTIC SERVICE AND DONATIONS

children received moveable assets whereas male children were more likely to get immoveable goods such as rented land and houses. In the fifty-eight living-will donations examined, men received entirely immoveable property in thirty-one and a combination of moveable and immoveable assets in a further fifteen contracts. For example, on the same day that he concluded a contract of marriage with Caterina, the daughter of the *llaurador* Pasqual Pont of Mislata (who brought a dowry of sixty pounds in cash, household goods and jewellery), Joan Stella (Jr), also a *llaurador*, was given by *donatio inter vivos* a rented house in the parish of St Joan, 1 *cafissada* of vineyards in the *horta* and another piece of arable land in Ramona from his father.[34] This kind of donation was equally true for men marrying under the *germanía* system. The *llaurador* Garcia Pereç received a donation from his parents Alvaro and Maria Pereç of 1 *cafissada* of arable land in Quart and a dovecote when he concluded a *germanía* contract with Beatrix, the daughter of a *llaurador* from Benaguasil in 1423 (Beatrix received a gift of forty-five pounds in cash, household goods and jewellery from her father on the same day).[35] In fact, *llauradors* such as Stella (Jr) and Pereç were much more likely to receive immoveable property, primarily a combination of rented arable land and houses, as a marital donation than artisan men. This form of property devolution is not surprising, given that the livelihood of these men was based on agricultural production, and they therefore needed some land to form the economic foundation of their new household; a factor also demonstrated by the prevalence of *llauradors* as the recipients of *donationes inter vivos* from their families.

Similarly, the trade of artisan men was based on the skills that they had acquired during their apprenticeships. In order to aid them in setting up their new households, and pursuing their new trades, these men were sometimes given tools as marital donations. For example, on 21 April 1423, the scribe Miquel Font provided his son Pere with all the tools necessary to set himself up as a barber on the occasion of Pere's marriage.[36] Another *donatio inter vivos* gave Bartolomé Tolia 110 pounds for his marriage to Johanna, the daughter of the blacksmith Pere de Lauguna in 1426. This gift consisted of fifty-five pounds in cash and a further fifty-five pounds in blacksmith tools. Bartolomé's donation was from his father Antoní Tolia who was also a blacksmith.[37]

In the case of Antoní Tolia, the donation of blacksmith tools indicates the graduation of his son from apprenticeship to the rank of journeyman. If their fathers were masters in this trade, such young men were groomed to take over the family workshop at a later stage. Even if his family were not of master status (which is the case of the Tolias), donating tools to a son at the time of his marriage served much the same purpose as giving land to a *llaurador* son. It helped to guarantee the economic prosperity of the newly married couple and secured the financial stability of the new household unit. In this manner, these donations were similar to dowries as they provided the economic foundation of the new conjugal union.

Marital donation: *donors*

Artisan and *llaurador* women received marital assets from a variety of familial and non-familial sources. While blood kin predominated as donors of this important property, numerous other non-familial donors were common, especially if we look at the property donated to labouring-status brides (see Table 5.1). Much like the amount and type of property brought by artisan and *llaurador* women to marriage, widowhood and deceased fathers influenced who acted as donors. For labouring-status men, marital donations came almost entirely from blood kin, emphasizing once again that such gifts were seen as a means of smoothly transferring property from one generation to the next (see Table 5.1).

For artisan and *llaurador* women who married under the dotal regime, *donzella* brides (those marrying for the first time) made up just under half of those providing the dowry in marriage contracts (see Table 5.2). Many of them worked as servants. Some received dotal assets from charitable bequests and through inheritance. Of labouring-status,

Table 5.1 Marital donation in *donationes inter vivos* and testaments, 1420–39 (total contracts: 94 *donatio inter vivos* and 102 testaments)

Donor	Men	Women	Total
Father	39	49	88
Mother	12	17	29
Brother	4	5	9
Mistress	0	13	13
Master	0	5	5
Sister	0	2	2
Parents together	4	2	6
Mother and brother	0	1	1
Extended family	2	21	23
Unknown man	1	5	6
Unknown woman	0	14	14
Total	62	134	196

EARNING THE DOWRY: DOMESTIC SERVICE AND DONATIONS

and often immigrants, such women relied upon the funds which they could cobble together from a variety of sources to provide sufficient dowries. Widows, on the other hand, almost exclusively donated their own dowries, indicating the independent status they had gained at their husbands' deaths.

Women who concluded *germanía* marriage contracts had an equally varied number of donors who provided them with assets to marry. Overall, most donors were blood kin but these women also received donations from employers, most often their salaries earned as domestic servants. Unlike dotal contracts, unless artisan and *llaurador* women who used the *germanía* regime received a donation as the time of their marriages, we have no way of knowing what type and amount of property they brought with them into the conjugal union, nor whence it came. Yet the *donationes inter vivos* contracts that are extant paint a similar picture to dowry donation, highlighting both familial involvement and the agency of these women to earn their own marital assets.

Although many different family members could provide funds to allow a woman to marry, fathers were still the central donors for artisan and *llaurador* women. The *Furs* did not compel a father to dower his daughter, unlike in Barcelona where a living father had to provide something for his daughter's dowry.[38] But for many artisan and *llaurador* men, generating the funds necessary for a suitable dowry was difficult, especially if they had numerous daughters. A journeyman mason would

Table 5.2 Marital donation in dowry contracts, 1420–39

Donor	Donzellas	Widows	Total
Woman	83	87	170
Father	83	2	85
Mother	24	1	25
Parents	9	0	9
Woman and relative	15	4	19
Brother	4	2	6
Extended family	12	0	12
Domestic service	18	0	18
Domestic service and family	6	0	6
Domestic service, family and other donors (non-familial)	16	0	16
Unknown male	0	1	1
Total	270	97	367

have to work forty-eight days to provide a twenty-pound dowry, approximately one-sixth of his annual income.³⁹ If he had three daughters, it would take a significant portion of his yearly wage just to provide them with a dowry that was at the low end of the scale for artisan and *llaurador* women. In addition, these figures do not taken into account the cost of living, but it can be seen overall that many artisan and *llaurador* men likely sought aid in providing their daughters with sufficient dotal funds.

Some women simply chose to marry under the *germanía* regime in cases where a dowry was not forthcoming. Still others were able to rely on mothers, siblings and extended kin to provide goods in addition to those given by fathers. Most commonly, the woman's mother added property to that already given by her husband. In some cases, this was done by testamentary bequest, usufruct rights over which the father often held until such time that his daughter married. For example in her testament of 30 March 1422, Caterina, the wife of the *llaurador* Jaume Fortea, left 3 *fanecades* of arable land to her daughter Isabel. The document stipulated that Jaume was to have usufruct rights over this property until such time that Isabel married.⁴⁰ In other cases, a woman's mother and father together donated dotal assets directly to the groom. This was the situation for Pasqual and Barbera Guerau of Mislata who endowed the wooldresser Joan Vianya with a sixty-pound dowry for their daughter Pasquala in 1422.⁴¹ Sometimes mothers were the central donors of their daughters' dowries, providing these assets directly to their children or even conferring them on grooms; however, this only took place if their husbands were deceased.

Interestingly, while the *Furs* does not regulate the donation of dowries by fathers, it does contain clauses that govern this kind of contribution by mothers. Specifically, it states that mothers do not have to provide their daughters with dowries out of their own property.⁴² The one caveat to this situation was if a father was unable to provide dotal assets, in which case, a mother was not to donate these funds out of her own dowry, unless expressly indicated in the dotal contract or stated before witnesses.⁴³ Fathers never had the power to donate dowries to their daughters from the goods of their wives without the latter's permission.

The clauses regulating maternal dotal donation raise several interesting points regarding the complex relationship between women and their dowries. To begin with, they demonstrate the ambiguous legal views regarding a woman's control of her dowry, while her husband was still alive. On the one hand, these laws reinforce the idea of the husband as merely the administrator, rather than owner, of this property. He could not alienate it for any reason without his wife's express consent, even to

EARNING THE DOWRY: DOMESTIC SERVICE AND DONATIONS

provide their daughter with a dowry. On the other hand, the *Furs* forbid the woman herself to alienate any part of her dowry, without his permission.[44] With its function to support the 'burdens of marriage', the dowry was seen as intrinsically tied to their marriage. Neither the husband nor the wife was able to dispose of it alone, demonstrating the key role of the dowry for the conjugal union.

Second, these legal articles recognize that women, even after they had children, still needed to retain their own dowries rather than dividing them among their offspring. While the dowry was used during the marriage to support the conjugal household, at its dissolution these assets became crucial for a woman's economic survival. A widow used dotal assets as a means of support and if she was compelled to give a share of them to her daughters, she could face serious financial limitations, especially if her own children were unwilling to take her in. For this reason, some women who did donate property to their daughters included stipulations in the dotal contract which gave them continued rights over this property. For example, in 1428, Ramoneta, the widow of the weaver Berenguer Ripoll, provided a dowry of sixty pounds to the shieldmaker Pere Garces for her daughter Johana. The property included a rented house located in the parish of St Joan de Mercat and Ramoneta stated that, as a condition of the donation, she was to have usufruct of this house until her death.[45] For other women, the maintenance of their dotal property after their husbands' deaths was important in case of remarriage, which was common for artisan and *llaurador* women

Third, the laws ensured that the rights of a woman's heirs were protected as the *Furs* mandated that her dowry was to be divided among her children. This included offspring from all of her marriages. If a woman's children had not reached the age of majority (20) at her death, this property was to be held in usufruct by their father or legal guardian.[46] If she had no living children, it was to devolve to her nieces, nephews or other kin.[47] The stipulations against using her dowry to provide dotal funds for her daughters therefore reflected the possibly complex devolution of these assets as there could be several different claimants to them.

Finally, beyond protecting the rights of husbands and heirs, the stipulations regarding maternal donation contained in the *Furs* recognize a mother's role as alternative head of the conjugal household. Depending on her husband's financial situation, or life span, it was possible for a mother to become the primary economic provider for her family. In that role, she would be responsible for providing the dowries of her daughters as well as supporting the household overall (including her husband). The *Furs* does state that a woman must support her husband and/or children out of her own property if he is impoverished for reasons beyond his control.[48] Even if her dowry was returned to her from her living husband by means of judicial restitution, if the reasons behind this legal action had been beyond his control, the woman had to provide support for her husband and family out of this property.[49] In this sense, she became the financial head of their household, which challenged gender norms and late medieval concepts of masculine honour. Yet the inclusion of these clauses in the *Furs* indicates that this was a situation which took place. In such instances, a woman's dowry could be the primary means of support, and assets from it were used to create greater opportunities for daughters.

Although there were restrictions on the ability of mothers to use their own dowries to provide dotal funds for their daughters, this was not the only property that they held. In some cases, these women had additional assets, usually inherited from kin that were equal to and even greater in value than their dowries. While the dowry was seen as a woman's share of the family patrimony, she could receive testamentary bequests from her parents above and beyond it.[50] In fact, due to the high mortality rate, some women were even made the central heirs of their fathers, giving them access to assets outside of their dowries which they could then bestow on their daughters as dotal bequests.

Valencian law termed all the property that a woman owned beyond her dowry *béns parafernals*, taken from the Roman legal term *parafernalia*. While *béns parafernals* were usually administered by the husband, alongside a woman's dowry, they were seen as separate and she was able to alienate them at any time and in any manner that she wished.[51] Her husband had no authority over this property, unless she transferred control of it to him by notarial instrument at the time of their marriage. For example, on the same day that he contracted marriage with Leonor, the daughter of the *llaurador* Jaume Uget of Patraix, Pere Teulada, *llaurador* of Beniparell, received administrative control over all of the property which his bride had inherited as the principal heir of her mother. This contract was drawn up between Teulada and his new father-in-law, transferring usufruct rights over Leonor's inheritance from one man to another.[52]

For women marrying under the *germanía* regime, fathers, more than any other blood kin, were the donors of marital property. As with dotal contracts, mothers could also provide *germanía* donations; however, in the contracts examined for this book, they only did so as widows. For the most part, these widows were acting as the executors of their husbands' wills, conveying property that had been bequeathed to their daughters. For example, Johana, the widow of the carter Martí Alvaro, as usufruct holder of her husband's property, and as his executor, gave a rented

EARNING THE DOWRY: DOMESTIC SERVICE AND DONATIONS

house in the parish of St Esteve and ten pounds in household goods to her daughter Ursola on the occasion of her marriage to Joan de Pina, a blacksmith.[53] While husbands often named their widows as executors of their estates, in defiance of Valencian law, even more frequently they made their spouses the guardians of their children. As discussed earlier in this book, in most cases, if these women remarried, they would lose their usufruct rights, as their deceased husbands did not want their property to come under the control of another man. This did not preclude guardianship, however, and the *Furs* allowed children to remain under the control of their mothers who simply had to support them from their own assets, rather than those of their deceased spouse.[54]

Beyond their parents, artisan and *llaurador* women received marital funds from numerous family members including brothers, sisters, aunts, uncles, step-parents and grandparents. Donations from kin were small amounts which were combined to create a single dowry or the entire dotal fund itself. Women with *germanía* contracts could also receive numerous gifts at the time they married, largely through *donationes inter vivos*. Dotal contributions came through direct donation to the husband, testamentary bequest and *donationes inter vivos*, sometimes from the donors' own property, at other times, from goods which they held as executors and tutors. On 9 September 1430 Bartolomeva, the daughter of a deceased *llaurador* from Valencia brought a dowry of fifty-five pounds to her marriage with the *llaurador* Bernat Balester. These assets were donated by her tutors, Guillem Pastor and Bernat Mart and they were left to Bartolomeva by her deceased father in his testament.[55] In this case, Pastor and Mart acted as conveyers of property which Bartolomeva's father had already earmarked for her dowry. Marrying the *llaurador* Martí de Mora of Albal by *germanía* contract, Elvira, the daughter of a *llaurador* from Callosa, received a donation of fifteen pounds from her brother Miquel Domingo from his own property. Unlike their father, who lived quite a distance from Valencia, Miquel also resided in Albal and appears to have helped his sister contract her marriage with Martí.[56]

The two women above were both *donzellas* when they married. Widows received donations as well, although less frequently. In 1432, Dominic Noguera, a cutler from Valencia, donated ten pounds in cash to his sister Isabel as dotal assets in her marriage to Pere Mala, a tailor from Onda. This property made up just under half of Isabel's twenty-five-pound dowry, allowing her to provide an average-sized dowry for a woman of labouring-status. Despite the fact that she had previously been married, Isabel's brother felt he still had familial responsibilities to help her conclude a suitable remarriage.[57]

Both male and female siblings provided gifts to their widowed sisters to help them remarry. It is possible that economic hardship forced these women to turn to brothers and sisters for help, especially if their parents were deceased or not in the city of Valencia. This aid could come in many forms, from food and shelter to marital funds. In some cases, siblings may have had less than affectionate reasons behind their donation of assets for remarriage. For example, on 4 May 1429, Clara, the wife of the tanner Gabriel Pardo, endowed Antoní Trullos, also a tanner from Nules, with a dowry for her sister Caterina, the widow of a tailor.[58] This dowry was seventy pounds in cash, more than double that of the average artisan woman. The first half of dotal contract closely followed the formula presented in all other marriage contracts examined for this book; however, it is the second half which makes it unique and raises questions about the widow Caterina and her marriageability. Clara stipulated that if the marriage between Antoní and Caterina lasted less than five years, Antoní only had to return half of the dowry. But if it endured beyond five years, the full value of the dotal fund was to be returned to Clara or her heirs. The widow-bride Caterina was not present at the drawing up of this marriage contract.

Given the unusual conditions included in this contract, one must wonder how attractive a spouse Caterina was as it appears that her sister Clara was providing the groom with financial incentives to marry her sister. In her actions, Clara disregarded legal precedent that held the dowry as belonging to the wife. While her husband had administrative rights over it, he never, at any time, had ownership. According to the *Furs*, at a woman's death, her dowry was to devolve to her direct descendents (children) or be returned, in full, to the original donor.[59] But in this case, if the marriage lasted fewer than five years, Antoní would receive thirty-five pounds of the dotal fund. This suggests that Caterina was an older widow; moreover, the contract does not consider possible offspring of the couple. As the *Furs* had strict rules of inheritance regarding a woman's dowry, stipulating its division between her children, it can be deduced that Caterina was beyond childbearing age.

The seventy-pound dowry, combined with the possibility of financial reward, made Caterina an attractive spouse for Antoní. Clara appears to have used her husband's trade connections to secure Caterina a suitable groom as both men were tanners; however, Antoní lived in Nules, 65 kilometres north of the city of Valencia. Marrying her sister to Antoní relieved Clara of the responsibility of taking care of Caterina who appears to have had little influence in this arrangement as she was not present at the drawing up of the contract. The fact that Clara was willing to provide a seventy-pound dowry for Caterina could indicate genuine concern for her sister's welfare. In this manner, the direct involvement of siblings and extended kin in bestowing dowries shows their desire to improve the situation of their female relatives by providing additional dotal funds to increase their chances on the marriage market.

Familial testamentary bequests represent further evidence of altruism by kin groups who provided their female relatives with the funds necessary for suitable dowries. In the testaments examined for this book, seventeen women and eight men left bequests to nieces, sisters, granddaughters, stepdaughters and even great-nieces. Stanley Chojnacki has argued that female kinsmen in Venice left more dotal bequests than male[60] and that they did so out of affection, rather than concerns for lineage.[61] While Chojnacki's evidence comes from the testaments of elite women, wills from Valencia suggest that women of labouring-status were also more likely to leave dotal bequests to their female relatives than their husbands. Although lineage may not have been as much of a concern for artisan and *llaurador* families, the honour and social status of their kin group was still important. The desire to help their female relatives find a spouse that would augment or reinforce this status influenced the familial motives behind testamentary dotal bequests. In addition, it is not so far fetched to assume that kin also wanted a suitable spouse for their female relatives, someone who would care for and support them, making affection a factor in their testamentary choices. While both men and women assisted their female kinsmen financially in choosing the best possible spouse, historians have argued that there was a distinct relationship among female relatives who gave dotal bequests and donations to create dowries that would attract a wider, and better, pool of grooms. As married women themselves, they understood the necessity of generating sufficient dotal funds for an honourable marriage.

Relying on testamentary bequests and donations from kin to generate marital funds may not have been an option for some women, such as those who had immigrated to Valencia and were without familial ties in the city, or those whose families were simply too poor. In addition, many labouring-status women were faced with the situation of having garnered some dotal assets, but not quite enough for a dowry appropriate to their status. Both orphaned girls and those whose fathers were still alive were faced with such circumstances, since providing dotal assets could be a significant problem for artisan and *llaurador* men who had many sons and daughters.[62] One of the most common charitable donations in the later Middle Ages across Europe was providing dowries for poor girls and there were various forms of charity available in Valencia to which impoverished women or their families could apply to for dotal aid.[63] This kind of assistance was given by hospitals, confraternities, the municipality and private individuals.

In Valencia, numerous guilds had ordinances which stipulated that members were to provide dowries for the daughters of those who were financially unable to. The ordinances from the guild of the tanners stated that 'those members who were poor or lacking in temporal goods, who had daughters of marriageable age…their guild brothers should help in this task'.[64] Providing dowries for the daughters of poor members helped guilds to retain the honour of their corporation, and went hand in hand with paying for the funerals of those that had become impoverished. This type of marital donation was largely available to the daughters of master artisans, who were least likely to need it. Although journeymen did have their own separate guilds/confraternities, they do not appear to have provided this kind of aid, possibly due to a lack of funds.[65]

Privately, people of all statuses, from nobles to patricians to master artisans and even those of labouring-status, left dotal money for young poor girls in their wills.[66] Members of the Valencian elite frequently left numerous small donations to poor girls as dotal aid in their testaments. For example, in a series of *apochas* from 1433, executors for the testament of *honrada* Johana, the wife of *honrat* Berenguer Molineri, provided dotal funds ranging from thirty pounds to 60 sous to twenty-two poor young women. Three-quarters of these donations were in the 60–150 sous range and all the girls who received assets had deceased fathers. While those of labouring-status were not able to leave the same number and amount of charitable bequests as an elite woman such as *honrada* Johana Molineri, nevertheless they too often donated funds to aid poor orphan girls in marrying. For example, in his testament of 4 July 1439, the tailor Joan Martí left 20 sous for orphan girls to marry.[67] In the same year, Johana, the wife of a *llaurador* from Ruçafa, left a bequest of ten pounds to be used as dotal assets for poor orphan girls.[68] Some of these donations went to the city's numerous parishes who then doled out dowry money to deserving girls in their catchment but Valencia also had a confraternity dedicated to providing orphaned girls with dowries. The '*almoina de les òrfenes a maridar*' was created in 1293 by ten merchants and became a confraternity in 1309.[69] With close ties to the mercantile community, this institution was in private and lay hands. It used funds gained from testamentary bequests and other donations, which were then invested in *censals*, to provide young orphaned girls with dotal assets.[70]

Orphaned girls were not the only females to received charitable donations for marriage. They were also given to girls whose fathers were financially unable, or who were immigrants to the city. In 1423, when Caterina, the daughter of a man from Castile, married Antoní de Vilamosa, a wooldresser from Valencia, she brought a dowry of fifty-five pounds, generated from three different sources. Twenty-five pounds had been left to her by the honoured citizen Joan Tolsa in his testament. A further twenty pounds was a bequest from Joan's brother Jaume Tolsa and the remaining ten pounds came by means of a *donatio inter vivos* from Francesca, the widow of the deceased master wooldresser Bernat Vallseguer.[71]

The series of documents that sets out the transfer of this property from the three donors to Caterina and her husband demonstrate the charitable actions of Valencians from different social statuses. The widow Francesca appears to have been the catalyst for these donations as it is she who eventually conferred the entire fifty-five-pound dowry on Caterina and Antoní in a *donatio inter vivos* drawn up one week after their marriage contract. Since there is no indication that Francesca and Caterina were blood relatives, it is likely that Caterina was Francesca's servant. Francesca, by collecting the various dotal bequests and conferring them as one sum on the couple, was performing a parental function that employers often did in the absence of family.[72] As Caterina's father, Francesc Çalbo, lived in Castile, he was not present to provide his daughter with a dowry. Moreover, Francesca's late husband was a master wooldresser, the same trade practised by Caterina's groom. As Antoní was a journeyman, it is possible that he worked in Bernat Vallseguer's workshop. It appears likely that Caterina met Antoní through the Vallseguers. The testamentary bequests from the brothers Tolsa are clearly charitable donations, possibly solicited by Francesca for her charge.

While many women received marital donations from a variety of sources, including familial and non-familial donors, as discussed earlier in this chapter, others earned these assets on their own. The prevalence of artisan and *llaurador* women as the central donors of marital assets is clearly influenced by immigration, widowhood and deceased fathers. The constantly shifting population of the city meant that few labouring-status families had large networks of blood kin present. This was especially true for women with *germanía* contracts as one third of them had immigrated to Valencia, some from as far away as Castile. While on the one hand, this could provide women with the agency to marry according to their own wishes, on the other hand the lack of familial presence may explain why some artisan and *llaurador* women did not marry under the dotal system, as they were not able to gain enough assets for suitable dowries. In the absence of family, immigrant women became responsible for providing their own marital property which often consisted of donations from a number of different sources.

In certain cases, these women relied on neighbours and friends to perform the functions that their relatives would in a smaller community. Artisan and *llaurador* women, in particular, left money as dotal gifts to the daughters of their social kin. These monetary bequests were relatively small, averaging 50–100 sous, but they demonstrate the close ties and neighbourhood solidarity that developed within a community where blood relatives were often absent. For example, Clara Mancosa, the widow of a tailor from Valencia, left 100 sous each to the daughters of a deceased tailor and a deceased tanner. Given that these young women were without fathers, Clara's small dotal bequests were essential. Providing multiple small donations to the surviving daughters of a friend or neighbour, such as Clara did, was common and helped to ease the burden that fathers with numerous daughters faced in bestowing suitable dowries.[73]

Like the testamentary dotal bequests left by women to their female relatives, marital donation by labouring-status friends and neighbours was a decidedly female action in early fifteenth-century Valencia. Of the nine bequests of this sort examined for this book, all but two were from women. Fully aware themselves of the importance that a sufficiently honourable dowry held, these women were sympathetic to the plight of their young female neighbours. Such concern is evident in testaments like that of Sansa Albast, the wife of a *llaurador* from Torrent. Not only did Sansa leave dotal bequests to the daughters of two neighbours, she also provided charitable dowry donations for poor orphan girls in two parishes of the city.[74] Women like Sansa were considerably freer than their husbands to dispose of their non-marital assets as this property was not governed by the Valencian laws of partible inheritance. Both men who made dotal bequests to the daughters of neighbours had no children themselves. For example, the shoemaker Antoní Morell left twenty pounds to Isabel, and a second twenty pounds to her sister Caterina, both daughters of Bernat Perez. Added to Morell's donations, was a further ten pounds that his first wife Johana, in her own testament, bequeathed to Isabel alone. This couple's childlessness contributed to the higher donations made by Morell who conferred the assets on Isabel and Caterina that he would have used for his own daughters' dowries.[75]

Not only did artisan and *llaurador* women receive dotal bequests from their friends and neighbours, they were also given such donations by their masters and mistresses. These additional gifts frequently came in the form of both testamentary bequests and *donationes inter vivos*. They were common across southern Europe.[76] For example, Maria, the daughter of a wooldresser from León, gave the mason Joan Alfons forty pounds as her dowry in 1424. Fifteen pounds of these assets were from her wages as a servant to Daniel Mascaros; however, twenty-five pounds was a testamentary bequest left to Maria by Mascaros's wife Margalita.[77] As the gift from Margalita was much higher than Maria's wages, it suggests that the two women had developed an affectionate relationship over the course of Maria's time as a servant in the Mascaros' household.

Mistresses were far more likely to provide dotal donations to their servants than masters and the size of these gifts ranged from 5 sous to twenty-five pounds.[78] Beyond extra dotal funds, masters and mistresses provided money for wedding expenses[79] and even held wedding feasts for their servants in their own homes.[80] As described in the introduction of this book, Maria Oviet, the wife of the ropemaker Francesc Oviet, testified in the dowry restitution case of her former servant, Teresa Dauder, that the couple's betrothal and wedding feast had taken place at her house. Although Teresa's parents were still alive at the time she married Tomàs Dauder, they lived in Sogorb, some distance from the city of Valencia. Maria and Francesc Oviet therefore acted as Teresa's surrogate parents.[81] Teresa had joined the Oviet household as a young girl, which was the case for many female servants who could be contracted at ages as young as 5 or 6 years. These girls worked for their employers for up to twelve years so it is not surprising that their masters and mistresses frequently went above and beyond their duty in providing marital aid.

Not surprisingly, widowhood greatly affected a woman's ability to provide her own dowry. Eighty-seven per cent of widows marrying in the documents examined for this book donated their own dotal assets. Only two of nineteen widows with *germanía* marriage contracts received marital donations, one from her mother and the second from two women whose relationship to the bride I was unable to determine.[82] Most widows were in control of their marital property from previous marriages, and able to freely donate it to a subsequent spouse, provided they remarried at least one year after their previous husband's death.[83] In addition, some widows inherited assets from their husbands, especially in the absence of children. This was the case for Johana whose husband the *llaurador* Pere Carbonell named her universal heir, giving Johana half of his property and usufruct rights to the other half for life, provided she did not marry again. The couple did not have any children, although Pere divided half of his assets among various members of his extended family which they were to receive at Johana's death.[84] Even if the couple did have offspring, a husband could divide his estate between his children and wife, who retained usufruct rights over all of this property until the children came of age, or she married again. Such was the case for the *llaurador* Bernat Martí of Morvedre who made his wife Jacmeta and two daughters, Isabel and Ursola, co-heirs of his estate. Jacmeta retained usufruct rights over the entire estate until her daughters married, provided that she remained a widow.[85] If a widow had previously married under the *germanía* system, she would have access to her half of the conjugal fund which could then be used to contract a new marriage. In some cases, widows would even receive the entirety of the couples' marital property if they did not have offspring, making them very attractive partners and, according to Paulino Iradiel, 'serious rivals of single virginal women in the marriage market of the time'.[86]

Just under half of *donzellas* who concluded their own dotal contracts had fathers who were deceased. The property that they brought as dowry was their share of the family patrimony and was equal to that inherited by their siblings because of partible inheritance laws followed in Valencia. There is evidence that, at least for labouring-status families, some patrimonies were equally divided between male and female children. For example, in his testament of 1421, the shieldmaker Alfons Ferran, while making his wife Elvira the executor of his estate, divided his property equally between his son Alfons (Jr) and his daughter Isabel.[87] Valencians' implementation of partible inheritance as dictated by the *Furs* appears to have differed from inhabitants in other areas of southern Europe, such as Marseilles, which theoretically had a system of partible inheritance but in practice equality between sons and daughters was rarely practised.[88] In Barcelona, sons tended to be preferred over daughters, particularly if a son was born to a second marriage, despite inheritance laws which stipulated that the family patrimony was to be equally divided among all living children.[89]

The testamentary bequests that labouring-status daughters received from their fathers were obviously earmarked for their dowries. For this reason, it is somewhat problematic to consider such funds as assets garnered by women themselves because, in reality, this dotal property was no different than that donated directly by still-living fathers. But the high infant mortality rate of late medieval Valencia (on average families had two surviving children) meant that some artisan and *llaurador* men had only one living child at their deaths. Whether male or female, that child would be made the universal heir of their father's estate. While part of the property they inherited was meant for their dowries, these heiresses decided themselves the amount and type of assets they conferred on their grooms. For example, the carpenter Lois Amoros left all of his property to his daughter Caterina, including a specific bequest of 100 pounds that was to be set aside for her dowry.⁹⁰ In another testament, the shoemaker Jaume Bella made his infant daughter Angelina universal heir of his estate, leaving her under the guardianship of her mother.⁹¹ Female offspring could also be made the central heirs of their mothers, in which case they would inherit the entirety of their mothers' marital assets, including dowry and *creix*. This was the case when Blanqua, the wife of a tailor, had her testament drawn up in October of 1428. While she named her husband Pere Sanxo as executor, and left ten pounds each to her brothers Bartolomé and Pere Cerda, the bulk of her estate went to her daughter Yolant.⁹²

Fewer *donzella* women marrying under the *germanía* regime had deceased fathers as only 20 per cent (13 out of 69) indicated that their father was no longer alive at the time that they married. Evidence demonstrates that three of these women were named the universal heirs of their fathers' estates and they therefore brought all of the property that they inherited as marital assets. This included the promise of future inheritance as was the case for Caterina, the daughter of the *llaurador* Bernat Cebria of Massalfassar, who concluded a *germanía* marriage contract with the *llaurador* Antoní Carbonell of Rafelbunyol on 18 February 1425. On the same day, Caterina's father Bernat drew up his testament, giving her sixty pounds in household goods and jewellery specifically for her marriage as well as making her the principal heir of his entire estate. It is interesting that Cebria made Caterina his heir, knowing that she was marrying Carbonell under the *germanía* regime and that therefore all of his property would, one day, be jointly owned by his son-in-law.⁹³ Cebria's trust was not misplaced as his daughter and her husband appear to have prospered after marrying, so much so that four years later, Caterina and Antoní Carbonell were able to provide a 175-pound dowry for Caterina's sister Ursola when she married the *llaurador* Jaume Ametler of Massamagrell.⁹⁴

The practice of naming daughters the universal heirs of their parents' estates was not uncommon elsewhere in Europe. In Marseilles, if there were no surviving sons, a father would almost always make a daughter his principal heir rather than a male relative.⁹⁵ Evidence from this Mediterranean city shows a high number of women providing their own dowries, which Daniel Smail argues, is an indication of their position as principal heirs to their fathers' estates. While sons were generally the preferred central heirs in Barcelona, if no male offspring survived, daughters were often named.⁹⁶ Daughters could be named principal heirs in Genoese testaments as well but rather than heiresses in their own right, they were viewed as simply transferring the family patrimony from grandfather to grandson. This type of property devolution was preferred to making one's son-in-law the central heir as it attempted to keep these assets within a woman's natal kin group. To ensure this happened, testaments included stipulations that if the woman died without offspring, these assets would revert to her relatives.[97]

The evidence discussed above clearly demonstrates that artisan and *llaurador* women were able to draw on a variety of sources in gathering marital assets. In many cases, the women themselves bestowed this property on their new spouses, earning wages as domestic servants and garnering small bequests from friends, neighbours and kin. The situation was different for labouring-status men who received marital donations through *donationes inter vivos* and testamentary bequests. All but one of the fifty-eight living-will donations given to men for marriage were from blood kin. In the single exception, the relationship between the groom and donor was not indicated. Although men received decidedly fewer testamentary bequests for marriage, all were from family members. Similar to women of the same status, artisan and *llaurador* men were often immigrants to the city of Valencia, but it is interesting to note that all of the men that received *donationes inter vivos* for their marriages had family that lived in the same location as themselves, whether in the *horta* or the city. In providing marital donations to their male kin, these families gave artisan and *llaurador* men an early share of the patrimony to be used in setting up their new conjugal household.

The primary donors of marital property to artisan and *llaurador* men were their fathers, followed by their mothers and their parents together. These donations acted as pre-mortem inheritances, advancing the division of the family patrimony. For example, on the same day that he concluded a contract of marriage with Ursola, the daughter of a *llaurador* from El Puig, Ramón Pujol received a *donatio inter vivos* from his father Antoní Pujol (Sr) of 9 *fanecades* of vineyards and another 9 *fanecadas* of wheat-producing land in the *horta*, plus twenty pounds in cash.[98] Five years earlier, the elder Pujol had given a donation to another son, Antoní (Jr), when he married Maria, the daughter of a baker.[99] This kind of pre-mortem division of the family patrimony was common in Valencia for families that had more than one surviving child. Although by law, Valencia followed partible inheritance, there was a tendency among *llaurador* families in particular to keep the majority of the land for one son and divide the rest among the remaining children when they married by means of *donationes inter vivos*.[100] This kind of inheritance pattern explains the exclusion of sons from testamentary marital bequests as they had already received their share of the familial estate.

By giving such donations to their sons for marriage, artisan and *llaurador* parents were helping to establish a firm economic foundation for the newly formed conjugal household. While it was common for elites to have extended family household structures, the predominant form for those of labouring-status was nuclear.[101] This was especially true of immigrant families.[102] But even for those whose families were from Valencia, when they married, they formed a new household that was distinct from the parental one.[103] This is partially a reflection of the later age at which artisan and *llaurador* couples married in comparison to those of elite status.[104] In addition, having served as apprentices and servants in a non-familial household for up to ten years, it is unlikely that these men desired to return to the paternal home.

Once they had taken a spouse, usually at the age of 25 or older,[105] *llaurador* men left the paternal home. Although married couples lived separately from their parents, *llaurador* families often continued to farm their scattered land parcels together. Kin groups organized their labour to cover all of the patrimonial lands, some of which were now owned by the children.[106] These collective familial farming practices were much like the *germanía* farming contracts used by poor *llauradors* who pooled their labour and resources with friends. Labour would be shared to work the plots and the profits from the land divided after all rents had been paid. In fact, some men who married under the *germanía* system likely already held the property they brought to the conjugal fund by this form. *Llaurador* families also tended to conduct land transactions among themselves in order to keep their property as coherent a unit as possible.[107] *Donationes inter vivos* from fathers to sons are one example of this attempt to preserve the integrity of familial holdings, as a counterbalance to the land division so characteristic of late medieval Valencia.

While the majority of *donationes inter vivos* between families and their male children for marriages involved *llauradors*, artisan men also received such donations. Similar to *llaurador* parents hoping to ensure the financial success of the new conjugal household, artisan parents donated property which they felt would be the most useful for their children. Hence, these donations were largely cash, artisanal tools and space in rented houses. If we can interpret the actions of *llaurador* fathers as attempting to consolidate control of familial landholdings, and help their sons establish their own agricultural careers, we can look at the donation of artisan fathers in a similar manner. Gifts of cash, tools and living spaces were all essential for the young artisan journeyman to set up his new household. In particular, gifts of tools demonstrated the passing on of familial trade skills as sons almost always practised the same trade as their fathers.[108]

In most cases, familial donations to grooms consisted of part of the family patrimony, whether pieces of land, cash or artisanal tools.

Occasionally, parents transferred all of their property to their married children, a move that was clearly intended to allow the new household to thrive.[109] This form of donation was practised by both artisan and *llaurador* parents who often attached stipulations to their gifts. For example, when her son Bartolomé Solat, a *llaurador* from El Puig, concluded a contract of marriage with Caterina, the daughter of a *llaurador* from the same town, the widowed Francesca Solat donated all of her moveable and immoveable assets to him, under the proviso that she retain usufruct rights to this property until her death.[110] Other conditions that appeared in these contracts were the provision of food, clothing and shelter for the lifetime of the donor.[111] Stipulations such as these were not unique to the marital donations of sons as daughters also received dotal gifts with similar conditions.

In the evidence examined for this book, overall, men who married under the dotal system received considerably fewer marital donations than their brides. Only 10 per cent of labouring-status grooms were given such gifts at marriage. In most cases, artisan and *llaurador* parents were themselves struggling to get by and were not financially able to provide for their sons in this manner. Like their female counterparts, labouring-status men worked to generate the income necessary to marry as journeyman artisans and day labourers. Once married, the couple together utilized her liquid dotal assets, and their combined income, to finance their household.

The situation was somewhat different for those couples with *germanía* marriage contracts. For couples using this marital property system, more women received *donatio inter vivos* than men (twenty-seven to twenty-one). Together, just over 50 per cent of *germanía* unions came with a donation of some kind. A higher percentage of grooms who married under the *germanía* regime received marital property donations than those marrying under the dotal system. This tendency was directly linked to their status as *llauradors*. Two-thirds of couples with *germanía* marriage contracts were of *llaurador* status. All of the grooms receiving donations whose social background was noted were *llauradors* and of those seven whose status is not known, three were married to daughters of *llauradors*. Given the pattern of marital endogamy followed by *llaurador* men (78 per cent married women of the same status);[112] it is likely that these men were also of farming background. A further three men were from the *horta* and received donations of rented land, an uncommon gift for artisan men. Overall, 35 per cent of *llauradors* marrying under the *germanía* system received a donation; in comparison, none of the artisans did. As stated earlier, as land was the basis of their livelihood, the reception of such marital property donations was essential for newly married young *llaurador* men in setting up their new households. It is not surprising, therefore, that a higher percentage of men marrying under the *germanía* regime received a gift of marital assets at marriage in comparison to those using the dotal system. Like those couples whose economic unions were founded on dowries, *germanía* couples utilized their combined assets to serve as the basis of their newly created households.

The social meaning of donation

Marital property was given to brides and grooms by donors for a variety of reasons that reflected the nature of their relationships. For some, these donations were simply altruistic, given as tokens of love, affection and friendship or to strengthen and perpetuate emotional bonds. Yet for others, these gifts had decidedly concrete purposes, designed to create important social, economic and political alliances. Whether or not their donors intended it, gifts of marital property served specific functions within late medieval Valencian society. Natalie Davis has examined the meaning of marital gifts in pre-modern societies in depth and raises three central functions: to express affection, compassion and/or gratitude among people who lived in the same parish, generating familiar affection; to reinforce the idea of marriage as an alliance, not only between the couple and their respective families, but also between the bride and groom and the community in which they lived;[113] to ensure that children conformed to the wishes of their parents in making marital choices.[114] Each of these purposes can be examined in light of the Valencian evidence to explore the social meanings behind marital property donation for those of artisan and *llaurador* background.

Notarial evidence from Valencia clearly demonstrates that marital property donations worked to express affection, compassion and/or gratitude among those that lived in the same neighbourhood. Testamentary bequests by women and men to the daughters of their neighbours reveal fond attachments created among those that lived in the same parish. The immigrant background of many Valencians furthered these feelings, supplanting blood kinship ties with those of social kin. Many of these donations were also given out of compassion, in an attempt to provide the largest dowry possible for those women whose families were unable to provide sufficient funds. This is supported by the popularity of charitable bequests, even among less well-off artisans and *llauradors*, to institutions which provided dowries for poor girls. Testamentary bequests from masters and mistresses to their servants for marriage show the gratitude of some employers for companionship given. The gift of 100 sous and a dress from the wife of a notary to her young servant Francesceta 'who was always at my side' indicates that close relationships could develop.[115] Servants often cared for ill employers up until their deaths and donations such as these were made in recompense for this care.

Marital donations also had a clear function for late medieval Valencian families: the exchange of property that characterized marriage was used to cement alliances between kin groups. As Mauss has argued that 'a gift that does nothing to enhance solidarity is a contradiction.'[116] Donations of marital property undeniably developed a web of connections between the families of bride and groom, provided they were present in the city. These essential links were not only created between the parents and the couple but, as the evidence from Valencia demonstrates, involved siblings, extended family and neighbours. Even for those artisan and *llaurador* couples that had immigrated to Valencia, marital donation worked to create ties within their own communities. Widows who provided their own dowries strengthened bonds created within particular parishes by marrying men who practised the same trade as their deceased husbands. *Donzellas* gave dotal assets earned as domestic servants to men who worked in a similar field to their masters. Labouring-status men and women left testamentary bequests of marital assets to young girls who lived nearby. All of these actions worked to strengthen the blood and social kin bonds within a given community.

Finally, Davis' argument that gift-giving could be used by parents to persuade their children into marrying those whom they deemed appropriate is clearly demonstrated by Valencian laws which allowed parents to disinherit daughters who went against their wishes. Interestingly, this law does not mention sons, and, given the low number of men who received *donationes inter vivos* at marriage from their families, it appears that these coercive measures had less effect on male offspring. But as labouring-status women were more involved overall than elite women in generating their own dowries, parents of the former had less of a say in whom their daughters married. This was strengthened by the immigrant status of many artisan and *llaurador* women whose families simply were not present to object.

Historians and anthropologists emphasize the reciprocal nature of gift-giving. Some have even described the obligation created as a heavy burden, which the recipient alone bore.[117] Historians whose work focuses on marriage in the medieval and early modern periods have largely used these theories to explore the nature of gifts given by husbands to their brides after marriage. Using records from Renaissance Italy, Christiane

EARNING THE DOWRY: DOMESTIC SERVICE AND DONATIONS

Klapisch-Zuber and Jane Fair Bestor have analysed the groom's counter-gift, known as the *antefactum* (the *creix* in Valencia) as well as the counter-trousseau of clothing and ornaments sometimes received. These authors argue that both gifts were given because of the demand for reciprocity created by the woman's donation of her dowry. Klapisch-Zuber and Bestor state, however, that the reciprocal nature of this exchange was more symbolic than real as these gifts were reappropriated by the husband, or his heirs, when the marriage dissolved, or the wife died.[118] According to Florentine law (the area studied by both Klapisch-Zuber and Bestor), any gifts a husband gave to his wife were only seen as loans that had to be returned.[119] Even the *antefactum* was eventually restored to the husband, or devolved to his heirs, at the time of the wife's death. The exchange of property that took place at marriage was therefore never truly reciprocal as the wife did not actually own the assets that had been given to her by the husband.

I feel that the narrow use of gift theory by Klapisch-Zuber and Bestor can be expanded to examine the larger web of connections created by marital property donation in late medieval Valencia. In doing so, more questions are raised than answered, but I believe that thinking about gifts of marital assets as part of a system of reciprocity can allow one to examine the power dynamics created among family, friends and neighbours in a given community during the later Middle Ages. As the analysis of Natalie Davis's arguments surrounding the functions of gifts has indicated, people provided marital property donations for specific reasons, linked to what they hoped to gain from the new alliance that was created.

At its most basic level, the exchange of property concluded at marriage demanded reciprocity between the bride who donated a dowry and the groom who responded with the *creix*. Yet it must be noted that the *creix* was valued at half of the dowry, leading one to question if the honour in bestowing this gift was reduced. Klapisch-Zuber argues that the amounts of the gifts was unimportant, rather the fact that they had been exchanged was the central symbolic aspect in terms of the new alliance created.[120] But this raises the issue of women who did not receive a *creix* from their husbands. After 1329, widows in Valencia no longer received a *creix*. Did the widow have greater power over her husband than a *donzella* bride? Popular literature has certainly portrayed her in this light. In his brilliantly satirical poem, Valencian author Jaume Roig has King Solomon decry the wicked and capricious nature of widows who live ostentatiously off their deceased husbands' estates, while simultaneously turning their new spouses into cuckolds.[121] Wealthier widows who brought more assets to the marriage than their husbands, perhaps having been named heirs of their deceased spouses, were often described in such terms by literary works.[122] Fears about the independence of widows often reflected anxieties present in late medieval society in regard to the lack of male authority over these women.

Germanía marriage contracts perhaps present the greatest example of reciprocity creating equality between the bride and groom at marriage. The very nature of this marital property regime demanded equal access for both spouses to the conjugal assets. But one must question if they can be described as contracts of gift exchange as couples did not actually give one another gifts but combined their property into one conjugal fund that they both enjoyed. In this manner, *germanía* contracts were less about reciprocity, and more focused on the future financial state of the conjugal union.

If we expand our analysis beyond the couple themselves to look at marital property donation by family members and neighbours, the ties of reciprocity and exchange become more intricate, demonstrating numerous layers of power relationships. The father-in-law who donated a dowry to the groom did not receive a gift in exchange at the time of the couple's marriage as the *creix* went to his daughter. According to Mauss's arguments, this debased the groom who accepted the dowry and placed him in the power of his father-in-law.[123] This kind of unequal relationship can be highlighted for all those who provided dowries, or other marital property donations, directly to grooms on behalf of their brides. In some cases, the groom may have reciprocated simply by taking the woman off the hands of the donor, as appears to be the case in the marriage of Caterina and Antoní Trullos mentioned above. In other situations, reciprocity was delayed until such a time that a favour was needed. For *llaurador* grooms whose families donated tracts of rented land to them by *donationes inter vivos*, the fact that husbands often continued to provide their labour to the family holdings after marriage helped to fulfil their obligations.

Overall, anthropological theories of gift-giving allow historians to think beyond the economic aspects of marital property donation to explore social networks that were created between donors and recipients. As donation contracts and testaments often do not indicate the reasons behind these gifts, anthropological theories of gift-giving permit considerations of their wider social implications and meanings. In this way, we can consider decisions made by those of artisan and *llaurador* status regarding marital property donation to blood and social kin in new ways, exploring the intricate web of relations created by this kind of gift-giving.

Whether they married under the dotal or *germanía* regimes, labouring-status brides and grooms were able to utilize a wide pool of

EARNING THE DOWRY: DOMESTIC SERVICE AND DONATIONS

donors willing to provide assets at the time that they married. Women received more donations from family members than any other group but also accessed neighbourhood networks, and their own labour, to provide adequate marital funds. Their ability to generate marital property on their own demonstrates the agency that artisan and *llaurador* women had in ensuring the sufficient funds necessary to marry according to their station. Men received fewer gifts of marital property than their brides, but those that did were almost always of *llaurador* background, gaining these gifts from their families who lived in the same location as they did. In this manner, and in light of the cooperative nature of farming for some families living in the *horta*, gifts to labouring-status men can be viewed as furthering the production of the family patrimony. When examined in light of anthropological theories of gift-giving, the idea of reciprocity created by these donations demonstrates the networks of power relations that existed between husband and wife, the couple and their parents, siblings, kin and neighbours. This dynamic becomes even more interesting when we next examine cases of dowry restitution, which returned marital property to brides who did not necessarily donate it themselves, further complicating power structures.

Notes

1 *Furs de València*, VI-IV-I; II; IV, pp. 146–147; Francisco Roca Traver, 'El Testamento', in *La jurisdicción civil del Justícia de Valencia, 1238–1321* (Valencia: Real Academia de Cultura Valenciana, 1992), p. 225.
2 *Furs de València*, VI-IV-XIV, pp. 153–154. The *Furs* did emphasize that witnesses always be male.
3 *Ibid.*, VI-IV-XVIII, p. 157.
4 *Ibid.*, VI-IV-IX, p. 150.
5 *Ibid.*, VI-III-IV, p. 137.
6 *Ibid.*, VI-III-VIII, p. 141.
7 *Ibid.*, VI-IV-XXI, p. 160.
8 *Ibid.*, VI-VIII-XX, p. 203.
9 *Ibid.*, VI-VIII-XXIV, p. 206.
10 *Ibid.*, VI-VIII-XIX, p. 202.
11 *Ibid.*, V-IV-I, p. 33; V-IV-II, p. 34. Initially Jaume I had forbidden the transfer of property between husbands and wives through written instrument. This law was expanded under Martí I in 1403 to include oral *donationes inter vivos* as well.
12 ARV Prot. 821, Bernat Estrellers, non-paginated (30 March 1422).
13 ARV Prot. 471, Berenguer Cardona, non-paginated (5 June 1430).
14 APPV Prot. 23404, Joan Peres, non-paginated (6 January 1430); (10 March 1430); (18 May 1430).
15 APPV Prot. 23409, Joan Peres, non-paginated (23 October 1433).
16 ARV Prot. 2613, Bernat Estrellers, non-paginated (15 January 1422).

17 Amparo Baixauli argues that in the seventeenth century, elite women had fewer donors of marital property than lower-status women and all of them were kin (*Casarse al'Antic Règime*, p. 82). Marriage contracts of elite women from the fifteenth century demonstrate that this was also the case two hundred years earlier. For example, *honrada* Elinor, widow of *honrat* Bernat Borell donated 2,200 pounds as dowry for her daughter Elionor, to Luis Çabata, baron of Castellnou in 1423. Of this, 700 pounds was a testamentary bequest to Elionor by her father, 300 pounds was donated by her aunt Clara and the final 1,200 pounds was from Elionor (Sr) APPV Prot. 23267, Joan de Pina, non-paginated (26 September 1423).
18 ARV Prot. 793, Martí Doto, non-paginated (19 January 1436).
19 ARV Prot. 792, Martí Doto, non-paginated (29 May 1434).
20 Traver, *La jurisdicción civil del Justícia de Valencia*, p. 173.
21 ARV Prot. 1266, Andres Julien, non-paginated (4 June 1422).
22 Traver, *La jurisdicción civil del Justícia de Valencia*, p. 200.
23 *Ibid.*, p. 201.
24 ARV Prot. 422, Juan de Campos (Sr), non-paginated (15 December 1432).
25 ARV Prot. 794, Martí Doto, non-paginated (14 February 1439).
26 Ann J. Kettle, 'Ruined Maids: Prostitutes and Servant Girls in Later Medieval England', in Robert R. Edwards and Vickie Ziegler (eds), *Matrons and Marginal Women in Medieval Society* (Woodbridge, UK: Boydell Press, 1995), p. 20.
27 Of course, not all domestic servants remained in their positions for the allotted time as laid out in their original service contract. Girls who abandoned their positions could face penalties, such as the loss of any assets earned. Whoever has concluded the original domestic service contract with the master/mistress on their behalf could also be sued for breach of contract and would thus lose the funds they pledged as a guarantee. These obligations fell on both sides and therefore masters/mistresses could not dismiss a servant without penalty. See Lora Serrano, 'El servicio domestic en Córdoba a fines de la Edad Media', p. 244 and Maria de Carmen García-Herrero, 'Mozas sirvientas en Zaragoza durante el siglo XV', in Cristina Segura and Angela Muñoz (eds), *El trabajo de las mujeres en la edad media hispana* (Madrid: Editorial Laya, 1988), p. 280. If both servant and master/mistress agreed to end the contract, no penalties were mandated. See ARV Prot. 2428, Vicent Zaera, non-paginated (2 March 1431; contract cancelled 1 October 1431).
28 Maryanne Kowaleski, 'Single Women in Medieval and Early Modern Europe: The Demographic Perspective', in *Single Women in the European Past, 1250–1800* (Philadelphia: University of Pennsylvania Press, 1998), pp. 39–40.
29 *Ibid.*, p. 42. Much of this evidence comes from Italy, where fuller evidence is extant for such demographic studies.
30 Guiral-Hadziossif, *Valence*, p. 458; Furió, *Història del País Valencià*, p. 198.
31 Dolores Guillot Aliaga, *El regimen económico de matrimonio en la Valencia foral* (Valencia: Biblioteca Valenciana, 2002), p. 50.
32 Guiral-Hadziossif, *Valence*, p. 455; Iradiel, 'Familia y función', p. 237.
33 Iradiel, 'Familia y función', p. 237.
34 ARV Prot. 10422, Martín Doto, non-paginated (29 October 1430).
35 ARV Prot. 11239, Desconocido, non-paginated (24 October 1423).
36 ARV Prot. 417, Joan de Campos (Sr), non-paginated (21 April 1423).
37 APPV Prot. 26371, Jaume de Sant Vicent, non-paginated (12 February 1436).

38 Vinyoles, *Les Barcelonines a les darreries de l'Edat Mitjana*, p. 86.
39 Hamilton, *Money, Prices and Wages*, pp. 275–276.
40 ARV Prot. 821, Bernat Estreller, non-paginated (30 March 1422).
41 ARV Prot. 1891, Andrés Puigmicha, non-paginated (22 February 1422).
42 *Furs de Valencià*, V-III-III, p. 29.
43 *Ibid.*, V-III-IV, p. 29.
44 *Ibid.*, V-III-IX, p. 33.
45 ARV Prot. 1094, Juan Garcia, non-paginated (20 June 1428).
46 *Furs de Valencià*, VI-IV-XX, pp. 159–160.
47 *Ibid.*, VI-V-I, pp. 192–196.
48 *Ibid.*, V-IV-IV, pp. 35–36.
49 *Ibid.*
50 But some women, once they had received their dowries, were excluded from their parents' estates. See ARV Prot. 2511, Bertrán de Boes, non-paginated (3 May 1420). In this testament, Elvira, the wife of Pere Ripoll, a wooldresser, states that she is excluding her daughter Ursola from her will (although making her an executor) because she had already received dotal funds from her mother when she married the wooldresser Antoni Agrit. Elvira then leaves her dowry and *creix*, which amount to 100 pounds, to her two sons Antoni and Jaume.
51 *Furs de Valencià*, V-III-VIII, pp. 32–33.
52 ARV Prot. 2427, Vicente Zaera, non-paginated (22 April 1430).
53 ARV Prot. 424, Juan de Campos (Sr), non-paginated (23 February 1431).
54 *Ibid.* If the children, or their relatives, did not want the surviving remarried spouse to retain guardianship, they could petition the court to have it removed and given to someone else.
55 ARV Prot. 10422, Martín Doto, non-paginated (3 September 1430).
56 ARV Prot. 791, Martín Doto, non-paginated (9 December 1431).
57 APPV Prot. 27356, Joan de Mas, non-paginated (25 November 1432).
58 ARV Prot. 2143, Juan Sarañana, non-paginated (4 May 1429).
59 *Furs de Valencià*, VI-IV-XXXI, pp. 166–167.
60 Chojnacki, 'Dowries and Kinsmen', p. 145. Also see Samuel K. Cohn Jr, *Death and Property in Siena, 1205–1800: Strategies for the Afterlife* (Baltimore: Johns Hopkins University Press, 1988), p. 207; Elaine G. Rosenthal, 'The Position of Women in Renaissance Florence: Neither Autonomy nor Subjection', in Peter Denley and Caroline Elam (eds), *Florence and Italy: Renaissance Studies in Honour of Nicolai Rubinstein* (London: Westfield Publications in Medieval Studies, 1988), p. 374.
61 Chojnacki, 'Dowries and Kinsmen', p. 151.
62 Teresa-Maria Vinyoles i Vidal, 'Ajudes a donzelles pobres a maridar', in Manuel Riu (ed.), *La Pobreza y la asistencia a los pobres en la Cataluña medieval: volumen miscelaneo de estudios y documents* (Barcelona: Consejo Superior de Investigaciones Científicas, 1980), vol. I, p. 296.
63 *Ibid.*
64 'que alguns de tals pobres e fraturajans de bens temporals que han filles grans de edad de maridar … requiring als dits confreres … fasen ajuda a maridar la filla de tal pobre et freturejen en bens' (quoted in Tramoyeres Blasco, *Instituciones gremiales*, p. 67).
65 Tramoyeres Blasco in his discussion of guilds providing dotal assets for the daughters of impoverished members, does not associate this practice with the numerous

journeymen confraternities that existed in Valencia (*Instituciones gremiales*, pp. 67–70). See also Piles Ros, *Estudio sobre el gremio de Zapateros*, pp. 53–54.
66 Vinyoles i Vidal, 'Ajudes a donzelles pobres a maridar', pp. 302, 325.
67 APPV Prot. 25474, Tomàs Argent, non-paginated (4 July 1439).
68 Ibid. (19 July 1439).
69 Agustín Rubio Vela, 'Infancia y marginación: en torno a las instituciones trecentistas Valencianas para el socorro de los huérfanos', *Revista d'Història Medieval*, 1 (1990), p. 122.
70 Ibid., p. 123.
71 Caterina and Antoni's marriage contract ARV Prot. 11239, Desconocido, non-paginated (23 January 1423). Other donation contracts to Caterina and Antoni: ARV Notal 2728, Vicente Zaera, non-paginated (13 July 1423) and ARV Prot. 2422, Vicente Zaera, non-paginated (30 January 1423).
72 Romano, *Housecraft and Statecraft*, p. 164.
73 ARV Prot. 2143, Juan Sarañana, non-paginated (18 May 1429); ARV Prot. 1094, Juan Garcia, non-paginated (30 August 1428); ARV Prot. 2421, Vicente Zaera, non-paginated (28 March 1420).
74 ARV Prot. 568, Bernat Centelles, non-paginated (17 November 1432).
75 APPV Prot. 23268, Joan de Pina, non-paginated (14 June 1421). The other testament which included this kind of dotal donation conformed to the smaller amounts left by artisan and *llaurador* women to the daughters of neighbours; however, in this case, it appears the testator was of considerably lower status than Antoní Morell. See ARV Prot. 3016, Marcos Barbera, non-paginated (27 September 1436).
76 For Florence, Herlihy and Klapisch-Zuber, *Tuscans and Their Families*, p. 225. For Genoa, Epstein, *Wills and Wealth*, p. 127. For Perpignan, Winer, 'Silent Partners?'. For Valencia, Iradiel, 'Familia y función', p. 241. Giovanna Benadusi, in her examination of wills from sixteenth-century Arezzo, Italy, has argued that testamentary dotal bequests by masters and mistresses to their female servants should not always be interpreted as evidence of affection. She points to the fact that these donations could simply be for unpaid wages, rather than as extra gifts of dotal funds. Benadusi states that 'Legacys of masters to their servants, then, should be read with cautiousness and their paternal [and maternal] generosity with a certain skepticism, especially in those cases when servants were young girls and when the bequest was intended as a dowry' ('Investing the Riches of the Poor', p. 823).
77 ARV Prot. 1893, Andrès Puigmicha, non-paginated (26 March 1424).
78 Of the eighteen testaments and living-will donations given to servants, thirteen were from mistresses.
79 Debra Blumenthal, 'Implements of labour, instruments of honor: Muslim, eastern and black African slaves in fifteenth-century Valencia' (Ph.D. dissertation, University of Toronto, 2000), p. 182 and *Enemies and Familiars: Slavery and Mastery in Fifteenth-Century Valencia* (Ithaca, NY: Cornell University Press, 2009). These kinds of bequests included funds for clothing. For example, Isabel, the wife of the notary Francesc de Monço left Francesceta, her servant, 'who was always at her side', 100 sous and a dress for her marriage (ARV Prot. 791, Martín Doto, non-paginated (16 June 1431)). See also Epstein, *Wills and Wealth*, p. 127.
80 Christiane Klapisch-Zuber, 'Female Celibacy and Service in Florence in the Fifteenth Century', in *Women, Family and Ritual in Renaissance Italy*, fn. 17, p. 174.

81 ARV Justicía Civil Peticiones 3723, m. 14, f. 35v. (30 September 1434).
82 APPV Prot. 27183, Lluis Guerau, non-paginated (14 March 1423) and ARV Prot. 471, Berenguer Cardona, non-paginated (28 December 1430).
83 The *Furs* stated that widows must remain chaste, and therefore unmarried, for one year after the death of their spouses. If they did not, they would lose their *creix* and any usufruct rights to their deceased husbands' property that they held. See *Furs de Valencià*, V-II-I to VI, pp. 18–22.
84 ARV Prot. 2143, Juan Sarañana, non-paginated (11 July 1429).
85 ARV Prot. 789, Martín Doto, non-paginated (20 May 1421).
86 Iradiel, 'Familia y función', p. 240. Giving usufruct rights to widows was practised elsewhere in the Crown of Aragon. Evidence from Barcelona demonstrates that just over one-third of widows gained these rights over their deceased husbands' property. See Equip Broida, 'La viudez ¿triste o feliz estado?', p. 33; Winer, 'Silent Partners?' p. 108; García-Herrero, *Las mujeres en Zaragoza en el siglo XV*, vol. I, p. 321.
87 APPV Prot. 23268, Joan de Pina, non-paginated (20 June 1421).
88 Francine Michaud, *Un signe des temps: Accroissment des crises familiales autour du patrimoine à Marseille à la fin du XIIIe siècle* (Toronto: Pontifical Institute for Medieval Studies, 1994), p. 83.
89 Equip Broida, 'La viudez ¿triste o feliz estado?', p. 34.
90 ARV Prot. 2866, Juan Peris, non-paginated (16 June 1424).
91 APPV Prot. 23267, Joan de Pina, non-paginated (13 March 1424).
92 ARV Prot. 505, Guillermo Cardona, non-paginated (14 October 1428).
93 ARV Notal 2525, Juan de Campos (Sr), non-paginated (18 February 1425).
94 ARV Prot. 421, Juan de Campos (Sr), non-paginated (7 February 1429).
95 Lord Smail, 'Démanteler le patrimoine', p. 350.
96 Equip Broida, 'La viudez ¿triste o feliz estado?', p. 34.
97 Epstein, *Wills and Wealth*, pp. 82–83.
98 ARV Prot. 1329, Pere Llorens, non-paginated (30 March 1429).
99 ARV Prot. 4206, Pere Llorens, non-paginated (2 January 1425).
100 Guiral-Hadziossif, *Valence*, p. 458.
101 For artisan family structure, see Iradiel, 'Familia y función', p. 232; for *llauradors*, see Furió, *Camperols del País Valencià*, p. 58.
102 There is evidence of some two-generation households in the *horta*, but they were far less common than nuclear ones (Furió, *Camperols del País Valencià*, p. 58).
103 Ibid.
104 Guiral-Hadziossif, *Valence*, p. 451.
105 Furió, 'Tierra, familia y transmisión de la propriedad', p. 321.
106 Ibid., p. 320.
107 Ibid., p. 327.
108 Navarro, 'L'Artisanat de la soie à Valence', p. 171; Tramoyeres Blasco, *Instituciones gremials*, pp. 367–369.
109 Guiral-Hadziossif, *Valence*, p. 455.
110 ARV Prot. 468, Berenguer Cardona, non-paginated (5 May 1426).
111 Guiral-Hadziossif, *Valence*, p. 455.
112 See Chapter 2 in this book.
113 Natalie Zemon Davis, *The Gift in Sixteenth-Century France* (Oxford: Oxford University Press, 2000), p. 47. The classic discussion of gift theory comes from Marcel Mauss's,

The Gift: The Form and Reason for Exchange in Archaic Societies, trans. W.D. Halls (London: Routledge, 1990), first published in 1923. This theory was then developed further by other anthropologists and sociologists such as Marshall Sahlins 'The Spirit of the Gift' and 'On the Sociology of Primitive Exchange', both in *Stone Age Economics* (Chicago: Aldine Publishing, 1972); Marilyn Strathern, *The Gender of the Gift: Problems with Women and Problems with Society in Melanesia* (Berkley: University of California Press, 1998); Helmuth Berking, *Sociology of Giving* (London: Sage, 1999).

114 Davis, *Gift in Sixteenth-Century France*, p. 110.
115 ARV Prot. 791, Martín Doto, non-paginated (16 June 1431).
116 Mauss, *The Gift*, p. vii.
117 Davis, *Gift in Sixteenth-Century France*, p. 16.
118 Klapisch-Zuber, 'Griselda Complex', p. 225; Jane Fair Bestor, 'Marriage Transactions in Renaissance Italy and Mauss' *Essay of the Gift*', *Past and Present*, 164 (1999), p. 8.
119 Bestor, 'Marriage Transactions in Renaissance Italy', p. 28.
120 Klapisch-Zuber, 'Griselda Complex', p. 224.
121 Jaume Roig, *Espill o Llibre de les dones*, ed. Jordi Tiñena (Barcelona: Laertes, 1988), p. 104. See also descriptions of the protagonist's mother who disinherits her son after her husband dies and takes up with a much younger man (pp. 53 and 56–57).
122 The most well known of these literary characters is the Wife of Bath from Geoffrey Chaucer's *Canterbury Tales*.
123 Mauss, *The Gift*, p. 63.

6

The right to property: dowry restitution in fifteenth-century Valencia

As has been demonstrated by the previous chapters, although the *Furs* gave control of all marital assets to husbands, this property was nevertheless always viewed as belonging to wives. Civil suits of dowry restitution brought by Valencian wives against their still-living husbands are the greatest manifestation of this control which, I will argue, represents the agency of women in protecting their marital property. The *Furs* recognized that although legally husbands had the right to control their wives' assets throughout their marriages, they did not always do so in an appropriate manner. Since women provided their husbands with a dowry in exchange for the necessities of life (food, shelter and clothing), men who did not fulfil this contract could also be faced with a suit of dowry restitution. While the *Furs* proclaims the theoretical right of women to have their dowries restored, extant evidence from dowry restitution cases demonstrates that this prerogative was in fact upheld. The overwhelming success of Valencian wives in dowry restitution suits indicates that courts recognized the inherent importance of this property by supporting the undeniable legal right of women to protect it from misuse by their husbands.

This chapter examines dowry restitution cases extant from two courts in Valencia: the Justícia Civil (court of the Civil Justice) and the Gobernació (court of the governor). It begins by investigating the reasons behind dowry restitution, looking at both articles contained in the *Furs* which allowed for this kind of litigation as well as how these played out in actual court cases. Next, this chapter will examine the structure of dowry restitution cases, the burdens of proof (witness testimony and documentary evidence) as well as the outcomes in each of the two courts. The evidence from these trials proves conclusively that the very laws that codified women's oppression in late medieval Valencia also gave them the means to negotiate a measure of control over their marital assets. Artisan and *llaurador* women were able to use the law to their own ends, demonstrating a wide knowledge of legal rights within Valencian society that cut across both status and gender lines.

Background: the Justícia Civil and the Gobernació

The primary court for dowry restitution in fifteenth-century Valencia was the tribunal of the Justícia Civil. For just the 1420–39 period, there are extant 220 cases of women suing for their dowries from their still-living husbands. Initially there was just one justice who dealt with both civil and criminal cases, but in 1321 two separate criminal and civil courts were established, each with its own justice.[1] The jurisdiction of the Justícia Civil was confined to the city of Valencia and its environs, with other towns maintaining their own separate civil courts. Although at first the civil justice was a royal appointee, by the fifteenth century he was elected by the municipal council.[2] Conditions were set stating that the justice must be a citizen of and live in Valencia; he could not be from the royal family, a cleric, moneylender, Jew or Muslim.[3]

While the Justícia Civil dealt with all civil cases in the first instance, the Gobernació was a court of appeal and treated cases with special circumstances. Presided over by the governor with jurisdiction throughout the kingdom of Valencia, this court's function in meting out the king's justice meant that, from its very inception, it acted to protect those deemed unable to take care of themselves: children, widows and others deemed '*miserabile personae*'.[4] Only four cases of women suing their still-living husbands for the restitution of their dowries are extant from 1420 to 1434. Much more common in this court were inheritance disputes involving widows seeking to have their dowries restored from the executors of their deceased husbands' estates. Those of upper social rank also used the court of the governor to determine their suits, preferring to air their differences before a representative of the Crown rather than of the municipality.

Although the *Furs* clearly outlined the separate jurisdictions of the criminal and civil justices as well as that of the court of the governor, there was still a great deal of conflict between them. Francisco Roca Traver has described the fourteenth century as a period of constant strife over jurisdiction between the *jurats* of the city of Valencia and the governor.[5] The king and his *Corts* issued laws reiterating the jurisdictional rights held by the courts in 1363, 1374 and 1390.[6] The Gobernació may have been relegated to handling appeals and cases of special circumstances by the *Furs* but evidence from dowry restitution suits demonstrates that it did stray beyond these confines.

The legal and contractual basis of dowry restitution

The right of a woman to sue for the restitution of her dowry from her living husband had precedence in Roman law. The *Corpus Iuris Civilis* allowed a wife to initiate a suit of dowry restitution when her husband became insolvent.[7] As a preferred creditor, the wife was able to make a claim against her husband's property before any other creditors;[8] however, she had to prove his complete insolvency before seeking the restitution of her dowry. Medieval jurists 'not only inherited and reaffirmed, but also amplified, the Roman law remedy that allowed wives to reclaim their dowries and other goods from insolvent husbands during marriage'.[9] In Italian juridical treatises, these laws were interpreted to allow for restitution if the husband merely inclined towards insolvency or if he was mismanaging his assets to the extent that 'if he satisfied his other creditors, he would not be able to satisfy his wife's claim'.[10]

The legal prescriptions regarding dowry restitution were integrated into the Valencian *Furs*, along with the rest of the Roman legal system of dowry. But the *Furs* increased the suitable grounds on which a woman could sue for restitution. Like Roman law, the *Furs* allowed the wife to seek restitution if her husband had become insolvent, but the *Furs* also stipulated that such a suit was possible if a woman's husband misused her property in any way, abandoned her, did not provide her with the necessities of life, or became a madman.[11] A wife whose marriage was dissolved through the fault of her husband – for example, because of adultery – was also able to initiate a suit of dowry restitution.[12]

Table 6.1 Reasons for dowry restitution, 1420–39 (total dowry restitution cases: 220)

Reason for restitution	Widows	Donzellas	Total
Debt/insolvency	17	154	171
Misuse of property	12	56	68
Poor administration of property	6	36	42
Not providing necessities of life (food, clothing, shelter)	2	73	75
Absence	6	33	39
Alienation of goods	3	45	48
Violence	3	10	13
Adultery	0	1	1
Domestic violence	0	1	1
Total	49	409	458

Although the *Furs* included a number of different reasons for initiating a suit of dowry restitution, the majority of the cases brought before the courts were linked to concerns about debt and insolvency (see Table 6.1). Out of the 220 cases, 171 women cited debt and/or insolvency as the reason behind their suit. In terms of insolvency, the *Furs* permitted a wife simply to prove that her husband was on the road to financial ruin as a valid reason for the return of her marital property, rather than requiring her to demonstrate his complete bankruptcy.[13] This clause allowed a wife who was concerned about the state of her husband's finances to use protective measures as a contingency plan. The greatest concern of the law was to guard a wife's assets from possible diminution, ensuring she had adequate funds to support herself in widowhood. To that end, wives who cited debt and insolvency as the reasons behind their suits stressed fears about the loss of their property to their husband's creditors. While the *Furs* mandated that a wife's dowry could not be seized by the creditors of her husband for the payment of his debts, evidence from the governor's court indicates that this did happen.[14] Although her suit was likely to be successful, a wife would then be faced with the legal headache of litigating against his creditors for the return of her property.

There was one caveat against a wife suing to regain her marital property from her currently, or soon to be, insolvent husband. As has been discussed in Chapter 3, the function of the dowry was to sustain the burdens of marriage. The *Furs* cited this as the reason why the husband should retain control of and administer these assets throughout the marriage. Insolvency demonstrated that the husband was incapable of successfully managing this property, and therefore he was seen as unable to support the family financially. When his wife regained control of these assets, it became her duty to sustain the burdens of marriage by providing for her husband and children out of the marital property. If the couple remained together after the wife had regained her dowry and *creix*, the *Furs* mandated that it was then her responsibility to support her family.[15] This clause clearly elucidates the dual purpose of the dowry which was connected to both the fortunes of the woman herself and her family.

Not only was the right to restitution enshrined in the prevailing legal code but it was also stipulated in every notarized dotal marriage contract. At the end of each contract, the husband solemnly promised to restore his wife's dowry 'at whatever time and for whatever reasons she wished, according to the laws of Valencia'. While this stipulation appears to have been merely formulaic, it was legally binding. Many of the petitions brought by wives support their claims by quoting this promise. Records of these lawsuits also occasionally include a copy of their marriage contract, used both to prove the validity of their marriage and the amount of the dowry donated as well as to demonstrate the promise of restitution sworn to by the husband.

The legal and contractual basis for dowry restitution in fifteenth-century Valencia was clearly laid out in the *Furs* and in marriage contracts. Judges in charge of determining the outcomes of dowry restitution suits had little trouble in interpreting the laws which allowed wives to sue their still-living husbands for the return of their marital property. In 152 out of the 155 dowry restitution cases from the court of the Justícia Civil whose outcomes are extant, the judge ruled that the wife should have her marital assets restored. In the remaining three cases, the judge asked for further investigation into the matter. The lack of legal ambiguity regarding dowry restitution meant that wives had little fear of losing their cases. In addition, the stipulation that all court costs be paid by the loser of the suit[16] meant that wives of all statuses had access to this kind of legal recourse.

Dowry restitution in the tribunal of the Justícia Civil: the case of Teresa Dauder against Tomàs Dauder

Valencian women who decided to sue their husbands for the restitution of their dowries made their primary claim with the Justícia Civil of the city. A suit of dowry restitution with this court had three stages: the initial claim, the presentation of evidence (witness depositions and documents) and the final sentence as determined by the judge. All aspects of the suit were recorded in Catalan in the book of the court (*Llibre de la Cort*) so that they could be used as evidence in case of appeal.[17] Although not extant for each year of the 1420s and 1430s, nineteen *Llibres de la Cort* survive from 1420 to 1439. Unfortunately, there is not a full record of all of the cases brought before the Justícia Civil for any one year; however, evidence indicates that approximately twenty to thirty suits of dowry restitution per annum involving wives and their still-living husbands were brought before this court.

Dowry restitution cases could also be initiated by widows seeking the return of their dowries from their husbands' reluctant heirs (in many cases their own sons), by the heirs of deceased women (usually their children) seeking their dotal inheritance from the executors of their mothers' estates or by husbands themselves seeking control of their adulterous wives' dowries in trust for their children. While the focus of this chapter is on the suits between wives and their still-living husbands, the other kinds of dowry restitution suits pleaded before the civil justice indicate the importance of dotal property to families. As Julius Kirshner has asserted, dowries helped to protect the welfare of the whole family, from the wife who needed control of this property to live an honourable life to her heirs who helped to transmit this patrimony to another generation.[18]

In order to illustrate how dowry restitution cases functioned in the court of the Justícia Civil, let us return to the case of Teresa Dauder against her husband Tomàs, a barber, introduced at the beginning of this book.[19] On Thursday 30 September 1434, Gabriel Bonet, a notary, acting on behalf of Teresa, came before the honourable justice Manuel Suau to plead a suit of dowry restitution against Teresa's husband Tomàs. This initial plea or *clam*, was written, rather than simply verbal, as the *Furs* stipulated that all civil suits must be presented in written form.[20] The use of a *procurator*, or legal representative, in this case Bonet, by Teresa followed the custom of most women making suits of dowry restitution. *Procurators* acted on behalf of their clients in all legal transactions and their use in court cases was extremely common, especially by women. While the law did not forbid women to act on their own behalf in court if the suit involved their property,[21] it is unlikely that many women had the legal knowledge to do so successfully. The importance of understanding the complexities of law in civil suits is underlined by the fact that most procurators were notaries.

The plea presented by Bonet on Teresa's behalf followed a formula set out by the justice for civil cases which contained two central aspects: an accurate description of the kind of property sought in the suit and the reasons why the petition for these assets was being made. As Teresa's suit was for her marital property, Bonet had first to indicate that the couple had indeed been married and that it was from their union that the assets in question derived.

> in the year 1429, a marriage was contracted, made, joined and solemnized in the holy mother church and afterwards consummated through carnal copulation between the said Tomàs Dauder and Teresa, daughter of Joan Dalarit, shieldmaker, inhabitant of the city of Sogorb.
>
> Moreover ... [after] the said marriage between Tomàs Dauder and Teresa was made and confirmed, those ones were and lived all the time together as husband and wife; they called themselves joined husband and wife and they are held, granted and joined as husband and wife from the said time ever since by all [their] familiars
>
> Moreover ... at the time of the contract of the said marriage, the said Teresa constituted and brought to the said Tomàs Dauder in and for her dowry according to the law of Valencia forty pounds of Valencian money and the said Tomàs Dauder [for] his marriage donation and *creix* [gave] to the said Teresa because of her virginity according to

the law twenty pounds of the said money. So thus the dowry and *creix* are sixty pounds of Valencian money which the said Tomàs Dauder secured for the said Teresa on and according to all his goods and rights to be held ... by the marriage contract that was made and confirmed by the above said in the power of Joan Caposa, notary on Sunday of the thirteenth day of the month of February of the year 1429.[22]

All suits of dowry restitution began in the same way as Teresa's, indicating that the couple had been married in accordance with canon law and then had exchanged property by means of a marriage contract. Some cases provide greater description of the dotal assets, stating that these consisted of household goods, jewellery, cash, *censals* or immoveable property; however, more commonly, the *clam* simply denoted the monetary value of the marital goods sought. While household goods and jewellery which women brought as dotal property may have been sentimentally significant, the monetary value of this property was far more important for women seeking to protect it or protect themselves from financial loss.

After indicating that a couple had indeed been legally married, and that property had been exchanged on the occasion of this union, the *clam* then turned to the reasons behind the suit of dowry restitution.

> Moreover...during the said marriage, Dauder incurred many and diverse debts and has diminished their goods so that now they are in poverty and their goods are valued at ten pounds ... and a lien has been made against the goods of Tomàs Dauder ...
>
> Moreover ... it is a case and place of restitution according to the law and the said Tomàs Dauder ought to be condemned to give, to return and to restore to the said Teresa, his wife, the said forty pounds of dowry and the twenty pounds of *creix*.[23]

Here, Bonet demonstrates that he is clearly aware of the law which stipulates that a woman ought to have her dowry restored if she fears the loss of this property to her husband's creditors. The assertions that Dauder had contracted 'many and diverse debts' and had 'diminished their goods so that now they are in poverty' along with the allegation that a lien had been placed on these goods presents a clear case of dowry restitution for the sake of current or impending insolvency. All suits of dowry restitution for insolvency contain the same language, emphasizing the uncertain number of debts owed (*moltes et diverses deutes*). Rarely does the *clam* indicate the identity of the creditors or the size of individual debts.

The claim that a lien had been placed on Dauder's goods worked greatly to Teresa's advantage in presenting her case to the Justícia Civil.

An *execució* was the act of executing a decision or sentence that had been passed by a judge.[24] In other words, if an *execució* had been made against Dauder's property, it meant that he had previously been taken to court by a creditor seeking the payment of debts owed. The creditor had won his case, and Dauder had yet to pay back his debts. The existence of an *execució* against her husband's property strengthened Teresa's case as it demonstrated that she was in danger of losing her dowry and *creix* to Tomàs's creditors. That a case had already been brought against Tomàs because of debt supported Teresa's assertion that Tomàs had financial problems, an important step in helping Teresa prove that she had a legally valid case of dowry restitution.

While the *clam* put forth by Bonet on Teresa's behalf simply indicates that Tomàs's indebtedness was the reason for her case, other dowry restitution suits provide more detailed explanations. Some state that the wife's goods had been misused and badly administered, others that her assets had been sold to pay off debts. Some cases, such as that of Yolant Arnau against her husband Lorenç, a carpenter, are much more forceful in their language. Yolant's *clam* states that Lorent 'abuses and has abused and has begun to abuse her property'.[25] Yolant further elucidates that Lorent has misused and diminished her property in case it was not clear from her initial argument. In thirty-nine cases, the *clam* indicates that the husband was absent from or had fled the city because of debts owed or violent crimes committed. These crimes were often detailed such as those of the shoemaker Berenguer Romeu whose wife Clara filed a suit of dowry restitution after he killed a man in a fight and then fled the city.[26]

In these cases, the *clam* emphasized the women's poor financial state by stating that they were not being provided with the necessities of life, i.e. food and shelter (*no fa sos ops ni alimenta*). In addition, they often indicated that their husbands' property had been seized by the court, further reducing their financial means. Tim Stretton, in his examination of civil court cases brought by women in Elizabethan England, has argued that wives emphasized their poverty in order to gain sympathy from the judge.[27] As used by women in medieval Valencia, this method worked well as a strategy in pleading their cases for it allowed wives to downplay the fact that they were challenging those whom the Catholic Church, and medieval society, saw as their natural rulers. An emphasis on poverty and on the husband's inability to provide his wife with food and shelter called into question the husband's right to control his wife's assets.

Overall, the reasons presented in the *clams* follow very closely the laws allowing for dowry restitution. This raises the question as to how these women knew that they were legally entitled to have their dowries

Table 6.2 Background of plaintiffs in dowry restitution cases, 1420–39

Background	Widows	Donzellas	Total
Artisan	8	77	85
Llaurador	3	13	16
Professional	1	21	22
Merchant	2	18	20
Honrat	6	16	22
Unknown	49	6	55
Total	69	151	220

restored for these reasons. Their procurators acted on their behalf before the courts, helping them to formulate the proper legal language to present their suits successfully. However, the seeds of their cases must have been sown within their own communities. For these women would not have sought out notaries to act as their procurators if they were not already aware of the laws surrounding dowry restitution. They may not have known the legal language with which to describe their situations, but they understood they held a legal right to protect their marital property.

One can only guess at where women of labouring-status gained this legal knowledge, but it is not hard to imagine them sharing this information through neighbourhood networks, through gossip and rumour between friends and neighbours. Valencian society was litigious. The numerous courts active in the later Middle Ages present a large amount of evidence for Valencians' efforts to resolve their disputes. Women of all statuses participated in many of these disputes as plaintiffs, defendants, and witnesses demonstrating their overall awareness of their legal rights in a variety of situations. Dowry restitution was only one of these, although it was the most significant, given the central importance of dotal property in women's lives.

Plaintiffs

While women of all backgrounds filed suits of dowry restitution against their husbands before the Justícia Civil, over 50 per cent of them were of artisan background (see Table 6.2). *Llaurador* women brought 10 per cent of these cases, women of merchant status 15 per cent, patrician women 12 per cent and the wives of professionals (notaries, doctors and court officials) 12 per cent. Artisan women predominated as litigants in dowry restitution suits for several reasons. To begin with, there were more artisans living in Valencia than any other social group because of the city's flourishing manufacturing sector. The prevalence of artisan women in dowry restitution suits was therefore representative of the social make-up of Valencian society. Second, as many artisan women immigrated to Valencia, either on their own as servants, or with their husbands, they were less likely to have familial support in case of financial hardship. This was the case for Teresa Dauder who had come to Valencia from Sogorb at the age of 12 to work as a servant in the house of Maria and Francesc Oviet. Teresa needed access to all of her dotal assets to support herself as her husband Tomàs was not doing so. Lastly, for *llaurador* women, the largely subsistence level of agricultural production and the nature of their dowries in late medieval Valencia made is less likely that these women would pursue a suit of dowry restitution. Survival for *llaurador* couples was directly linked to the land they farmed, some of which may have been part of the wife's dowry. While artisan dowries comprised mainly liquid wealth, *llaurador* ones more often included immoveable assets. The separation of a wife's landed property from the husband's would benefit neither member of the marital couple as both would be left financially unable to sustain themselves.

Although they comprised one-quarter of women marrying in Valencia, previously widowed women only represented 13 per cent of dowry restitution suits brought before the Justícia Civil. As this was at least their second marriage, it was much more likely for them to be widowed again before dowry restitution became necessary. These women tended to recognize fairly quickly that their assets needed protection from their debt-ridden husbands. Twelve out of the twenty-five previously widowed women seeking dowry restitution filed their suits within eight years of marriage. Nine out of these twelve did so within the first five years of their unions. In comparison, the suits of *donzella* brides were predominantly brought after ten to forty years of marriage. Eighty-four out of 139 suits were filed after ten or more years of marriage, thirty-seven of these cases took place after the couple had been married for more than twenty years. Although we have no way of knowing how long they were widowed previous to marrying again, it is apparent that the experience of widowhood made women more aware of the need to protect their assets. Having previously struggled to support themselves on their marital property, widows were fully aware of the possibilities of financial hardship that widowhood presented and therefore took steps to prevent the loss of their primary means of support.

Evidence: witnesses

Once the property being sought and the reasons behind the suit had been laid out in the *clam*, the court then named the judges and the case began. The *Furs* stated that all cases had to be concluded within thirty days of the initial suit unless extenuating circumstances made that impossible.[28] Each judge was named specifically for a case, usually because he specialized in that area of law. Litigants had the right to refuse a particular judge if they were concerned about impartiality.[29] Once the *clam* had been filed with the court, the defendant was informed of the proceedings and had ten days to respond. If he did not respond, the plaintiff won her case automatically and the defendant was also ordered to pay all of the expenses of the suit.[30] If the defendant was absent from the city, as was the case for all of the husbands who had fled because of debt or violent actions, he was able to name a procurator to act on his behalf. Even if he remained in the city, the defendant could still use a procurator to help him to navigate the legal intricacies of the court. This was the case for Teresa's husband Tomàs who had Francesc Oviet, a ropemaker, and Teresa's former employer, respond to the *clam* for him. Other men had their fathers,[31] and friends[32] respond on their behalf.

For a suit of dowry restitution to be legally valid, the wife had to prove both that the dowry had been handed over and that the other claims of her case were sound. Two types of evidence were used to fulfil these requirements: witness testimony and relevant documents. Overall, the court preferred witness testimony to documents as a measure of proof, largely because of the oath sworn by witnesses to tell the truth in the presence of God. While documents could be forged, court officials felt the religious oath sworn by witnesses would encourage them to provide truthful and accurate testimony.[33] In case their religious convictions did not prove strong enough, false testimony was also discouraged through secular means: the *Furs* stipulated that those who lied in their depositions could lose their own property.[34] If deceitful witnesses failed to pay this debt, the *Furs* ordered that their tongues be burned with a hot iron, and that they be run around the town,[35] both punishments for infamous actions,[36] demonstrating the severity of bearing false witness. All witnesses were to be examined in the presence of the justice or his representative.[37] The sole exception to this rule was for witnesses who lived far away; they could be examined by a local justice. Their testimony would then be sealed and sent to the civil justice in Valencia.[38]

The number of witnesses deposed varied by case but the *Furs* stated that civil suits needed two to three witnesses to provide sufficient evidence to successfully prove a claim.³⁹ The dowry restitution suits examined for this book averaged four to six witnesses each. In her case against her husband Tomàs, Teresa Dauder had four witnesses testify on her behalf. Only twelve of the cases examined had more than six witnesses and, overall, these cases were more complex or involved higher monetary sums than the rest. For example, in 1421 Johana Dabella sued her husband Narcis, a shoemaker, for the restitution of her 120-pound dowry and her sixty-pound *creix*. Johana's *clam* was exhaustive in its accusations against Narcis. It argued that he had badly used and administered her property, had contracted many debts since they married, had been implicated in the death of a carpenter and subsequently fled the city, and that the criminal justice had since seized his property. The eight witnesses who testified in Johana's suit were necessary in order to provide evidence for the various aspects of this complex case.⁴⁰ In another example, *honrada* Isabel de Partasa had eleven witnesses testify in her suit against her husband *honrat* Luis de Partasa. She was attempting to recover her 1,500-pound dowry and 185 pounds of *bens parafernals*, assets which she claimed were in jeopardy as Luis had fallen into poverty and caused numerous debts.⁴¹ The specifics of this case and the sizable value of the property increased the number of witnesses needed as conclusive proof.

Although wives were the central actors in dowry restitution suits, both litigants were able to use witnesses to testify on their behalf in civil court;⁴² however, in the cases examined, even the infrequent witnesses who appeared on behalf of the husband, confirmed rather than challenged the claims made by the wife in the original suit. The one anomaly is a witness in the case of Clara Aspiti against her husband Joan, a wooldresser. In her initial *clam*, Clara alleged that Joan had misused and badly administered her property, that he was in poverty and debt, had left the city fleeing his creditors, and because of his absence, was not providing her with the necessities of life.⁴³ One of Joan's relatives, Miquel Aspiti, disputed Clara's version of these events in his deposition. He stated that Clara has taken her children and left Joan before he fled the city, arguing that she instigated the couple's separation, not Joan.⁴⁴ Miquel does not contest Joan's insolvency, but asserts that Clara herself, by leaving Joan, precipitated her own difficult financial state. As the other witnesses in this case relate a different story, Miquel's statements become suspect. As he was a relative of Joan, it is possible that he slightly altered his version of the events to protect the honour of his family. A man who abandoned his wife and children to a life of want and poverty was clearly dishonourable in late medieval society. Joan had reneged upon the contract he signed with Clara which gave him control over her dowry to bear the burdens of their union. In not providing the necessities of life for his wife and children, Joan Aspiti failed as a husband, and as a man in a society where masculinity was defined by the ability to provide for one's family.[45] His relative Miquel knew 'the dishonourable conduct of one reflect[ed] upon the honour of all',[46] and therefore may have been attempting to downplay Joan's shameful actions in order to protect his family's reputation.

It is unclear why husbands failed to contest their wives' claims for dowry restitution. Perhaps they suspected their challenges would be fruitless given the clarity of the laws on these matters as well as the high success rates for wives seeking the return of their marital assets. Another possibility is the collusion of spouses seeking to protect a measure of their property from creditors. Julius Kirshner has demonstrated that Italian jurists feared husbands and wives were using dowry restitution for this purpose.[47] Their answer was to try to make the couple's insolvency public, creating shame which would 'hopefully' act as a deterrent.[48] It is difficult to prove conclusively whether the cases brought before the Justícia Civil were fraudulent or legitimate. Dowry restitution certainly was a useful tool for couples beset by creditors to retain some assets. As the *Furs* stipulated that a husband's creditors could not seize his wife's dowry in payment for debts owed,[49] dowry restitution allowed debt-ridden couples to escape with some measure of property with which to support themselves. The lack of defence mounted by husbands is one possible proof that these actions were used in this manner.

Depositions generally began by recording the oath sworn by the witness, as well as identifying their name and place of residence. For example, the first witness deposition in Teresa Dauder's case read:

> Thursday September the thirtieth, in the year from the birth of the lord, 1433
> Maria, wife of Francesc Oviet, ropemaker, inhabitant of the city of Valencia, living in the parish of St Bartomeu in the street of the ropemakers, a witness produced and given on behalf of the said Gabriel Bonet … who swears before God and the four holy gospels … that she owes the truth in her deposition concerning that which she knows.[50]

In addition to their sacred oath, witnesses also swore a secular one mandated in the *Furs* that the information they related had been given freely, i.e. not for money, power, ill will, future promises, gifts, love or lack of love.[51] This oath was used to prevent the manipulation of the courts by witnesses to settle personal scores.

The choice of witnesses by litigants was extremely important in the successful pursuit of their cases. Wives had to ensure that they followed legal restrictions regarding licit witnesses, met the judge's expectations as to who was suitable to fill this role and had people who would support their story with clear and believable evidence. Given the role that family members played in the creation of many Valencian artisan and *llaurador* marriages, one would expect them to be actively involved when wives attempted to regain control of their dotal property during their marriages. As has been discussed, dowries were important not only for wives, but also their families, as they were one aspect of the family patrimony. Maintaining the financial integrity of the dowry was therefore important to a wife's natal family as well as to herself. For the families of husbands, dowries were often integrated into their familial wealth once couples married and husbands gained control over them. Christiane Klapisch-Zuber's work on Florence argues that marital families fought strongly to prevent a woman from regaining control of her dowry once widowed, urging her instead to remain living within the confines of their households.[52] Strategies such as these worked to their advantage as they would be able to maintain control over the widow's lucrative dotal property until such time that her heirs (members of their kin group) came of age. Evidence from the Justícia Civil demonstrates the reluctance of marital families to give up control of a woman's dowry once she was widowed, as many widows were forced to go to court against their deceased husbands' relatives in order to have their dowries restored.[53]

Neighbours and friends: non-familial witnesses

Appearing as witnesses in dowry restitution suits gave family members on either side an active role in protecting this property. But family members of both husbands and wives appeared infrequently as witnesses in these civil cases. Instead, neighbours and those of the same social background as the couple predominated, especially for those litigants of artisan and

Table 6.3 Relationship of witnesses to plaintiffs/defendants in dowry restitution cases, 1420–39 (total dowry restitution cases: 220)

Background	Neighbour	Same status	Family
Artisan	55	96	9
Llaurador	6	17	5
Merchant	4	6	1
Honrat	6	10	6
Professional	7	14	4
Total	78	143	25

llaurador background (see Table 6.3). For artisans, 25 per cent of witnesses identified themselves in their testimony as neighbours of the couple and an additional 44 per cent were of the same background. With *llauradors*, 14 per cent of witnesses were neighbours and 40 per cent of the same background. This is in comparison to family members who consisted of only 4 per cent of witnesses in dowry suits involving artisans and 12 per cent of those involving *llauradors*.

The greater presence of neighbours and people of the same background as witnesses in artisan and *llaurador* dowry restitution cases, was, in part, determined by the *Furs* and by the desires of the Justícia Civil. The Valencian *Furs* had very strict rules about who could and could not act as witnesses in civil suits. The central regulations forbade any plaintiff or defendant to testify on his or her own behalf.[54] This is the reason why neither husbands nor wives testified in these cases. Equally important was the related legal precept which disallowed the testimony of someone for or against anyone who lived in the same house and who ate at the same table.[55] This therefore excluded the testimony of son for or against father, of wife for or against husband, in essence, of anyone who lived in the house of the defendant at the time that the suit was made. This meant that possible key witnesses to the suit, those that were living in the couple's house and had witnessed many of the actions that led to the wife asking for the restitution of her dowry, were unable to participate in the case itself.

The *Furs* was concerned about the nature of the relationship between the witness and litigants and how this might affect the testimony presented. Judges felt that close familial ties and hierarchical relations might generate overly prejudicial evidence.[56] To this end, servants and slaves could not testify in favour of or against their masters.[57] This did not prevent masters or mistresses from testifying on behalf of their former servants. The first witness to appear in Teresa Dauder's suit was her former mistress. Maria Oviet's testimony indicates that Teresa had been a servant in her house at the time of her marriage to Tomàs. Overall, the judge wanted to be fully aware of the connections between witnesses and litigants, whether they were family, worked in the same occupation, were friends or neighbours. This would allow him to determine whether or not the witness' testimony had to be more closely scrutinized for possible biased information.

The second reason for the prevalence of neighbours and people of the same background as witnesses in Valencian dowry restitution suits lay in the value accorded to the testimony of these groups by the court. Jurists from both Valencia and Italy agreed that the best witnesses in dowry restitution cases were the couple's neighbours.[58] For, as one Italian jurist put it

'If there are men under the sun who know their neighbours' secrets, they are neighbours.'[59] In a society where conceptions of public and private were radically different from our own, especially among artisan families whose workshops were located in their homes, neighbours, quite simply, were always present and could see and hear things that others would not.[60] In Teresa's case, Maria Oviet was not only her former mistress, she was also her current neighbour. Two other witnesses who appeared on her behalf, the ropemaker Miquel Bou and the wooldresser Francesc Riudaura, were also neighbours of the couple. The fourth witness, Francesc Adubell, was a barber, the same trade as Tomàs Dauder.

The value of the testimony of such witnesses lay in their proximity to the litigants. The civil court felt that the best testimony was from a person who had actually been present during the events of the case.[61] Maria Oviet testified that she had personally witnessed the betrothal and the creation of the marriage contract between Teresa and Tomàs Dauder as both of these events had taken place in her house. She reinforced her statements by naming the notary who drew up the marriage contract (Joan Caposa) and indicating that her husband and many of their neighbours in the parish of St Bartomeu could corroborate her testimony.[62] Francesc Adubell, the barber, testified in his deposition that while he had not been present at the couple's wedding, he had seen the couple 'living together as husband and wife in one house and room continually for about three years'.[63] Of even greater import to Teresa's case was Adubell's testimony that he had been present when Tomàs agreed to pay debts owed to two of his creditors.[64] A third witness in Teresa's case, the wooldresser Francesc Riudaura, was especially valuable. He lived across the street from the couple and testified that he had been in their house many times. He was able to provide evidence of the couple's poverty, and therefore evidence of Tomàs's mismanagement of their assets, stating that their house 'had very few linens and moveable goods ... that all the goods that are in the house were not worth 10 sous'.[65]

Being able to testify that they had seen and heard what had taken place increased a witness' importance greatly in the eyes of the justice. Witnesses that only testified that they had heard about the circumstances, but were not actually present themselves, did not hold as much evidentiary weight.[66] Like most areas, rumours ran rampant through the streets of each parish in Valencia, funnelling gossip from household to household. For example, the *llaurador* Martí Comes, testifying in Ursola Pasqual's case against her husband Bartomeu, reported that there was a rumour in the city that Bartomeu had committed unknown crimes and fled the city.[67] In another example from 1421 involving Caterina and Pere

Saragoça, the tanner Miquel Segarra stated that 'he had heard it said by many people that … Pere Saragoça had lost all of his property'.⁶⁸ Both of these witnesses emphasized that they had heard this information through the parish grapevine. Some witnesses tried to support their 'hearsay' testimony by stating that the information was *'publica fama'*, publicly known, in the neighbourhood. If they could provide the names of other people who were also aware of this information, or the name of the person from whom they had heard it, their testimony held greater weight.⁶⁹ Although rumour, to the justice, was not as valuable as concrete fact, nevertheless it did provide him with a window into the mood of the parish and the reputation of the husband among his neighbours. Setting the atmosphere could be especially important if the circumstances of the case were vague as they helped to provide the justice with the context in which to set the evidence.⁷⁰

The third reason for the predominance of neighbours and people of a similar background as witnesses was related to the influx of immigrants to the city of Valencia during the first half of the fifteenth century. Teresa Dauder herself fell into this category since she had come from Sogorb as a young girl to work as a domestic servant in the Oviets' house. As has been indicated in earlier chapters, the population of the city of Valencia grew substantially in the fifteenth century in direct connection to its expanding economy. Many immigrants to Valencia were like Teresa, from other areas of the kingdom seeking to benefit from the greater economic opportunities available in the city. Among those of labouring-status, the most mobile of the social classes as they often owned little immoveable property and had valuable transferable skills, the population was constantly shifting and relatives came to play less of a daily role in one another's lives.

Diane Owen Hughes, in an article looking at medieval Genoa during a time of similar economic and demographic expansion, has found that women of the labouring classes did not have many family members actually living in the city, stating 'For humbler women … the move to the city had meant an abrupt loss of kin'.⁷¹ Instead of the usual reliance on kin to act as counsel in a legal capacity, such as testifying on their behalf in court cases, these women turned to their neighbours for support.⁷² Given the fact that artisans and others of labouring-status likely immigrated to the city after marriage, or like Teresa, had even come before marrying, fulfilling an apprenticeship or service contract, it is likely that some of the women and men involved as litigants in dowry restitution suits did not have any close kin with whom they frequently interacted. In addition, for artisans, it was the household, not the kin group, that was essential to their lives.⁷³ Neighbours and those of the same background were better witnesses as they could testify to the current state of the couple's relationship and the husband's finances.

The lack of kin involvement as witnesses in dowry restitution cases certainly adds to the image of artisan and *llaurador* women's greater legal and economic control of their assets. This is supported if we compare witnesses from the dowry restitution cases of labouring-status women with those who appeared in the suits of patrician women. Only eight out of the twenty-two patrician dowry restitution cases extant for this period contain full witness testimony. In half of these cases, at least one witness was a family member of either the husband or wife. For example, in this case, of *honrada* Simona Dodena against her husband *honrat* Dionis Dodena mentioned earlier, family members had a much greater presence as witnesses than in the suits of labouring-status women. Three out of the eight witnesses deposed for this case were related to the litigants: one to Dionis and two to Simona.[74] In another case brought by a woman whose family was of *honrat* status but who was married to a silversmith, two witnesses out of six were family members, both related to the wife.[75]

Although this evidence is limited, it can allow one to make some tentative conclusions regarding the use of familial witnesses by women of patrician background. Unlike artisans, whose family ties in the city of Valencia were limited or non-existent, patricians had intricate networks of blood kin, extending far beyond the nuclear family. These ties were essential in their attempts to consolidate and maintain political, economic and social control in the city. With the constant competition for power that characterized Valencia's political system, familial supporters were key for patrician families.[76] In addition, patrician dowries were considerably higher than artisan ones with most valued from 500 to 1,500 pounds. This property represented a large investment for patricians in the future of their families since marriage alliances played a central role in their consolidation and maintenance of power. Third, as Joanne Ferraro has argued for Venice, the living arrangements of patrician women meant that their neighbours would not have provided particularly insightful evidence. Their vast homes created privacy which hid their husbands' bad behaviour from the public.[77] The appearance of family members in patrician dowry restitution suits, therefore, was not surprising given the ready-made pool of kin support these women had available to them, and their interest in preventing the diminution of important dotal assets.

Before ending a discussion of witness identity in late medieval Valencian dowry restitution suits, a few remarks about their gender must be made. The first witness to testify in Teresa's case was a woman, her former mistress, Maria Oviet. The law certainly allowed women to appear as witnesses in civil court cases; however, evidence from dowry restitution suits shows that they did so infrequently. Although women testified in 32 per cent of these cases, they only made up 11 per cent of the total witnesses being deposed. Dowries may have been perceived as distinctly female property but law and litigation were largely male spheres of activity. Women did appear as litigants in civil cases on a frequent basis but less commonly acted in the capacity of witnesses. They testified to the canonical and legal validity of the couple's marriage but rarely gave first person details of the events behind the suit of dowry restitution.

The majority of female witnesses were deposed in the dowry restitution trials of artisan and *llaurador* women. Female witnesses who appeared in the cases of non-labouring-status women (the wives of patricians, professionals and merchants) usually did so alongside their husbands. For example, in this suit between Francesca de Tornay and her husband Jaume, a mercer, two of the four witnesses deposed were women but each of them testified alongside their husband. In contrast, female artisan and *llaurador* witnesses provided their evidence independently of their husbands. Most female witnesses appeared in the suits of artisan women, which was related to their prevalence as litigants in dowry restitution cases. This fact also illustrates the community relationships formed between artisan women as many of them identify themselves as the couple's neighbours, or had husbands who practised a similar trade. Artisan women often had no family present in the city of Valencia to whom they could turn for support; instead they looked to their neighbours. For example, Blanqua Dalearaç, the wife of a weaver, testified in Dolça de Heredia's case against her husband Bonanat, a tailor, that she had frequently taken Dolça in when she was locked out of her house.[78] Monica Chojnacka, in examining Inquisition records from early modern Venice, found that women often went to their female neighbours as a source of comfort during difficult times.[79] Artisan women, much more so than women of a higher status whose lifestyles enclosed them within familial circles, would have come into daily contact with the women of their neighbourhood. Their inclusion of these women as witnesses in dowry restitution cases elucidates some of the community ties that existed within fifteenth-century Valencian parishes.

The structure of witness testimony

Regardless of the relationship between witnesses and litigants, all depositions given before the civil justice in late medieval Valencia followed a similar pattern. After swearing an oath to tell the truth, witnesses were then asked to respond to each section of the wife's petition. As all the witnesses were responding to the same statements, their answers were very similar. In his work on the Elizabethan Court of Requests, Tim Stretton has discussed the problems inherent in using witness depositions from civil cases as historical evidence as much of the testimony given is formulaic. Stretton points out the strong possibility that witnesses were coached to provide testimony that would work to the litigants' greatest possible advantage.[80] In fifteenth-century Valencian dowry restitution suits, the witness testimony is often almost identical, not just within a particular case but between suits brought by different litigants.

There was a distinct formula for deposing witnesses in these kinds of cases that elicited answers that were nearly indistinguishable in language and structure. This language reflected that used in the wife's initial *clam*. For example, the first question put to all witnesses regarded the validity of the couple's marriage, mirroring the opening statements made by the wife in her petition. The words of the ropemaker Miquel Bou, the second witness to testify in Teresa Dauder's case, follow almost identically that of the 505 other witnesses that were deposed in dowry restitution cases between 1420 and 1439.

> The said witness regarding the first, second and third questions of the said request ... says that he knows that Tomàs Dauder, a barber, and Teresa, named above, are husband and wife because he was present in the neighbourhood and heard the betrothal through their words in the present tense which were done at the house of Francesc Oviet, a ropemaker, and he went to their nuptial mass which was at the parish church of St Bartomeu of the city of Valencia and after [the witness said] that he had seen them being and living together as husband and wife in the said city.[81]

Other aspects of a couple's relationship were discussed in equally similar language. For example, the third witness in Teresa's case, Francesc Adubell stated, 'The said Tomàs Dauder called the said Teresa wife and the said Teresa called Tomàs's husband and as husband and wife they were held and reputed in the city of Valencia.'[82]

Witness after witness in dowry restitution cases used the exact same language to describe their knowledge of the couple's marital relationship. They followed the language used in the wife's petition but also expanded upon it to add their own comments and details. The similarity of answers demonstrates that the courts were looking for specific kinds of information to determine the legal validity of the couple's marriage. The justice wanted to know that their union had been concluded according to both canonical and secular norms. Knowledge that a nuptial mass had taken place, that a marriage contract had been drawn up and that the couple was perceived in their neighbourhood as husband and wife, through cohabitation and interaction, was important. Details such as the name of the parish church in which they married, the location of their wedding feast, the date when they were married and the name of the notary who drew up the marriage contract, added to the overall picture of late medieval Valencian conjugal relationships. For example, in Francesc Adubell's testimony, we learn that Teresa and Tomàs had been married for three years.[83] Francesc Riudaura relates that the couple lived across the street from him in the Plaça del Abeurador near the Torres de Serranos.[84] Demonstrating the close nature of her relationship with Teresa and Tomàs, Maria Oviet provides the most details including the name of the notary that drew up the couple's marriage contract, the fact that it had taken place in her house, that her husband Francesc had provided twenty-five pounds of the dowry in fulfilment of Teresa's service contract and, extremely key in a suit of dowry restitution, that Caposa had also drawn up a receipt indicating that the dowry had been paid in full to Tomàs.[85]

As was discussed in Chapter 1 of this book, the answers given by witnesses in dowry restitution create an image of the ways in which Valencians defined marital relationships in the late medieval period. The indication that a nuptial mass had taken place and that a marriage contract had been drawn up fulfilled the legal requirements of the case. Testimony that the couple lived together in one house and that they called one another husband and wife demonstrated the social aspects of marriage. The similarity of witness testimony in these aspects does point to the possibility that witnesses were, in fact, coached to provide the best possible answers; however, it also elucidates the social markers of marriage, not only for the witnesses testifying but also for the justice hearing the case.

While the first series of responses made by witnesses focused on the couple's marital relationship, the second turned to the events that had led to the suit of dowry restitution. It is in this aspect of the witnesses' depositions that their testimony deviates the most, yet the language used and information provided is often remarkably similar within a given case. The ways in which witnesses answer the questions posed to them by the procurators all reflected the reasons for dowry restitution given by the wife in her original *clam*. For example, in Teresa Dauder's suit, the witness depositions discuss Tomàs's indebtedness, with varying amounts of detail. Maria Oviet affirms that Dauder had many debts, was lacking in temporal goods and that his property was not worth ten pounds. To emphasize his poor financial state, and the threat to Teresa's dowry, Oviet states 'she knows for certain that the said Tomàs, beyond the dowry of his wife, owes and is obligated to pay his creditors more and a greater amount of money than the goods in his house are worth.[86] Francesc Adubell reiterates that Tomàs was indebted to many people but indicates to whom specifically his debts were owed as well as their value, 'he is held to pay to the honrat Pere Andreu, citizen of Valencia, 100 sous of Valencian money ... and the said Tomàs is held to pay to the lady Agnes all the 100 sous which the said Tomàs confessed in the presence of the said witness [that he owed]'.[87]

The structure of witness testimony in cases of insolvent husbands is similar to the above examples. Witnesses emphasize the husband's 'many and diverse debts' (*molts et diverses deutes*), give details as to whom he owed money and often indicate whether or not an *execució* had already been made against his property. The best possible witnesses in these cases were the court officials who provided evidence of additional civil suits for unpaid debts in progress against the husband, a clear illustration of his insolvency. For example, the notary Andreu Mir testified in Ursola Ferrer's case against her husband Francesc that he had gone to the couple's house to estimate the value of Francesc's goods at the behest of the civil justice. Mir then listed four people who had brought a civil suit against Francesc for debts owed.[88]

In general, witness testimony in dowry restitution cases supported and illuminated the reasons cited for the suit in the *clam*. This evidence helped the justice to determine the husband's reputation among his fellow Valencians. In addition, witness depositions demonstrate how a husband's behaviour towards his wife, and her assets, was viewed by members of his own community. Actions that were looked upon with disapproval by witnesses included the misuse and bad administration of marital property (particularly when the husband alienated these assets to pay his own debts) and the refusal to provide the wife with food and shelter.

The alienation of a wife's dowry by her husband was strictly forbidden by the *Furs*. The law stated that if a husband sold his wife's property without her permission, the sale was not valid.[89] The merchant Ramon Perelada flagrantly disregarded this law when, according to the witness Jacme Bengut, he made many contracts using his wife Guillomena's property as collateral, resulting in the seizure of these assets by his creditors when the debts remained unpaid.[90] Bengut provided the justice with details as to the nature of these contracts (for the purchase of *censals*), and the people with whom they were concluded. A subsequent witness indicated that Perelada's own property was about to be seized by the civil court for other debts.

The refusal of a husband to provide food and shelter for his wife drew strong criticism from witnesses in dowry restitution suits. Neighbours testifying in Caterina Garo's case against her husband Antoni stated that Antoni had thrown Caterina out of their house and prevented her from returning, forcing her to seek shelter with her mother and sister. Bartomeu Pax testified that, along with others in the village of Alboraia where the couple lived, he had gone to Antoni to urge him to give Caterina the necessary means of support or, barring that, to restore her dotal assets.[91] Other witnesses corroborated Pax's testimony showing their open disapproval of Garo's behaviour.[92] According to their social norms, a husband was to provide his wife with shelter and nourishment and if he did not do so, he was not entitled to her dowry.

In general, witnesses tended to frown upon any threats made to a wife's marital assets either through debt or other financial abuses. The use of a wife's property to pay gambling debts was particularly nefarious. The case of Johana Dabella against her husband Narcis, discussed earlier in this chapter, illustrates these concerns.[93] The testimony of eight witnesses painted an unflattering picture of a husband who gambled at dice and other games where he accrued large debts, who was implicated in the death of a carpenter's son and who then fled the city, abandoning Johana with no means to support herself. Gambling was seen as the root of Narcis's, and by association, Johana's problems. Joanne Ferraro argues that gambling was greatly disapproved of by witnesses in her cases of sixteenth-century Venetian marital discord, particularly those husbands who gambled away gifts earmarked for their wives.[94] In incurring great debts due to gambling problems, Narcis Dabella also put in jeopardy the *creix* promised to Johana at the time of their marriage as it appeared that he had lost the majority of his property.

Surprisingly, witnesses in cases which involved violent actions on the part of the husband rarely condemned him for this behaviour. As the work of Mark Meyerson has demonstrated, violence was a regular part of late medieval Valencian life.[95] Twelve cases of dowry restitution present the violent behaviour of the husband as one aspect of the wife's suit. In all of these, the key aspect for witnesses was not the husband's violent actions but the abandonment of his wife without financial support. The focus by witnesses on the wife's resources is related to the nature of the court in which these cases appeared; that of the civil justice. The issue at hand was property, not crime. For example, witnesses in the case of Johana del Spital against her husband Joan testified that Joan was absent from Valencia because of debt and his involvement in violent personal feuds. Pasqual Camayes, who identified himself as Joan's 'good friend' (*gran amich*), admitted that Joan badly used his wife's property, struck Guismar, the wife of his neighbour, and subsequently fled the city, leaving Johana without the necessary means to support herself.[96] Camayes, although a good friend of Joan's, disapproved of Joan's behaviour towards his wife and appeared as a witness on her behalf in her quest for financial stability.

All witness testimony, while often formulaic and repetitive, helped the wife to form and support a case against her husband. She, and/or her *procurator*, made sure to choose witnesses that would present her suit in the best possible light. Again, this raises the issue of the genuineness of the witnesses' testimony. Did the wife's procurator tell the witnesses what to say in order to successfully prove her case? Was Gabriel Bonet coaching Maria Oviet, Miquel Bou, Francesc Adubell and Francesc Riudaura in their use of language and information which would influence the judge, Manuel Suau, to award Teresa Dauder her marital property? Suits involving conjugal collusion seemed particularly ripe for witness instruction. Although it is likely that this kind of manipulation did happen in fifteenth-century Valencian dowry restitution cases, there is no evidence to prove conclusively that it did. Tim Stretton found cases in Britain's Court of Requests which alleged the coaching of witnesses, but this was not overt proof that it actually took place.[97] The similarity of answers by witnesses could simply reflect that they were asked identical questions.

Their use of the same language to describe aspects of the suit was influenced, in part, by how their testimony was written down by scribes who may have interpreted their words to fit a specific juridical model. This does raise the issue of the layers of interpretation placed on witness depositions at the time they were recorded. The initial petition of the wife would have influenced their statements in the determination of which questions should be asked. The choice of words by the scribe also influenced the way this testimony was written down. While one has to be aware of these influences when interpreting the witness testimony from dowry restitution cases, they still do not cloud the central issue. Despite medieval patriarchal norms that gave husbands a great deal of power over their wives, these women were able to use dowry restitution as a means of controlling their marital property. Their rate of success demonstrates their ability to choose witnesses that worked to their advantage. Perhaps coached by their procurators, perhaps not, this witness testimony was key in allowing wives to protect their assets whenever they felt this property was threatened.

Evidence: documents

The best way for a wife to corroborate the testimony of her witnesses was to include documentary evidence that was relative to her suit. The most common types of documents used in dowry restitution cases were notarial, that is, marriage contracts and records of financial transactions. In presenting Teresa Dauder's case to the civil justice, her procurator Gabriel Bonet included a copy of the couple's marriage contract.[98] For the justice, this documentation proved central details such as the monetary amount and type of property that made up the dowry and *creix*. For the historian, the inclusion of dotal contracts in dowry restitution cases helps to provide additional information about the couple litigating. For example, the contract of marriage drawn up between Teresa and Tomàs Dauder provides further evidence of the close relationship between the couple and Teresa's former employers. Teresa, who concluded the dotal contract with Tomàs herself, indicated that she was doing so with the consent of her father, Joan Dalarit, as well as that of Francesc Oviet and his wife Maria.[99] In the absence of her father, who lived in Sogorb, Teresa relied upon the Oviets for counsel in marrying Tomàs. Maria Oviet's appearance as a witness in Teresa's dowry restitution suit eight years after her marriage, and Francesc's role as Tomàs's procurator, demonstrates the close relationship created between the two couples.

Another key document in dowry restitution cases was the *apocha*, or receipt, drawn up by a notary indicating that the dowry had been paid. The *apocha* was important as husbands could claim they had not received the dotal property, either in part or in full, from their wives as a method of defence. If the justice was unsure whether or not the dowry had been paid, he could order greater investigation into the circumstances of the suit before making a definitive ruling. This was the provisional ruling passed in Caterina Gerat's suit against her husband Joan in 1434.[100] Caterina had accused Joan of misusing her property and contracting numerous debts after their wedding. Her *clam* stated that she felt Joan did not have the ability to take care of her property in an appropriate manner. Before any witnesses were deposed in this case, the justice ordered greater investigation into the matter, as he was not fully convinced that Caterina's dowry had in fact been paid to Joan. In this case, an *apocha* for the received dowry would have alleviated the justice's concerns; however, it does not appear that Caterina produced one.

The Justícia Civil was fully aware that documents could be forged and therefore it was an asset to the wife's suit if she had the notary who wrote them act as a witness.[101] The notary could testify both to the details of the marriage contract as well as whether or not the dowry had in fact been transferred to the husband's control. In the case of Caterina Caroja against her husband Lorenç, the notary Antoni Joan produced their marriage contract and *apocha* to help Caterina prove her case.[102] Other kinds of documents useful in proving dowry restitution cases were notarial contracts that demonstrated the husband's misuse and maladministration of his wife's property. For example, in the suit of Elionor Bonjoch against her husband Jacme, a tanner, four witnesses testified to the validity of the couple's marriage and the misuse of Elionor's dotal property by Jacme.[103] At the end of this testimony, a series of contracts was included which clearly indicated all of the debts owed by Jacme as well as his alienation of Elionor's property.[104] With such overwhelming oral and written evidence, it would have been extremely difficult for Jacme to mount an adequate defence against Elionor's claim. Although documentary evidence could be extremely useful in helping a woman prove a suit of dowry restitution, it was used infrequently by litigants. Only 59 out of the 220 suits presented some form of documentation as judicial proof. Oral testimony, therefore, was key in proving dowry restitution cases.

Sentencia

The final aspect of dowry restitution cases was the judgment, or *sentencia* determined by the justice who, in making his decisions, consulted with the '*honrats, jurats, prohomes et consellors de la present ciutat*',[105] the politically important men of the city. At least that is what the sentences of all dowry restitution cases claimed. It seems more likely that this phrase was formulaic, included to give the justice's sentence greater weight and authority. There were two forms of sentencing permitted in Valencian law: the definitive judgment, which ruled in favour or against the wife's petition, and the interlocutory sentence, which ruled on aspects of the case and asked for further investigation into the matter.[106] The use of interlocutory sentences reflected the *Furs* mandate that the justice had to have sufficient legal proofs to rule definitively on any given suit.[107] If he felt the wife's suit was justified, but that she had presented insufficient evidence, he could ask for greater investigation into the matter. This kind of ruling also allowed the justice to consider whether or not this suit was legitimate, that is, if the husband and wife were colluding to escape paying their creditors.

Each sentence passed by the justice reiterated the important facts of the suit and then presented what Roca Traver has called an 'excessive abundance' of reasons why he had ruled in a particular manner.[108] The sentence in Teresa Dauder's suit read:

As through the depositions of the witnesses and justly produced below ... to be the contract of marriage between the said Tomàs Dauder and the said Teresa and she gave to him as her dowry forty pounds and he promised to restore to her this [dowry] with the twenty pounds of *creix* in case the dowry is to be restored. And much later the said Tomàs Dauder fell into insolvency through such from his penury and declare [this] to be a case and reason for restitution of the dowry and *creix* and with the present [sentence the justice] condemns the said Tomàs Dauder and for such from him to give and to pay to the said Teresa, his wife, forty pounds of dowry and twenty pounds of *creix*.[109]

Dowry restitution sentences always repeated the judicial proofs entered (in this case the witness testimony and the couple's marriage contract) and then summarized the details of the suit as supported by this evidence. The sentence ended with the justice's ruling, inevitably as in Teresa Dauder's suit, ordering the return of the wife's marital assets to her control.

The *Furs* stated that in cases with more doubts than proofs, the justice had to rule in favour of the defendant.[110] Some sentences ended with the statement 'as for us, it cannot be any more certain' (*com a nos, no pusca esser cert bastantment*) to demonstrate the justice's absolute certainty in making his ruling.[111] This was necessary as all those litigating in civil court had the right of appeal, although a definitive sentence must have been made by the justice in order for these to proceed.[112] The use of appeal was widespread in Valencian society. To stem the rising tide of appeal cases, in 1307 Jaume II promulgated a new law that forbade the introduction of new information unless this was done to clarify some of the evidence already presented.[113] Only certain judges were able to preside over appeals and it was up to them to determine whether or not these appeals were legitimate or being used as a delaying tactic.[114]

There are no surviving appeals made by husbands unwilling to hand over control of marital property in the Justícia Civil records from this period. This indicates that husbands were clearly guilty of misusing and maladministering their wife's property. We must remember that dowry restitution was a last resort for women, desperate to protect their marital assets from financial harm. These women would only have pursued a suit of dowry restitution if they were clearly able to prove their husband's guilt. Most wives were probably reluctant to sue their husbands and it is unlikely that all or even most women went to court when their marital property was endangered.

One road that some husbands took was simply to refuse to hand over their wives' marital assets, regardless of the justice's ruling. Although 220 suits of dowry restitution are extant from the Justícia Civil from 1420 to 1439, I discovered a mere six notarial contracts of restitution from the same time period. In each of these contracts, the husband was restoring marital assets to his wife as ordered by the civil justice. Four out of the six contracts give an indication of the amount of time elapsed between the end of the suit and the actual restoration of the wife's property. For example, a contract from 11 February 1430, between the silversmith Bernat Doties and his wife Vicenta, was drawn up approximately two weeks after the husband had been ordered to restore his wife's dowry and *creix*.[115] A second contract, also from 1430, between the carpenter Gabriel Fuster and his wife Francesca, was drawn up on 27 November, just four days after a definitive sentence of dowry restitution had been made.[116] Vicenta Doties's *clam* was presented on 7 January, and approximately one month later, she regained her dotal assets. Bernat Doties had been ordered to restore both Vicenta's dowry and *creix* but the contract from 11 February only detailed the return of her dotal property. Francesca Fuster had brought her petition of dowry restitution before the civil justice on 20 September and it took just over two months for the sentence to be decided. However, two other dowry restitution contracts indicate that it sometimes took several months for the wife to have her assets restore. Leonarda, the wife of the draper Jacob Ferrer presented her petition before the civil justice sometime in late 1432. The justice ruled in her favour on 5 January 1433 but her dowry and *creix* were not restored until 19 June 1433.[117] In the other case, it took Maria, wife of the *llaurador* Joan Viander of Valencia almost six months to have her dotal property returned.[118]

These notarial contracts provide important information as to the ways in which marital assets were restored to the wife after pleading a successful suit of dowry restitution. In both cases, the husbands gave their wives a combination of immoveable property (rented houses and land) and moveable assets (household goods). These contracts do not indicate whether or not this was the actual property that they had received as part of their dowry and/or *creix*. Given the high percentage of artisan women who brought household goods as part of their dowries, it is likely that these items were the same or similar as that which she had brought into the marriage. The difference lay in the fact that whereas the dotal contract simply stated that the dowry was made up of the ambiguous 'household goods', the contract of restitution was very specific in describing this property and its value. For example, Francesca received pots, dishes, a measure of wine and a paella dish, all valued at 976 sous. Bernat Doties provided Vicenta with a wooden table, a bench, plus several wooden chests with a total worth of 1,000 sous.

It is surprising, given the number of dowry restitution suits extant from this period that more notarial contracts of restitution do not survive. It is possible that many couples simply chose not to have a contract of restitution drawn up to record the return of the wife's marital assets. This would be especially true for those couples who had colluded to file a false suit of dowry restitution. We also must remember that although wives were almost guaranteed to have their marital assets returned by the court, this did not necessarily mean that their husbands were actually willing to give up control over this property. Evidence from the governor's court demonstrates that wives, despite a ruling in their favour by the civil justice, sometimes had difficulty enforcing that favourable judgment. It is to these cases, and others from the governor's court, that we now turn.

Dowry restitution in the Gobernació

Whereas the involvement of the civil justice in marital disputes was limited to cases of dowry restitution, the court of the governor had much wider jurisdiction. As the highest court in the kingdom of Valencia, the Gobernació dealt primarily with appeals from cases initially tried by local criminal and civil justices. The suits brought before the Gobernació were second appeals of cases which had already been reviewed by lower court judges. For example, Nadal Roselló appealed the sentence passed by the civil justice of Valencia which had awarded his wife Jacmeta control of her non-dotal assets. In this, his second appeal, Nadal argued that this property belonged to the couple together; however, he was unsuccessful in convincing the governor of this fact.[119]

The second role of the Gobernació was to enforce sentences already passed by local justices. All but one of the four cases of dowry restitution between wives and their still-living husbands pleaded in the governor's court were brought to enforce earlier rulings. This provided those women whose husbands refused to return their marital property, despite being ordered to do so by the civil justice, with another way to retrieve control over their assets. For example, Margalida Domingo had won a suit of dowry restitution against her husband, the *llaurador* Joan Domingo, in the court of the Justícia Civil. Joan had returned some of Margalida's assets but not all and she therefore came before the governor's court asking for the civil court sentence to be fully enforced.[120] Whereas civil court cases of dowry restitution were non-specific in their descriptions of property sought, Margalida's case in the governor's court noted the exact items she wanted: a bed, a straw mattress, a table, a cabinet and a white blanket. Frustrated with her husband's refusal to restore the monetary amount of her property, Margalida was forced to name specific items which added up to the same value.

A third area in which the Gobernació held jurisdiction was in suits of litigants who had been named '*miserabiles personae*' or '*miserabiles pobres*', that is, those so destitute that both the Catholic Church and the Crown were obligated to protect them.[121] The legal status of these people entitled them to use the governor's court as their debility and poverty made them special cases worthy of the king's protection.[122] In particular, the *Furs* singled out children (primarily orphans) and widows as people who needed special assistance. Being declared a *miserabile pobre* in Valencia entitled one to special rights under the law. Fiscally, these people were exempt from paying taxes and they were perceived as not having sufficient income to be taxable.[123] Legally, they had recourse to 'legal aid' from the *procurador dels miserables* and the ability to plead suits in the Gobernació that were not appeal cases.[124] Legal advocates such as these were common in southern Europe throughout the fifteenth century.[125]

Widowhood could place women at a serious economic disadvantage in late medieval society. Difficulty in regaining their marital assets from their husband's heirs and/or executors was not an uncommon situation. The *Furs* stipulated that widows were to receive their dotal property a year and a day from their husband's decease. During this period, known as '*l'any de plor*', the year of mourning, widows held usufruct rights over their husbands' patrimony as a means of support.[126] In some cases, the deceased husband's heirs and executors refused even this to the widow, pushing her into greater poverty. The Gobernació provided these women with protection and help in seeking their usufruct rights, along with their dotal property. For example, Constanca Tamarit of Morvedre brought a suit against her husband's three brothers in the governor's court. Her *procurador* described Constanca as a poor widow (*pobre vidua*) and named her one of the miserable poor. Constanca was seeking financial support in her widowhood as, according to her *procurador*, she was penniless and her deceased husband's siblings had refused to come to her aid. In his sentence, the governor ordered the brothers to hand over the fruits of some vineyards from her husband's estate to be used as financial sustenance.[127]

Those of higher status, especially the Valencian patriciate, also appeared frequently as litigants in this court. Unlike the itinerant Aragonese and Catalan courts, the Valencian Gobernació was a permanent institution in the capital city.[128] The *honrats* of the city took advantage of this geographical proximity and used the Gobernació to present petitions normally pleaded before the municipal justices. For example, *honrada*

Orfisina, wife of the *honrat* Joan Bonfill, brought her suit of dowry restitution before the Gobernació, rather than the Justícia Civil.[129] Orfisina's case does not indicate why she chose not to plead her suit before the lower court but one can assume that Orfisina felt her patrician status entitled her to use the highest court in the kingdom to present her legal actions.

Due to the diverse nature of the suits brought before the Gobernació, their structure varied widely. This variance depended on whether the case presented was a first suit, an appeal or the enforcement of a previous sentence. Some cases followed that of the Justícia Civil with the litigants pleading their case, presenting evidence in the form of witness testimony and documents, and then receiving a sentence from the governor.[130] Other suits were much briefer, containing merely the litigant's petition and the governor's judgment. Not surprisingly, those cases upholding a previous judgment were the most succinct, presenting simply the plea and the governor's ruling that the earlier sentence be upheld.[131] Most appeal cases were also concise, unless the governor had evidence from the previous suit written into the record or allowed new evidence.

The suits brought by *miserabiles pobres* and others under the Crown's protection were much longer and contained judicial proofs similar to those of the Justícia Civil. As in civil cases, the witnesses appearing in these suits testified to the facts of the case, answering to each aspect of the wife's initial petition. For example, in Gonstanca de Mir's case against her abusive husband Dalmau, witnesses testified to the severity of the beatings and wounds she received.[132] Appearing as witnesses in this case were five female neighbours of the couple as well as a barber-surgeon who had examined Gonstanca's wounds. In the suit of the widow Antonia Pont, declared *miserabile pobre*, who was seeking her dowry and *creix* from her husband's executors, witnesses testified to her poverty, enforcing both her status as one of the miserable poor and the economic necessity of dowry restitution.[133]

Unlike sentences passed in the court of the Justícia Civil, which reiterated the central points of the suit, those of the Gobernació were to the point, stating only that the governor had ruled in favour or against the litigant. Overall, records of dowry restitution in this court are much sparser, providing fewer cases and less detail. These suits are, however, important because they demonstrate that wives had access to another level of juridical action to protect their marital assets from diminution and abuse by their husbands. Dowry restitution suits in the Gobernació may not have been common, but this court did allow those unable, for whatever reasons, to plead suits in the Justícia Civil, such as the *miserabiles pobres*, the chance to assert their legal rights and regain property that could allow them a modicum of financial stability.

Germanía restitution

While Valencian women exercised agency in negotiating control over their marital property, this was limited to those women that had married under the dotal system. The Justícia Civil abounds with cases of wives seeking the restitution of their dowries, but not one suit involving a couple who married with a *germanía* contract is extant in our sample. What recourse did these women have in protecting their assets from the mismanagement and abuse of their husbands? Under the *germanía* system, the couple's assets were combined, unlike the dotal regime which prescribed the separation of property. Wives who had married with a *germanía* contract also had an interest in maintaining the integrity of the conjugal fund as it greatly affected their own financial welfare.

But as *germanía* contracts did not follow the legally recognized regime of marital property, wives who married under this system were less likely to use the courts to protect their share of the conjugal fund. The Gobernació does have a single appeal case from a woman in Castellnou seeking control over her half of the marital property.[134] Johana Nanyes had already brought a suit against her husband Lorent in the civil court of Castellnou where she claimed he had contracted numerous debts which threatened the financial integrity of their jointly held assets.[135] The justice of Castellnou denied Johana's petition, even though the couple were no longer living together and actually resided in separate towns. The governor was equally unconvinced of the legitimacy of Johana's request and denied her appeal. Unfortunately, he did not state his reasons for this sentence but one can speculate about his concern for this kind of legal action.

For justices at the local level, and for the governor in appeals, the validity of any suit was determined by Valencian law. Petitions brought by wives against their husbands who had married under a *germanía* regime fell outside their jurisdiction. The refusal of the local justice in Castellnou and the governor in Valencia to support Johana's petition, reflected legal constraints which allowed officials to act only within the laws laid out by the *Furs*. Those laws, while explicitly stating the procedure and rules around dowry restitution, were silent regarding *germanía* contracts. This left women such as Johana unprotected if their husbands diminished the conjugal fund, and gave them few options in maintaining their economic resources.

There is one piece of evidence that can provide us with some clues as to the legal options available to wives seeking to have their share of the *germanía* fund restored. This is a notarial contract drawn up between the wooldresser Joan Mingot and his wife Johanna on 6 March 1431.[136] In

16 Roca Traver, *La jurisdicción civil del Justícia de Valencia*, p. 43.
17 Roca Traver, *El Justícia de Valencia*, p. 157.
18 Kirshner, 'Wives' Claims', p. 302.
19 ARV Justícia Civil Peticiones 3723, m. 14, f. 8 r., sig. f. 35 r. a 38 (30 September 1434).
20 *Furs de Valencià*, II-V-IX, p. 66.
21 Roca Traver, *El Justícia de Valencia*, p. 145.
22 ARV Justícia Civil Peticiones 3723, m. 14, f. 8 r. (30 September 1434).
23 ARV 3723 Manus 14, folio 34 verso a 35 recto.
24 Mn. Antoni Ma. Alcover, *Diccionari Català-Valencià-Balear* (Palma de Mallorca: Eno-Form, 1953), vol. V, p. 649.
25 ARV Justícia Civil Peticiones 3718, m. 2, f. 41r. (23 February 1431).
26 ARV Justícia Civil Peticiones 3717, m. 2, f. 17r. (26 February 1428).
27 Tim Stretton, *Women Waging Law in Elizabethan England* (Cambridge: Cambridge University Press, 1998), pp. 180–182. In her examination of marital disputes in sixteenth- and seventeenth-century Venice, Joanne Ferraro explores how women used narratives of abandonment in cases against their husbands to win sympathy from the judge. These women focused on the hardships they faced because their husbands had left them without means. See *Marriage Wars in Late Renaissance Venice* (Oxford: Oxford University Press, 2001), pp. 120–133.
28 *Furs de Valencià*, III-I-VII, p. 8.
29 Roca Traver, *La jurisdicción civil del Justícia de Valencia*, p. 31.
30 *Furs de Valencià*, VII-II-XXII, p. 35.
31 ARV Justícia Civil Peticiones 3715, m. 11, f. 13v. (17 October 1424); ARV Justícia Civil Peticiones 3718, m. 3, f. 8r. (1 March 1431).
32 ARV Justícia Civil Peticiones 3723, m. 18, f. 15r. (15 December 1434).
33 Roca Traver, *La jurisdicción civil del Justícia de Valencia*, p. 67.
34 *Furs de Valencià*, IV-IX-XVIII, p. 53.
35 *Ibid.*
36 Roca Traver, *La jurisdicción civil del Justícia de Valencia*, pp. 69–70.
37 *Ibid.*, p. 68.
38 *Ibid.*, p. 69.
39 *Furs de Valencià*, IV-IX-X, p. 50. In petitions where the value of the goods sought was less than 50 sous, the litigants only needed one witness to provide testimony. See above.
40 ARV Justícia Civil Peticiones 3711, m. 2, f. 18 r. i v. (6 March 1421).
41 ARV Justícia Civil Peticiones 3726, m. 5 f. 31r. sig. f. 46v. sig. m. 6 f. 31r. a 35v. (7 May 1436).
42 Roca Traver, *La jurisdicción civil del Justícia de Valencia*, p. 75.
43 ARV Justícia Civil Peticiones 3711, m. 8., f. 8r i v. (18 August 1421).
44 *Ibid.*, m. 9, f. 27v. a 28r. (18 August 1421).
45 Vern L. Bullough, 'On Being a Male in the Middle Ages', in Clare A. Lees (ed.), *Medieval Masculinities* (Minneapolis: University of Minnesota Press, 1994), p. 34.
46 Jean G. Peristiany, 'Honour and Shame', in J.G. Peristiany (ed.), *Honour and Shame: the Values of Mediterranean Society* (London: Weidenfeld & Nicolson, 1965), p. 35.
47 Kirshner, 'Wives' Claims', p. 297.
48 *Ibid.*, p. 298.
49 *Furs de Valencià*, IV-V-III, p. 34.50 ARV Justícia Civil Peticiones 3723, m. 14, f. 35v. (30 September 1434).

51. ARV Justícia Civil Peticiones 3723, m. 14, f. 36r. (30 September 1434).
52. Klapisch-Zuber, "'Cruel Mother'", pp. 121–122.
53. There are numerous cases of widows seeking the restitution of their dowries from their marital families. For example see ARV Justícia Civil Peticiones 3711, m. 10, f. 20r. sig. m. 15, f. 7r. (23 October 1421).
54. *Furs de Valencià*, IV-IX-II, p. 45.
55. *Ibid.*, IV-IX-III, p. 46.
56. Roca Traver, *La jurisdicción civil del Justícia de Valencia*, p. 71.
57. *Furs de Valencià*, IV-IX-I, p. 45.
58. Kirshner, 'Wives' Claims', pp. 270–273; Ferraro, *Marriage Wars*, p. 122.
59. Kirshner, 'Wives' Claims', p. 271.
60. Roca Traver, *La jurisdiccón civil del Justícia de Valencia*, p. 73.
61. *Ibid.*
62. ARV Justícia Civil Peticiones 3723, m. 14, f. 35v. a 36r. (30 September 1434).
63. *Ibid.*, f. 36v.
64. *Ibid.*
65. *Ibid.*, f. 37v.
66. Roca Traver, *La jurisdicción civil del Justícia de Valencia*, p. 74.
67. ARV Justícia Civil Peticiones 3718, m.6 f. 14r. (2 May 1431).
68. ARV Justícia Civil Peticiones 3711, m. 6 f. 42v. (20 May 1421).
69. For example, see ARV Justícia Civil Peticiones 3711, m. 4, f. 40v. (6 March 1421).
70. Roca Traver, *La jurisdicción civil del Justícia de Valencia*, p. 74.
71. Diane Owen Hughes, 'Urban Growth and Family Structure in Medieval Genoa', *Past and Present*, 66 (1975), p. 21.
72. *Ibid.*
73. Owen Hughes, 'Domestic Ideals and Social Behaviour', p. 126.
74. ARV Justícia Civil Peticiones 3717, m. 7, f. 2r. a 3v sig. f. 9r. a 12r. sig., m. 10 f. 36r. a 46r. (31 May 1428). The familial witnesses that appeared in this case were Dionis' nephew and two relatives of Simona's who only indicated that they were members of her kin group.
75. ARV Justícia Civil Peticiones 3716, m. 1, f. 21r. sig. f. 42r. a 46v. (23 January 1425).
76. Narbona Vizcaíno, 'Vida pública y conflictividad urbana en los reinos hispánicas', pp. 555–568 and *Valencia, municipio medieval*, p. 176.
77. Ferraro, *Marriage Wars*, p. 126.
78. ARV Justícia Civil Peticiones 3716, m. 5 f. 38r. (9 May 1425).
79. Chojnacka, *Working Women of Early Modern Venice*, p. 62.
80. Stretton, *Women Waging Law in Elizabethan England*, pp. 16–17.
81. ARV Justícia Civil Peticiones 3723, m. 14, f. 36r i v. (30 September 1434).
82. *Ibid.*, f. 36v. (30 September 1434).
83. *Ibid.* (30 September 1434).
84. *Ibid.*, f. 37v. (30 September 1434).
85. *Ibid.*, f. 35v. a 36r. (30 September 1434).
86. *Ibid.*, f. 36r. (30 September 1434).
87. *Ibid.*, f. 37r. (30 September 1434).
88. ARV Justícia Civil Peticiones 3716, m. 1, f. 44v. (23 January 1425).
89. *Furs de Valencià*, IV-XVIII-XXX, p. 156 and IV-XIX-I, pp. 157–158. The same law applied if a wife alienated any of her husband's property without his permission.

90 ARV Justícia Civil Peticiones 3723, m. 1, 38v. a 39r. (1 February 1421).
91 *Ibid.*, m. 12, f. 44v. (23 June 1433); *ibid.*, f. 45r. (25 June 1433).
92 See testimony of Ramon Serreces, *llaurador* of Alboraya, *ibid.*, f. 45v. (25 June 1433) and Jacme Perez, *llaurador* of Alboraya, *ibid.*, f. 45v. a 46r. (25 June 1433).
93 ARV Justícia Civil Peticiones 3711, m.4, f. 40r. a 44v. (6 March 1421).
94 Ferraro, *Marriage Wars*, p. 122.
95 Meyerson, 'Bloodshed and baptism'.
96 ARV Justícia Civil Peticiones 3717, m. 1, f. 46r. (28 January 1428).
97 Stretton, *Women Waging Law in Elizabethan England*, fn. 67, p. 16.
98 ARV Justícia Civil Peticiones 3723, m. 14, f. 38r. (30 September 1434).
99 *Ibid.*
100 *Ibid.*, m. 14, f. 4r. a 34r. (27 September 1434).
101 Roca Traver, *La jurisdicción civil del Justícia de Valencia*, p. 79.
102 ARV Justícia Civil Peticiones 3711, m. 1, f. 6v. a 7r. (9 January 1421).
103 ARV Justícia Civil Peticiones 3715, m. 19, f. 43r. a 45r. (3 July 1424).
104 *Ibid.*, f. 45v. a 46r. (3 July 1424).
105 ARV Justícia Civil Peticiones 3723, m. 14. f. 38r. i v. (2 October 1434). This language was used in every sentence passed by the Justícia Civil.
106 Roca Traver, *La jurisdicción civil del Justícia de Valencia*, p. 90.
107 *Ibid.*, p. 92.
108 *Ibid.*
109 ARV Justícia Civil Peticiones 3723, m. 14, f. 38v. (2 October 1434).
110 *Furs de Valencià*, VII-V-IV, p. 59.
111 Roca Traver, *La jurisdicción civil del Justícia de Valencia*, p. 92.
112 *Ibid.*, p. 94.
113 *Ibid.*, p. 96.
114 *Ibid.*, p. 94.
115 ARV Prot. 2270, Bernat Vallseguer, non-paginated (11 February 1430).
116 ARV Prot. 471, Berenguer Cardona, non-paginated (27 November 1430).
117 APPV Prot. 23409, Joan Peres, non-paginated (19 June 1433).
118 ARV Prot. 3011, Esteban Queralt, non-paginated (17 October 1436).
119 ARV Gobernació Litium 2227, m. 11, f. 21r. a 22v. (7 August 1421).
120 ARV Gobernació Litium 4842, m.5, f.8r. i v. (19 April 1421).
121 Rubio Vela, 'Infancia y marginación', p. 112.
122 *Furs de Valencià*, I-III-CXII, p. 241; III-V-LVIII, pp. 105–106.
123 Michel Mollat, *The Poor in the Middle Ages: An Essay in Social History*, trans. Arthur Goldhammer (New Haven, CT: Yale University Press, 1986), p. 174.
124 From the mid-fourteenth century, the city of Valencia instituted a special office, the *procurador dels miserables*, that acted in a legal capacity on behalf of all those deemed *miserabiles personae* (*ibid.*, p. 145).
125 *Ibid.*
126 *Furs de Valencià*, V-V-VI, p. 42
127 ARV Gobernació Litium 4842, m. 2, f. 15r. iv. (11 February 1421).
128 Lalinde Abadia, *La Gobernación General en la Corona de Aragon*, p. 374.
129 ARV Gobernació Litium 2228, m. 13, f. 34r. i v., sig. m. 16, f. 46r. (31 August 1422).
130 For example, see ARV Gobernació Litium 2228, m. 13, f. 5 r. y v., sig. m. 16 f. 13r. (13 August 1422).

131 ARV Gobernació Litium 4842, m. 5, f. 8r. i v. (19 April 1421).
132 ARV Gobernació Litium 2228, m. 13, f. 5r. i v., sig. m. 16 f. 13r. (13 August 1422).
133 ARV Gobernació Litium 4578, m. 2, f. 26r. i v. (17 April 1422).
134 One other case involving *germanía* restitution appears in the Justícia Civil records. In it, Francesca de Barbastro claims that her husband, Lop, destroyed their marriage contract but despite this fact, claims that his poor treatment and neglect of her demonstrates that she should be granted her half of the communal property. This case is completely different from any other civil case I have read in the Valencian archives as the only two witnesses who testify are the couple themselves. In the end, the justice does not rule on the case. See ARV Justícia Civil Peticiones 3731, m. 10, f.5r. sig. ARV Justícia Civil Peticiones 3730, m. 13, f. 25r. a 31v. (28 June 1438).
135 ARV Gobernació Litium 4842, m. 3, f. 45r. i v. (12 April 1421).
136 ARV Prot. 54, Antonio Altarriba, non-paginated (6 March 1431).
137 *Ibid.*

Conclusion

Teresa Dauder won her suit of dowry restitution against her husband Tomàs. The evidence she presented, both in the form of witness testimony and notarial instruments, clearly demonstrated that Tomàs had failed in his role as administrator of her assets. Less obvious in this record is the implication of Teresa's suit for the couple's marriage. Did Teresa and Tomàs Dauder remain living together after she won her suit of dowry restitution? Or did Teresa petition the ecclesiastical court for a separation? Canon law stated that marriages were indissoluble but evidence from other areas of southern Europe indicates that couples were granted legal separations.[1] As church court records for the diocese of Valencia do not survive, we are unable to ascertain whether Teresa took the next step in dissolving her marriage to Tomàs. Those wives whose husbands committed a violent crime, and fled the kingdom, likely sought a writ of separation from the ecclesiastical court. Their husbands' criminal activity, and absence, alongside their victory in civil court, would have assisted these women greatly in their petitions. Those couples who colluded to reserve one aspect of their assets from creditors would obviously have remained together, although one must wonder about the implications of these actions in terms of the husband's and his wife's social honour.

In looking at the impact of dowry restitution suits, were 'admonitions that women live under the control of men compromised if women could bring lawsuits against men?'.[2] What effect did these cases have on a husband's authority over his wife? Certainly the hierarchical medieval social structure that placed the husband as the head of his wife would have been disturbed if she could challenge openly aspects of that authority. But, as this book has demonstrated, the marital relationships of artisan and *llaurador* couples rarely fit within the confines of prescriptive legal, religious and social texts. Artisan and *llaurador* women used the legal apparatuses available to them in order to protect their marital assets. The laws and institutions present in late medieval Valencia provided them with the ability to do so.

The key factors that gave these women the manoeuvrability that they exercised were their immigrant and labouring-status background. Having moved to Valencia on their own, likely as servants, these women had great influence and freedom in their marital choices. Removed from the sphere of their natal kin, labouring-status women who immigrated to Valencia contracted their own marriages, provided their own dotal assets, and challenged their husbands' authority over this property in dowry restitution cases when things went wrong. As labouring-status women, they were less affected by the desires of their families to utilize marriage as a means of creating important social, economic and political alliances. However, this does not mean that the kin groups of artisan and *llaurador* women were entirely without concern regarding their marital choices. Rather, the evidence presented in this book demonstrates that we must reconsider how those of labouring-status defined 'kin' in the urban communities of late medieval southern Europe.

Cities that were built on immigration had neighbourhoods that contained a constantly moving population, as those of lower status moved in and out, in search of economic opportunities. In such a constantly shifting society, people came to rely on bonds other than those of blood to support one another in their daily lives. For labouring-status women in late medieval Valencia, friends and neighbours became centrally important in their marital choices. These social kin helped them to choose their spouses, provide adequate dowries and support their claims of restitution as witnesses in their court cases. As Katherine Lynch has argued, individuals in urban communities used extrafamilial bonds to add to or replace functions that families usually provided.[3] This was certainly the case for Teresa Dauder, as her master and mistress hosted her wedding feast and provided assets towards her dowry. Indeed, it was Teresa's friends and neighbours who gave the necessary testimony that allowed her to win her suit of dowry restitution.

In her examination of pre-modern urban communities, Lynch states that higher rates of mortality (due to population density and poor sanitation), combined with migration worked to reduce the size of households and weaken familial bonds.[4] In late medieval Valencia, while we are unable to examine the relative size of households at the lower levels of society, it is clear that the conditions of urban life produced a much different view of kin groups than was evident in rural areas. One aspect of Lynch's argument that is particularly interesting for the issues raised by this book is her suggestion that women in urban communities had stronger relationships with their neighbours than men did. She feels that as women were more 'spatially circumscribed' than men, they developed longer and greater connections with those that lived in the same area.[5]

Evidence from Valencia certainly supports the idea that strong ties existed between women and their neighbours. Testaments indicate that neighbours often left bequests to one another; marriage contracts show them supplementing women's dowries; and court records present neighbours as frequent witnesses in one another's suits of varying kinds. One aspect of these documents that is particularly compelling in light of Lynch's argument is the fact that it was largely female neighbours that provided support to other women. Testimony from dowry restitution cases demonstrates that female neighbours often took other women into their homes, giving them a place to live if their husbands refused to do so. Female neighbours were also far more likely to leave dotal bequests in their testaments to other women than men were. In addition, mistresses more often than their husbands donated dowry funds above and beyond that earned by their servants. All of this evidence points to the idea that ties of social kinship were particularly strong between women in neighbourhoods. While an examination of connections between labouring-status men of the same neighbourhood needs to be done in order to explore whether or not women had stronger relationships with their neighbours than men did in fifteenth-century Valencia, it is evident that female neighbours did form close associations with one another.

In its examination of the relationship between labouring-status wives and their dowries in early fifteenth-century Valencia, this book has complicated and nuanced our understanding of women's influence and ability to shape their own lives from a number of different perspectives. Through the analysis of notarial evidence and court records, it is clear that socio-economic status and immigration influenced married women's access to and control of marital property in late medieval Valencia. Thus although the law encoded a system which appeared to impose and reinforce gender ideologies, at the same time, that legal discourse in practice created grey areas which allowed women to negotiate agency within limits.[6] Labouring-status women therefore worked within legal and social norms to protect and maintain their marital assets, negotiating patriarchal structures to their advantage.

Notes

1 Ferraro, *Marriage Wars*; Kirshner, 'Wives' Claims'; Linda Guzzetti, 'Separations and Separated Couples in Fourteenth-Century Venice', in Trevor Dean and K.J.P. Lowe (eds), *Marriage in Italy, 1300–1650* (Cambridge: Cambridge University Press, 1998), pp. 249–274.
2 Stretton, *Women Waging Law in Elizabethan England*, p. 51.
3 Katherine A. Lynch, *Individuals, Families, and Communities in Europe, 1200–1800: The Urban Foundations of Western Society* (Cambridge: Cambridge University Press, 2003), p. 1.
4 *Ibid.*, p. 2.
5 *Ibid.*, p. 63.
6 Kelleher, *Measure of Woman*, p. 14.

Appendix

Dowry Restitution Case (ARV Justícia Civil Peticiones 3723 m. 14, f. 8r. sig. f. 35r. a 38v. (30 September 1434).

In the year of the lord mccccxxxiv Thursday 30 September before the honourable justice Manuel Suau of the city of Valencia in the civil court. Case between Gabriel Bonet, notary who was nominated as written below and Francesc Oviet, ropemaker, legal representative for Tomàs Dauder.

Before the presence of your honourable Manuel Suau, civil justice of Valencia is presented Gabriel Bonet, notary and legal representative of dona Teresa, wife of Tomàs Dauder, barber of the said city who petitions and demands against the said Tomàs, her husband and against any other person who represents him legally concerning the issues below.

First ...in the year 1429, a marriage was contracted, made, joined and solemnized in the holy mother church and afterwards consummated through carnal copulation between the said Tomàs Dauder and Teresa, daughter of Joan Dalarit, shieldmaker, inhabitant of the city of Sogorb.

Moreover ... [after] the said marriage between Tomàs Dauder and Teresa was made and confirmed, those ones were and lived all the time together as husband and wife; they called themselves joined husband and wife and they are held, granted and joined as husband and wife from the said time ever since by all [their] familiars ...

Moreover ... at the time of the contract of the said marriage, the said Teresa constituted and brought to the said Tomàs Dauder in and for her dowry according to the law of Valencia forty pounds of Valencian money and the said Tomàs Dauder [for] his marriage donation and *creix* [gave] to the said Teresa because of her virginity according to the law twenty pounds of the said money. So thus the dowry and *creix* are sixty pounds of Valencian money which the said Tomàs Dauder secured for the said Teresa on and according to all his goods and rights to be held ... by the marriage contract that was made and confirmed by the above said in the power of Joan Caposa, notary on Sunday of the thirteenth day of the month of February of the year 1429 ...

Moreover ... during the said marriage, Dauder incurred many and diverse debts and has diminished their goods so that now they are in poverty and their goods are valued at ten pounds ... and a lien has been made against the goods of Tomàs Dauder ...

Moreover ... it is a case and place of restitution according to the law and the said Tomàs Dauder ought to be condemned to give, to return and to restore to the said Teresa, his wife, the said forty pounds of dowry and the twenty pounds of *creix*.

[numerous lines reminding the participants to present true witnesses to the court with details as to when and where; it is at this point that we learn Tomàs Dauder is not present in Valencia which is why Francesc Oviet is acting as his legal representative]

Witness one: Thursday 30 September 1434

Maria, wife of Francesc Oviet, ropemaker, inhabitant of the city of Valencia, living in the parish of St Bartomeu in the street of the ropemakers, a witness produced and given on behalf of the said Gabriel Bonet ... who swears before God and the four holy gospels ... that she owes the truth in her deposition concerning that which she knows.

And in response to the first question of the petition, the witness says that she knows it is true. And when asked how she knows it is true, she states because dona Teresa, wife of Tomàs Dauder named in the question when she was 12 years old, more or less, entered the house of the witness and Francesc Oviet, ropemaker, her husband [as a servant]. And the said Teresa was joined in marriage with Tomàs and the witness was present at the conclusion of the marriage contract and the betrothal of the couple and these were done in the house of the witness. Afterwards, the witness went to the nuptial mass and the wedding feast of the couple [which was held in the witness's house] and she and her husband ate and drank there. After the wedding, the witness saw the couple acting and living together as husband and wife in one house and one room. And Tomàs called Teresa wife and she called Tomàs husband. Many other people can attest to these facts including Joan Caposa, the notary and the witness's husband Francesc Oviet as well as many of their neighbours in the street of St Bertomeu in Valencia.

And in response to the second question of the petition, the witness states that these are true. She states she has seen this many times and been to the house of the couple and that many others, including her husband, have seen these things.

And in response to the third question, the witness states that these are true and that she was present when the marriage contract was concluded and received by the notary Joan Caposa in the witness's house. She states that her husband Francesc Oviet paid the dowry of Teresa to Tomàs Dauder in the amount of 25 pounds of Valencian money. And the witness was present and heard this happen.

And in response to the tenth question, the witness states these are true. After Tomàs and Teresa Dauder were married, Tomàs caused many and diverse debts and has lost most of his goods and has been made poor in temporal belongings so much so that what he has left is not worth 10 pounds of Valencian money. The witness knows for certain that Tomàs does not have enough to guarantee the dowry of his wife and pay the obligations he has to his creditors. And that the goods in his house are worth nothing.

And the witness swears she has told the truth and that there is no hatred among her and the defendant.

Witness two: the same Thursday 30 September in the year of the lord 1434

Miquel Bou, ropemaker, living in the city of Valencia in the parish of St Bertomeu, a witness produced and given on behalf of the said Gabriel Bonet...who swears before God and the four holy gospels ... that he owes the truth in his deposition concerning that which he knows.

And in response to the first question and the third question of the petition, the witness states that these are true. He knows that Tomàs Dauder, barber and Teresa in the named question are husband and wife. And he knows this because he was present in the neighbourhood and heard the wedding of the couple and the exchange of consent between them in the house of Francesc Oviet, ropemaker. The witness went to the nuptial mass of the couple in the parish church of St Bartomeu of the city of Valencia and afterward he saw the couple living together as husband and wife in the said city. As husband and wife they had a reputation among those that knew them. The witness states that this happened about three years ago and that many other people know this, but he doesn't remember who.

And concerning the fifth question, the witness knows nothing.

And the witness swears he has told the truth and that there is no hatred between him and the defendant.

Witness three: on the aforesaid day, Thursday 30 September, in the year of the lord 1434

Francesc Adubell, barber, living in the city of Valencia. A witness produced and given on behalf of the said Gabriel Bonet ... who swears before God and the four holy gospels ... that he owes the truth in his deposition concerning that which he knows.

And concerning the first, second and third questions of the petition, the witness states that they are true. He states he was not present at the betrothal or wedding of Tomàs Dauder, the barber and Teresa but he has seen them living together as husband and wife in one room and house continually for three years, more or less. And he has heard Tomàs Dauder call Teresa his wife, and Teresa call Tomàs husband. And that as husband and wife, the couple has a reputation in the city of Valencia among those that know them.

And concerning the fifth question of the demand, the witness states that it is true. He has heard it said by many people and it is well known that Tomàs Dauder has caused many and diverse debts and has many and diverse creditors including the honourable Pere Andreu of Valencia to whom he owes 100 sous of Valencian money ... And to dona Agnes, Tomàs Dauder owes 100 sous. The witness has also seen that Tomàs Dauder is poor in temporal goods. This is all the witness knows concerning this question but he states that it is true and that many other people know these facts.

And the witness swears he has told the truth and that there is no hatred between him and the defendant.

Witness four: Friday 1 October, in the year of the lord 1434

Francesc Riudaura, wooldresser, living in the street of Morvedre in the plaza of the Abredors, near the Gate of Serranos. A witness produced and given on behalf of the said Gabriel Bonet ... who swears before God and the four holy gospels ... that he owes the truth in his deposition concerning that which he knows.

And concerning the first, second and third questions of the demand, the witness states these are true. He said he knows the couple named, Tomàs Dauder and his wife Teresa because they are the neighbours of this witness and for around three years, he has seen them being and living together as husband and wife in one house and room. And Tomàs calls Teresa wife and she calls Tomàs husband. The couple has a reputation as husband and wife in the city among those that know them.

And concerning the fifth question, the witness states that these are true. He has heard it said among many people and it is publicly known that Tomàs Dauder has caused many debts and is a debtor to many people. The witness states that Tomàs Dauder is a poor person and lacking in temporal goods and he knows this because he is a neighbour to the couple who lived in a house behind that of the witness. Many times, the witness went into the house of Tomàs and Teresa Dauder and saw the few goods they had and that nothing is worth more than 10 sous.

Marriage contracts [included in the court record]

In the name of the lord, I Teresa, daughter of Joan Dalarit, shieldmaker of the city of Sogorb with the will of my father and of Francesc Oviet, ropemaker of the city of Valencia and his wife Maria, in contemplation of the marriage between myself and you Tomàs Dauder, barber of Valencia, I give and concede to you Tomàs for my dowry 40 pounds of Valencia money.

Namely, 20 pounds that was given to me by Francesc Oviet and his wife Maria as payment for my work as a domestic servant. And 10 pounds that was given to me by my father Joan which he promised for marriage. The remaining 10 pounds of this 40 pounds will be given by Francesc Oviet in his last will and testament.

And I Tomàs, knowingly and gratefully accept this dowry in this form. And on account of your virginity, I give to you Teresa as *augmentum* or donation on account of marriage, 20 pounds.

Thus in dowry and *augmentum* there is 60 pounds of Valencian money. I promise to return your dowry to you Teresa, for any reason or event, at any time that you wish, according to the laws of Valencia.

Sentence: Saturday 2 October 1434

Before the honourable justice with Gabriel Bonet representing one side and Francesc Oviet the other.

And the honourable justice having conferred with the honourable jurists, leading men and councillors of the present city presents the following sentence.

As through the depositions of the witnesses and justly produced below … to be the contract of marriage between the said Tomàs Dauder and the said Teresa and she gave to him as her dowry forty pounds and he promised to restore to her this [dowry] with the twenty pounds of *creix* in case the dowry is to be restored. And much later the said Tomàs Dauder fell into insolvency through such from his penury and declare [this] to be a case and reason for restitution of the dowry and *creix* and with the present [sentence the justice] condemns the said Tomàs Dauder and for such from him to give and to pay to the said Teresa, his wife, forty pounds of dowry and twenty pounds of *creix*.

Marriage contracts

APPV 26341, Thursday 26 June 1427

In the name of the Lord, amen. Let it be known to all that we, Pere Ramon (son of Guillem Ramon, once a farmer in the village of Benifaraig in the *horta* of Valencia and his wife Dulcia) and Caterina (a virgin girl, daughter of Guillem Vilana, farmer in the place of Alfara in the *horta* of Valencia) make between us a contract of marriage. I, the said Pere Ramon do so with the consent of my mother and the consent of other friends and relatives. And I, the said Caterina, do so with the consent and will of my father Guillem Vilana and the consent of my family and friends. We [Pere and Caterina] make and contract between us fraternity and *germanía* for all the time of our lives. And we hold in common all goods and rights that we have.

Thus after one of us dies, the one remaining alive gets half of the property. If we have no children, the one remaining alive receives all of the property. And we obligate each other's goods as surety for the other half.

Witnesses: Joan Andreu, notary; Bernard Roqua, carpenter; and Joan Sparch, all living in Valencia.

APPV 23404, Sunday 7 August 1429

I Johana, a virgin woman living in Valencia, with the consent of my family and friends, join myself in marriage with you, the blacksmith Jacob Andreu of Valencia. Presently, I promise and constitute to you in and for my dowry, 30 pounds of Valencian money in cash and household goods. And on account of the aforesaid [dowry] I obligate all of my goods to you.

And I the said Jacob Andreu accept you, the said Johana as my future wife. I confess to have held the said dowry … And since according to the laws of Valencia I ought to give to you an *augmentum* for virginity, therefore I give to you, the said Johana present, an *augmentum* of 15 pounds of

Valencian money. Thus for dowry and *augmentum* is 45 pounds which I promise to restore to you in any case or event of dowry restitution. And I, the aforesaid Jacob, obligate all of my goods, according to the laws of Valencia.

Witnesses: Joan de Nou, tavern owner and Jacob Cambrils, dyer both of Valencia.

APPV 23409, Sunday 4 January 1433

In the name of the Lord, amen. Let it be known to all that I, Griselda, living in Valencia, with the will of my family at the time of marriage, I constitute or give in and for my dowry 100 *solidos* [5 pounds] of Valencian money in cash to you the weaver Joan Marti, living in the place of Quart. I obligate all my goods as surety.

And therefore I the said Joan Marti accept you Griselda as my future wife. I confess and recognize to you promised to me the said 100 *solidos*. I promise to restore this property to you for any reason or event of dowry restitution. And I obligate all my goods as surety, according to the laws of Valencia.

Witnesses: Pere Gasto, courier and citizen of Valencia and Dominic Guille, blacksmith of Quart.

Bibliography

Primary sources

Archival sources

Archivo del Reino de Valencia (ARV)

Protocolos (181 volumes from 54 different notaries)
Paolo Agustí: 3169
Pedro Agusti Veses: 2333
Antoni Altarriba: 10410, 696, 2569, 2570, 2572, 54, 55
Joan Amalrich: 63, 4341
Joan Aymes: 15
Marcos Barbèra: 199, 3016, 200
Bertran de Boes: 2511, 312, 10419
Nicholau Bonet: 3153
Vicent Çaera: 2421, 2727, 2422, 2724, 4228, 2729, 2424, 2425, 2731, 2423, 2426, 2427, 2428, 2429, 2430, 2432
Joan de Campos (Sr): 416, 417, 2524, 2525, 419, 420, 421, 424, 411, 425, 423, 426, 418, 428, 429, 427, 430, 431, 432, 433, 435, 436, 438
Joan Cañada: 10420
Berenguer Cardona: 2533, 468, 2534, 469, 2535, 470, 471, 472, 466, 467, 473, 474, 475, 476, 477, 478, 479, 484
Guillem Cardona: 505
Vicent Castronovo: 517
Francesc Cavaller: 2477
Bernat Centelles: 567, 568
Pere Clemens: 584
Desconocido: 11231, 11235, 11237, 11238, 11239, 11242, 11182
Joan Domingo: 4159
Martí Doto: 789, 790, 10422, 791, 3093, 792, 793, 794, 795, 796, 798, 799, 800, 10434, 4168, 801, 803, 805, 806, 807, 808
Guillem Durando: 811
Bernat Estrellers: 821
Bernat Falchs: 2873, 4377, 3101
Sancho Falco: 852
Jaume Ferran: 2581, 2582, 2584
Bernat Flores: 934, 935
Joan Forner: 947
Bernat Fuster: 3239
Joan Garcia: 1094, 1095
Andreu Gasull: 4376
Joan Gil: 3006

Pedro Guitart: 1217
Juan Jimenez: 3120, 3196
Miquel Joan: 1243
Antoni Jover: 3091
Andreu Julian: 2612, 1267, 1268,
Pere Llorens: 4206, 1329, 1330, 2865, 1331
Bartolomé Matoses: 2635
Nicholau Menor: 3122, 10423
Jaume Molner: 1539
Francesc Monço: 2850, 1559, 3150
Bernat Montesano: 1548
Joan Peris: 2864, 2866
Andreu Puigmicha: 1889, 1891, 1893, 1895, 1896, 1897 1898, 1899, 1892, 1894, 1890, 1900
Esteban Queralt: 3011
Joan Sarañana: 2142, 2143, 2144
Bartolomé Tolosa: 2711
Jaume Tolosa 3211
Francesc Tomàs: 3199
Luis Torres: 2253
Bernat Vallseguer: 2270
Bernat Vidal: 2773
Jaume Vidal: 3100, 2357
Miquel Villafarta: 2367

Justícia Civil

Peticiones: (22 volumes)
3710 (1420); 3711 (1421); 3712 (1421); 3713 (1422); 3714 (1423); 3715 (1424) 3716 (1425); 3717 (1428); 3718 (1431); 3719 (1431); 2720 (1432); 3721 (1432) 3722 (1433); 3723 (1434); 3724 (1434); 3725 (1435); 3726 (1436); 3727 (1436); 3729 (1437); 3730 (1438); 3731 (1438); 3733 (1439)

Gobernació

Litium: (24 volumes)
4840 (1420); 2224 (1420); 2225 (1420); 4841 (1420); 4842 (1421); 2227 (1421); 2226 (1421); 4578 (1422); 2228 (1422); 2229 (1422); 2230 (1422); 2231 (1422); 2232 (1423); 4843 (1424); 2233 (1424); 2234 (1425); 2235 (1425); 2236 (1426); 2237 (1426); 2238 (1427); 2239 (1429); 2240 (1429); 2241 (1430); 2242 (1430)

Archivo de Protocolos del Patriarca de Valencia (APPV) (54 volumes from 33 different notaries)

Martí de Alago 25304
Ambrosi Alegret: 1109
Joan d'Aragó: 18417

Pere Andreu: 6332
Tomàs Argent: 25474
Gabriel Bonet: 21504
Joan Capdevilla: 1275
Dionis Cervera: 16383, 1370, 28643
Martí Coll 19784, 14402, 19785, 25089
Joan Comes: 22096
Bertomeu Esteve: 27286
Joan Eiximeno: 14472
Joan Ferrer: 25990, 25988, 22350
Miquel Gali 26341, 26342, 26343
Joan Gallart 21670, 21669
Bertomeu Gueralt: 1091
Lluis Guerau: 27183
Felip Lleopart: 23685
Joan Marromà: 26181
Bertomeu Marti: 69
Joan del Mas: 27356
Arnal de Montello: 23930
Tomàs Oller 24096
Francesc Pelegri: 6582
Joan Peris: 22842, 22852, 23404, 22121, 23408, 22735, 23409 23407, 22097, 22098, 23414
Joan de Pina: 23268, 23267
Miquel de Ripoll: 22110
Joan de Sant Feliu: 25845
Jaume de Sant Vicent: 26371
Bernat Teixidor: 22476
Joan Tamarit: 24335
Pere Todo: 25745
Jaume Venrell: 14403

Printed sources

Constitucions i alters drets de Catalunya. Barcelona: Base, 1973.
Consuetudines Dertosae. Tarragona: Institucio de Estudios Tarraconenses Ramon Berenguer IV, 1972.
Corpus Iuris Civilis. P. Krueger and T. Mommsen (eds). Zurich: Weidmann, 1973.
Corpus Iuris Civilis: Codex Iustinianus. Paul Kreuger (ed.). Berlin: Weidmannsche Verlagsbuchhandlung, 1963.
Eiximenis, Francesc. *Lo llibre de les dones: Volum I i II*. Barcelona: Biblioteca Torres Amat, 1981.
Ferrer, Vicent. *Sermons: Vols I–V*. Josep Sanchis Sivera and Gret Schib (eds). Barcelona: Editorial Barcino, 1934–1984.

Fori Antiqui Valentie. Manuel Dualde Serrano (ed.). Madrid–Valencia, 1950–67.
Fueros de Aragon: según el ms. del Archivo Municipal de Miravete de la Sierra. Zaragoza: Anubar, 1992.
Fueros de Cuenca. Rafael Ureña y Smenjaud (ed.). Madrid: Tipografia de Archivos, 1935.
Fueros de Teruel. José Castañé Llinas (ed. and trans.). Teruel: Ajuntamiento de Teruel, 1994.
Furs de Valencià Vols 1–VI. Germà Colon and Arcadia Garcia (eds). Barcelona: Editorial Barcino, 1970–94.
Roig, Jaume. *Espill o Llibre de les dones.* Jordi Tiñena (ed.). Barcelona: Laertes, 1988.
Las Siete Partidas. Samuel Parsons Scott (ed.). Chicago: Commerce Clearing House, 1981.
The Usatges of Barcelona: The Fundamental Law of Catalonia. Donald Kagay (ed.). Philadelphia, University of Pennsylvania Press, 1994.

Secondary sources

Alcover, Mn. Antoni Ma, *Diccionari Català–Valencià–Balear* Vols I–X. Francesc B. De Moll (ed.) (Palma de Mallorca, 1926–62).
Amparo Baixauli, Isabel, *Casar-se al'Antic Règime: Dona i família a la València del segle XVII* (Valencia: Universitat de Valencia, 2003).
Amt, Emilie (ed.), *Women's Lives in Medieval Europe* (New York: Routledge, 1993).
Arjawa, Antti, *Women and the Law in Late Antiquity* (Oxford: Clarendon Press, 1996).
Ashley, Kathleen and Robert L.A. Clark (eds), *Medieval Conduct* (Minneapolis: University of Minnesota Press, 2001).
Aventín i Puig, Mercè, *La societat rural a Catalunya en temps feudals: Vallès Oriental, segles XIII–XVI* (Barcelona: Columna Edicions, 1996).
Aznar Gil, F.R., *La institutción matrimonial en la Hispania Cristiana bajomedieval (1215–1563)* (Salamanca: Publicaciones de la Universidad Pontificia de Salamanca, 1989).
Badia, Juan Ferrando, *El historico Reino de Valencia y su organización foral* (Valencia: Generalitat Valenciana, 1995).
Baum, Hans-Peter, 'Annuities in Late Medieval Hanse Towns', *Business History Review*, 59 (1985), pp. 24–48.
Belda, M. Angeles, 'La economica familiar valenciana en el codigo de Jaime I (Furs de Valencia) y su proyección en el llamado privilegio marital', in *VI Congreso Historia de la Corona de Aragón*, pp. 393–402 (Cerdaña, 1953).
Belda Soler, M. Angeles, *El régimen matrimonial de bienes en los 'Furs de València'* (Valencia: Editorial Cosmos Valencia, 1965).
Belenguer Cebrià, E., *València en la crisi del segle XV* (Barcelona: Edicions 62, 1976).
— (ed.), *Història del País Valèncià. Vol. II: De la Conquesta a la Federació Hispànica* (Barcelona: Edicions 62, 1989).
Benadusi, Giovanna, 'Investing the Riches of the Poor: Servant Women and Their Last Wills', *American Historical Review*, 109(3) (June 2004), pp. 805–826.

Bennett, J., E.A. Clark and J.F. O'Barr (eds), *Sisters and Workers in the Middle Ages* (Chicago: University of Chicago Press, 1989).
Bennett, Judith M., 'The Tie that Binds: Peasant Marriage and Families in Late Medieval England', *Journal of Interdisciplinary History*, 15 (1984), pp. 111–129.
— *Women in the Medieval English Countryside: Gender and Household in Brigstock before the Plague* (Oxford: Oxford University Press, 1987).
— 'History That Stands Still: Women's Work in the European Past', *Feminist Studies*, 14 (1988), pp. 269–283.
— 'Medieval Women, Modern Women: Across the Great Divide', in David Aers (ed.), *Culture and History 1350–1600: Essays on English Communities, Identities and Writing* (London: Harvester Wheatsheaf, 1997), pp. 147–175.
— 'Theoretical Issues: Confronting Continuity', *Journal of Women's History*, 9(3) (autumn 1997), pp. 73–94.
— 'Writing Fornication: Medieval Leyrwite and Its Historians', *Transactions of the Royal Historical Society*, 6(13) (2003), pp. 131–162.
— *History Matters: Patriarchy and the Challenge of Feminism* (Philadelphia: University of Pennsylvania Press, 2006).
Bensch, Stephen, *Barcelona and Its Rulers, 1096–1291* (Cambridge: Cambridge University Press, 1994).
Berking, Helmuth, *Sociology of Giving* (London: Sage, 1999).
Bestor, Jane Fair, 'Marriage Transactions in Renaissance Italy and Mauss's Essay on the Gift', *Past and Present*, 164 (August 1999), pp. 6–46.
Blumenthal, Debra, 'Implements of labour, instruments of honor: Muslim, eastern and black African slaves in fifteenth-century Valencia' (Ph.D. dissertation, University of Toronto, 2000).
— *Enemies and Familiars: Slavery and Mastery in Fifteenth-Century Valencia* (Ithaca, NY: Cornell University Press, 2009).
Boix, Vicente, *Apuntes históricos sobre los fueros del antiguo reino de Valencia* (Valencia: Liber Paris-València, 1982).
Bonnassie, Pierre, *La organización del trabajo en Barcelona a fines del siglo XV* (Barcelona: Consejo Superior de Investigaciones Cientificas, 1975).
Bossy, John, *Christianity in the West, 1400–1700* (Oxford: Oxford University Press, 1988).
Botticini, Maristella, 'A Loveless Economy? Intergenerational Altruism and the Marriage Market in a Tuscan Town, 1415-36', *Journal of Economic History*, 59(1) (March 1999), pp. 104–121.
Bresc, Henri, 'Europe: Town and Country (13th to 15th Century)', in A. Burguiére, Christiane Klapisch-Zuber, Martine Segalen and F. Zonabend (eds), *A History of the Family Volume I: Distant Worlds, Ancient Worlds* (Cambridge: Polity Press, 1996), pp. 430–466.
Broida, Equip (Olga Bravo Ortega, Pilar Gallego Garces, Margarida González i Betlinski, Montserrat Marsiñach i Tirvio, Nuria Muñoz i Soria, Anna Rubio i Rodon, Elisa Varela Rodriguez and Teresa-María Vinyoles), 'La viudez ¿triste o feliz estado? (Las últimas voluntades de los barceloneses en torno al 1400)', in C. Segura Graiño (ed.), *Las mujeres en las ciudades medievales* (Madrid: Seminario de Estudios de la Mujer, Universidad Autónoma de Madrid, 1984), pp. 27–41.

Brooke Christopher, N.L., *The Medieval Idea of Marriage* (Oxford: Oxford University Press, 1989).
Brown, Judith, 'A Woman's Place Was in the Home: Women's Work in Renaissance Tuscany', in Margaret Ferguson, Maureen Quilligan and Nancy Vickers (eds), *Rewriting the Renaissance: The Discourses of Sexual Difference in Early Modern Europe* (Chicago: University of Chicago Press, 1986).
— and Jordon Goodman, 'Women and Industry in Florence', *Journal of Economic History*, 10(1) (1980), pp. 73–80.
Brundage, James, *Law, Sex and Christian Society in Medieval Europe* (Chicago: University of Chicago Press, 1987).
Bullough, Vern L., 'On Being a Male in the Middle Ages', in Clare A. Lees (ed.), *Medieval Masculinities: Regarding Men in the Middle Ages* (Minneapolis: University of Minnesota Press, 1994), pp. 31–45.
Burns, Robert I., *The Crusader Kingdom of Valencia* (Cambridge, MA: Harvard University Press, 1967).
Carcel Orti Vicente, 'Sinodos Medievales Valentinos', in *Hispania Christiana: Estudios en honor del Professor José Orlandis* (Pamplona: Ediciones Universidad de Navarra, 1988), pp. 429–447.
Carlé, Maria del Carmen, *La Sociedad Hispano-Medieval: La ciudad* (Barcelona: Gedisa, 1984).
— 'Apuntes sobre el matrimonio en la Edad Media Española', *Cuadernos de historia de España*, 63–64 (1980), pp. 115–177.
Caro Baroja, Julio, 'Honour and Shame', in Jean G. Peristiany (ed.), *Honour and Shame: the Values of Mediterranean Society* (London: Weidenfeld & Nicolson, 1965), pp. 79–139.
Carpenter, Jennifer and Sally-Beth MacLean, 'Introduction', in Jennifer Carpenter and Sally-Beth MacLean (eds), *Power of the Weak: Studies on Medieval Women* (Chicago: University of Illinois Press, 1995), pp. xi–xix.
Castañeda Alcover, Vicente, 'Organación familiar en el derecho valenciano', *Revista de Archivos, Bibliotecas y Museos* (1908), pp. 259–262.
Castiglione, Caroline, 'Adversarial Literacy: How Peasant Politics Influenced Noble Governing of the Roman Countryside during the Early Modern Period', *American Historical Review*, 109(3) (June 1994), pp. 783–804.
Cavallo, Sandra and Lyndan Warner, 'Introduction', in Sandra Cavallo and Lyndan Warner (eds), *Widowhood in Medieval and Early Modern Europe* (New York: Longman, 1999), pp. 3–23.
Cerutti, Simona, *La ville et les métiers: Naissance d'un langue corporatif (Turin, 17e–18e siècle)* (Paris: Éditions de l'École des hautes études en sciences socials, 1980).
Chabas Lloréns, Roque, *Génesis del derecho foral de Valencia* (Valencia, 1902).
Chabot, Isabelle, 'Widowhood and Poverty in Late Medieval Florence', *Continuity and Change*, 3 (1988), pp. 291–301.
— 'Lineage Strategies and the control of widows in Renaissance Florence', in Sandra Cavallo and Lyndan Warner (eds), *Widowhood in Medieval and Early Modern Europe* (New York: Longman, 1999), pp. 127–144.
Chaline, Jean-Pierre and C. Vicent, 'Convivialité, commensalité: De la cohésion sociale à la civilisation des mœurs', in M. Aurell, O. Dumoulin and F.

Thelamon, *La sociabilité à table: Commensalité et convivialité à travers les âges* (Rouen: Publications de l'Université de Rouen, 1992), pp. 253-259.

Chojnacka, Monica, 'City of women: gender, family, and community in Venice, 1540-1630' (Ph.D. dissertation, Stanford University, 1994).

— *Working Women of Early Modern Venice* (Baltimore: Johns Hopkins University Press, 2001).

Chojnacki, Stanley, *Women and Men in Renaissance Venice: Twelve Essays on Patrician Society* (Baltimore: Johns Hopkins University Press, 2000).

Codina, Jaume, *Contractes de Matrimoni al Delta del Llobregat (XIV a XIX)* (Barcelona: Fundació Noguera, 1997).

Cohn Jr, Samuel K., *Death and Property in Siena, 1205-1800: Strategies for the Afterlife* (Baltimore: Johns Hopkins University Press, 1988).

Collins, James, 'The Economic Role of Women in Seventeenth-Century France', *French Historical Studies*, 16 (1989), pp. 436-470.

Coolidge, Grace E., *Guardianship, Gender, and the Nobility in Early Modern Spain* (Burlington: Ashgate, 2011).

Corbett, Percy Ellwood, *The Roman Law of Marriage* (Oxford: Clarendon Press, 1979).

Cordoba de la Llave, Ricardo, 'La Femme dans l'artisanat de la péninsule ibérique', *Razo*, 14 (1993), pp. 103-114.

Cruilles, El Marques de, *Los Gremios de Valencia: Memoria sobre su origen, vicistitudes y organización* (Valencia: La Casa de Beneficencia, 1883).

Cuesta, Maria Luzdivina, 'Notes on Family Relationships in Medieval Castilian Narrative', in C. J. Itnyre (ed.), *Medieval Family Roles: A Book of Essays* (New York: Garland, 1996), pp. 197-224.

d'Arms, J. H., 'Control, Companionship, and Clientela: Some Social Functions of the Roman Communal Meal', *Échos du monde classique/Classical Views*, 28(3) (1984), pp. 327-348.

Davis, Natalie Zemon, 'Boundaries and the Sense of Self in Sixteenth-Century France', in Thomas C. Heller, Morton Sosna and David E. Wellberg, *Reconstructing Individualism: Autonomy, Individuality, and the Self in Western Thought* (Stanford: Stanford University Press, 1986), pp. 53-63.

— *The Gift in Sixteenth-Century France* (Oxford: Oxford University Press, 2000).

Dayton, Cornelia Hughes, 'Rethinking Agency, Recovering Voices', *American Historical Review*, 109(3) (June 2004), pp. 827-843.

Dean, Trevor and K.J.P. Lowe, 'Introduction: Issues in the History of Marriage', in Trevor Dean and K.J.P. Lowe (eds), *Marriage in Italy, 1300-1650* (Cambridge: Cambridge University Press, 1998), pp. 1-23.

Dillard, Heath, *Daughters of the Reconquest: Women in Castilian Town Society, 1100-1300* (Cambridge: Cambridge University Press, 1984).

Donahue Jr, C., 'The Canon Law on the Formation of Marriage and Social Practice in the Later Middle Ages' *Journal of Family History*, 8(2) (1983), pp. 144-158.

Emigh, Rebecca Jean, 'Property Devolution in Tuscany', *Journal of Interdisciplinary History*, 33(3) (2003), pp. 385-420.

Epalza, Míkel de and Enrique Llobregat, 'Hubo mozárabes en tierra valencianas? Proceso de islamización del Levante de Peninsula (Sharq al-Andalus)', *Revista del Instituto de Estudios Alicantinos*, 36 (1982), pp. 7-31.

Epstein, Steven, *Wills and Wealth in Medieval Genoa* (Cambridge, MA: Harvard University Press, 1984).
Farr, James, *Hands of Honor: Artisans and their World in Dijon: 1550–1650* (Ithaca, NY: Cornell University Press, 1988).
— *Artisans in Europe, 1300–1914* (Cambridge: Cambridge University Press, 2000).
Ferraro, Joanne, *Marriage Wars in Late Renaissance Venice* (Oxford: Oxford University Press, 2001).
Figueras, Lluís To, *Familia i Hereu a la Catalunya Nord-Oriental (segles X–XII)* (Barcelona: Publicaciones de l'Abadia de Montserrat, 1997).
Finch, A.J., 'Sexual Relations and Marriage in Later Medieval Normandy', *Journal of Ecclesiastical History*, 47(2) (April 1996), pp. 232–256.
Font y Ruis, José Maria, *La ordenación paccionada del régimen matrimonial de bienes en el derecho medieval hispánico* (Madrid: Instituto Editorial Reus., 1954).
Furió, Antoni, *Camperols del País Valencià: Sueca, una communitat rural a la tardor de l'Edat Mitjana* (Valencia: Edicions Alfons el Magnànim, 1982).
— 'Tierra, Familia y Transmisión de la propriedad en el pais valenciano durante la baja edad media', in Reyna Pastor (ed.), *Relaciones de poder, de producción y parentesco en la Edad media y moderna* (Madrid: Consejo Superior de Investigaciones Científicas, 1990), pp. 305–328.
— 'La Baixa Edat Mitjana (segles XIV i XV)', in Milagro Gil-Mascarell, Thomas F. Glick, Antoni Furió et al. (eds), *Història del País Valencià* (Valencia: 3i4 Papers Bàsics, 1992), pp. 85–134.
— 'Crédito y endeudamiento: el censal en la sociedad rural valenciana (siglos XIV–XV)', in Esteban Sarasa Sánchez and Eliseo Serrano Martín (eds), *Señorío y feudalismo en la Peninsula Iberica (ss. XII–XIX)* (Zaragoza: Institucion Fernando el Católico, 1994), vol. I, pp. 501–534.
— *Història del País Valencià* (Valencia: Edicions Alfons el Magnànim, 1995).
Gámez Montalvo, María Francisca, *Régimen Jurídico de la Mujer en la Familia Castellana Medieval* (Granada: Editorial Comares, 1998).
García García, Honorio, 'El exovar o exouar y el *creix*', *Boletín de la Sociedad Castellonese de Cultura*, 3 (1922), pp. 237–239.
— 'Las bienes de la mujer', *Boletín de la Sociedad Castellonese de Cultura*, 4 (1924), p. 234.
— 'Régimen económico conjugal', *Boletín de la Sociedad Castellonese de Cultura*, 4 (1924), pp. 153–155.
— 'Más sobre el *creix* y el *exovar*', *Boletín de la Sociedad Castellonese de Cultura*, 8 (1927), pp. 316–317.
— 'La germanía', *Boletín de la Sociedad Castellonese de Cultura*, 9 (1928), pp. 170–173.
— 'Más sobre la germanía', *Boletín de la Sociedad Castellonese de Cultura*, 10 (1929), pp. 76–79.
— 'Derechos de la mujer indotada', *Boletín de la Sociedad Castellonese de Cultura*, 12 (1931), pp. 22–26.
— 'Estudios de derecho foral valenciano: El consentimiento dela esposa para el matrimonio', *Boletín de la Sociedad Castellonese de Cultura*, 17 (1936), pp. 357–363.

— 'Estudios de derecho foral: La germanía', *Boletín de la Sociedad Castellonese de Cultura*, 21(1945), pp. 23–35.
— 'Possibilidad de un elemento consuetudinario en el Código de Jaime I', *Boletín de la Sociedad Castellonense de Cultura*, 23 (1947), pp. 428–450.
García-Herrero, María, 'Mozas sirvientas en Zaragoza durante el siglo XV', in Cristina Segura and Angela Muñoz (eds), *El trabajo de las mujeres en la edad media hispana* (Madrid: Editorial Laya, 1988), pp. 275–285.
— *Las mujeres de Zaragoza en el siglo XV*, 2 vols (Zaragoza: Ayuntamiento de Zaragoza, 1990).
— 'Viudedad foral y viudas Aragonesas a finales de la edad media', *Hispania: Revista Espanola de Historia*, 184 (1993), pp. 431–450.
— 'La misa aplazada: un compromiso matrimonial anómalo a finales de la Edad Media', in *Aragón en la Edad Media: XVI Homenaje al Professor Emérito Angel Sanvincente Pino* (Zaragoza: Universidad de Zaragoza, 2000).
Garcia-Oliver, Ferran, *Terra de feudals: el Pais Valencià en la tardor de l'Edat Mitjana* (Valencia: Edicions Alfons el Magnànim, 1991).
Gaudemet, Jean, *Les Communautés familiales* (Paris: M. Rivière et Cie, 1963).
Gibert, Rafael, *Historia general del derecho español* (Madrid: M. Huerta, 1981).
Godding, Philippe, *Le droit privé dans les Pays-Bas meridionaux du 12e aux 18e siècle* (Brussels: Académie royal de Belgique, 1987).
Goldberg, P.J.P., '"For Better, for Worse": Marriage and Economic Opportunity for Women in Town and Country', in P.J.P. Goldberg, *Woman is a Worthy Wight: Women in English Society, c.1200–1500* (Wolfeboro Falls: Alan Sutton, 1992).
— 'Migration, Youth and Gender in Later Medieval England', in P.J.P. Goldberg and Felicity Riddy (eds), *Youth in the Middle Ages* (York: York Medieval Press, 2004).
González Arce, José Damián, 'Las corporaciones laborales agrarias como formes de identidad, cohesion y representación en Castilla medieval', *Congreso de Historia Agraria*, Córdoba, 2008, pp. 1–32.
Goody, Jack, *The Development of the Family and Marriage in Europe* (Cambridge: Cambridge University Press, 1983).
— *The European Family: A Historico-Anthropological Essay* (Oxford: Blackwell, 2000).
— and S.J. Tambiah. *Bridewealth and Dowry* (Cambridge: Cambridge University Press, 1973).
Gual Camerena, Miguel, 'El regimen matrimonial de bienes en los Fueros de Valencia', *Anuario de historia del dercho español*, 37 (1967), pp. 553–561.
Guillot Aliaga, Dolores, *El Regimen Económico de Matrimonio en La Valencia Foral* (Valencia: Biblioteca Valenciana, 2002).
— and Juan Alfredo Obarrio Moreno, 'La voz *Donatio propter nuptias, sponsalitium, creix* en el Derecho medieval de Valencia y Cataluña', *Boletín de la Sociedad Castellonese de Cultura*, 75 (enero–diciembre 2000), pp. 75–90.
Guinot Rodriguez, Enric, *Feudalismo en expansion en el norte valenciano: antecedents y desarrollo del senorio de la Orden de Montesa, siglos XIII y XIV* (Castellón: Diputación de Castellón, 1986).
Guiral-Hadziiossif, Jacqueline, *Valence: Port méditerranéen au XVe siècle (1410–1525)* (Paris: Publications de la Sorbonne, 1986).

Guzzetti, Linda, 'Separations and Separated Couples in Fourteenth-Century Venice', in Dean and Lowe (eds), *Marriage in Italy, 1300-1650*, pp. 249-274.
Hajnal, J., 'European Marriage Patterns in Perspective', in D. V. Glass and D.E.C Eversley, *Population in History* (London: E. Arnold, 1965), pp. 101-143.
Hallissy, Margaret, *Clean Maids, True Wives, Steadfast Widows: Chaucer's Women and Medieval Codes of Conduct* (Westport, CT: Greenwood Press, 1993).
Hamilton, Earl J., *Money, Prices and Wages in Valencia, Aragon and Navarre, 1351-1500* (Cambridge, MA: Harvard University Press, 1936).
Hanawalt, Barbara A. and Anna Dionzek, 'Women in Medieval Urban Society', in Linda E. Mitchell (ed.), *Women in Medieval Western European Culture* (New York: Garland, 1999), pp. 31-45.
Heinsch, Bridget Anne, *Fast and Feast: Food in Medieval Society* (Pennsylvania: Penn State University Press, 1976).
Herlihy, David, 'The Medieval Marriage Market', *Medieval and Renaissance Studies*, 6 (1976), pp. 3-27.
— *Medieval Households* (Cambridge, MA: Harvard University Press, 1985).
— *Women, Family and Society in Medieval Europe: Historical Essays, 1978-1991* (Providence, RI: Berghahn Books, 1995).
— and Christiane Klapisch-Zuber, *Tuscans and Their Families: A Study of the Florentine Catasto of 1427* (New Haven, CT: Yale University Press, 1985).
Hilaire, Jean, *La régime des biens entre époux dans la region de Montpellier du début du XIIIe siècle à la fin du XVIe siècle* (Montpellier, 1957).
Hinojosa Montalovo, José, *Diccionario de historia medieval del Reino de Valencia*, vols 1-4 (Valencia: Biblioteca Valenciana, 2002).
Howell, Martha, *The Marriage Exchange: Property, Social Place and Gender in Cities of the Low Countries* (Chicago: University of Chicago Press, 1998).
— 'The Social Logic of the Marital Household in Cities of the Late Medieval Low Countries', in Myriam Carlier and Tim Soens (eds), *The Household in Late Medieval Cities: Italy and Northwestern Europe Compared* (Louvain: Garant, 2001), pp. 185-202.
Iradiel, Paulino, 'Familia y función económica de la mujer en actividades no agrarias', in Yves-René Fonquerne and Alfonso Esteban (eds), *Condición de la mujer en la Edad Media* (Madrid: Casa de Veláquez/Universidad Complutense, 1986), pp. 222-259.
— 'L'Evolució Econòmica', in *Història del País Valencià Volum II: De la Conquesta a la Federació Hispània*, pp. 267-324.
— (ed.), *València i la Mediterrànian medièval: societas i economies en contacte al segle XV* (Valencia: Department d'Historià Medieval de la Universitat de València, 1992).
— 'Corporaciones de oficio, acción política y sociedad civil en Valencia', in *Cofradías, Gremios y Solidaridades en la España medieval* (Pamplona: Gobierno de Navarra, Departamento de Educación y Cultura, 1993), pp. 253-284.
Itur, Santiago Cebrión, *Los fueros de Valencia. Apuntes preliminares para su exposición y estudio* (Valencia, 1925).
Jacob, Robert, *Les époux, le seigneur et la cité: Coutume et pratiques matrimoniales des bourgeois et paysans de France du Nord au moyen âge* (Brussels: Publications de Facultés Université St Louis, 1990).

Johnson, Walter, 'On Agency', *Journal of Social History*, 37(1) (2003), pp. 113–124.
Jordan, William C., 'Communal Administration in France, 1257–1270: Problems Discovered and Solutions Imposed', *Revue belge de philologie et d'histoire*, 59 (1981), pp. 292–311.
— *Women and Credit in Pre-Industrial and Developing Societies* (Philadelphia: University of Pennsylvania Press, 1993).
Kelleher, Marie, *The Measure of Woman: Law and Female Identity in the Crown of Aragon* (Philadelphia: University of Pennsylvania Press, 2011).
Kertzer, D.I., 'Anthropology and Family History', *Journal of Family History*, 9 (1984), pp. 210–216.
Kettle, Ann J., 'Ruined Maids: Prostitutes and Servant Girls in Later Medieval England', in Robert R. Edwards and Vickie Ziegler (eds), *Matrons and Marginal Women in Medieval Society* (Woodbridge, UK: Boydell Press, 1995), pp. 19–32.
Kirshner, Julius, *Pursing Honor While Avoiding Sin: The Monte delle Doti of Florence* (Milano: A. Giuffré, 1978).
— 'Wives Claims against Insolvent Husbands in Late Medieval Italy', in Julius Kirshner and Suzanne F. Wemple (eds), *Women of the Medieval World: Essays in Honor of John H. Mundy* (Oxford: Basil Blackwell, 1985), pp. 256–303.
— and Anthony Molho, 'The Dowry Fund and the Marriage Market in Early Quattrocento Florence', *Journal of Modern History*, 50(3) (September 1978), pp. 403–438.
Klapisch-Zuber, Christiane, *Women, Family and Ritual in Renaissance Italy* (Chicago: University of Chicago Press, 1985).
— 'Women Servants in Florence during the Fourteenth and Fifteenth Centuries', in Barbara Hanawalt (ed.), *Women and Work in Preindustrial Europe* (Bloomington: Indiana University Press, 1986), pp. 56–80
— 'The Medievalist: Women and the Serial Approach', in Michelle Perrot (ed.), *Writing Women's History* (Oxford: Blackwell, 1992), pp. 25–33.
Kowaleski, Maryanne, 'Single Women in Medieval and Early Modern Europe: The Demographic Perspective', in Judith M. Bennett and Amy M. Froide (eds), *Single Women in the European Past, 1250–1800* (Philadelphia: University of Pennsylvania Press, 1998).
Kuehn, Thomas, *Law, Family and Women: Toward a Legal Anthropology of Renaissance Italy* (Chicago: University of Chicago Press, 1991).
— 'Understanding Gender Inequality in Renaissance Florence: Personhood and Gifts of Maternal Inheritance by Women', *Journal of Women's History*, 8(2) (summer 1996), pp. 58–80.
— 'Daughters, Mothers, Wives and Widows: Women as Legal Persons', in Anne Jacobson Schutte, Thomas Kuehn and Silvana Seidel Menchi (eds), *Time, Space and Women's Lives in Early Modern Europe* (Kirksville, MO: Truman State University Press, 2001), pp. 97–115.
Ladero Quesada, Manuel F., *Las ciudades de la corona de Castilla en la Baja Edad Media (XVII al XV)* (Madrid: Arco Libros, 1996).
Lalinde Abadia, Jesus, *La Gobernación General en la Corona de Aragon* (Madrid-Zaragoza: Consejo Superior de investigaciones cientificas, 1963).
Landès-Mallet, Anne-Marie, *La famille en Rouergue au moyen âge, 1239–1345: Étude de la practique notariale* (Rouen: Université de Rouen, 1985).
Le Roy Ladurie, Emmanuel, *Les Paysans de Languedoc* (Paris: Mouton, 1966).

López Beltrán, María Teresa, 'La Accesibilidad de la Mujer al Mundo Laboral: El Servicio Domestico en Malaga a finales de la Edad Media', *Estudios Historicos y Literarios Sobre la Mujer Medieval* (Malaga: Diputacion Provincal, Servicio de Publicaciones, 1990).

López Elum, Pedro, *La Conquista y Repoblación Valenciana Durante el Reinado de Jaime I* (Valencia: Federico Domench, 1995).

— and Mateu Rodrigo Lizondo, 'La mujer en el código de Jaime I de los Furs de Valencià', in *Las mujeres medievales y su ámbito jurídico* (Madrid: Seminario de estudios de la mujer, Universidad Autonoma de Madrid, 1982), pp. 125–135.

Lynch, Katherine A., *Individuals, Families and Communities in Europe, 1200–1800: The Urban Foundations of Western Society* (Cambridge: Cambridge University Press, 2003).

Mackenney, Richard, *Tradesmen and Traders: The World of the Guilds in Venice and Europe, c.1250–1650* (London: Croom Helm, 1987).

McNamara, JoAnn and Suzanne Wemple, 'The Power of Women through the Family in Medieval Europe, 500–1100', in Mary Erler and Maryanne Kowaleski (eds) *Women and Power in the Middle Ages* (Athens: University of Georgia Press, 1988), pp. 83–101.

Martínez Llopis, Manuel M., *Historia de la gastronomía española* (Madrid: Alianza Editoral, 1989).

Mauss, Marcel, *The Gift: Forms and Functions of Exchange in Archaic Societies*, trans. W.D. Halls (London: Routledge, 1990).

Meek, Christine, 'Women between the Law and Social Reality in Early Renaissance Lucca', in Letizia Panizza (ed.), *Women in Italian Renaissance Culture and Society* (Oxford: Legunda, 2000), pp. 182–193.

— and Catherine Lawless (eds), *Studies on Medieval and Early Modern Women: Pawns or Players?* (Dublin: Four Courts Press, 2003).

Meyerson, Mark D., 'Bloodshed and baptism: Christian, Muslim, and Jewish violence and the transformation of Spain', paper presented at Friends of the Library of the Pontifical Institute for Medieval Studies 2003 Lecture, (24 October 2003).

— *The Muslims of Valencia in the Age of Fernando and Isabel: Between Coexistence and Crusade* (Berkeley: University of California Press, 1991).

— *Jews in an Iberian Frontier Kingdom: Society, Economy and Politics in Morvedre, 1248–1391* (Leiden: Brill, 2004).

Michaud, Francine, *Un signe des temps: Accroissment des crises families autour du patrimoine à Marseille à la fin du XIIIe siècle* (Toronto: Pontifical Institute for Medieval Studies, 1994).

Millo Casas, Llorenç, *Gastronomia Valenciana* (Valencia: Generalitat Valenciana, 1997).

Molho, Anthony, *Marriage Alliance in late medieval Florence* (Cambridge, MA: Harvard University Press, 1994).

Mollat, Michel, *The Poor in the Middle Ages: An Essay in Social History*, trans. Arthur Goldhammer (New Haven, CT: Yale University Press, 1987).

Narbona Vizcaíno, Rafael, *Valencia, municipio medieval. Poder politico y luchas ciudadanas, 1239–1418* (Valencia: Ajuntament de Valencia, 1995).

— *Precedentes y configuración institucional del Consejo municipal de gobierno*

(1239–1420) (Valencia: Institut Valencia d'Administració Publica, 1992).
— *Pueblo, Poder y Sexo: Valencia Medieval (1306–1420)* (Valencia: Diputació de València, 1992).
— 'Familias y poder municipal en Valencia', in *Consell de Valencia de Cultura* (Valencia, 1994), pp. 13–24.
— 'Vida pública y conflictividad urbana en los reinos hispánicas (siglos XIV–XV)', in Juan Ignacio Ruiz de la Peña Solar (ed.), *Las sociedades urbanas en la España Medieval* (Pamplona: Gobierno de Navarra, Departamento de Educación y Cultura, 2003), pp. 541–589.
Navarro, Germán, 'L'Artisanat de la soie a Valence a la fin due moyen age', *Razo: Cahiers du centre d'études médiévales de Nice*, 14 (1993), pp. 163–175.
Nicholas, David, *The Domestic Life of a Medieval City: Women, Children and the Family in Fourteenth-Century Ghent* (Lincoln, NE: University of Nebraska Press, 1985).
O'Callaghan, Joseph F., 'Kings and Lords in Conflict in Late Thirteenth-Century Castile and Aragon', in P.E. Chevedden, D.J. Kagay and P.G. Padrilla (eds), *Iberia and the Mediterranean World in the Middle Ages: Essays in Honor of Robert I. Burns, S.J. Volume II* (New York: E.J. Brill, 1996), pp. 117–135.
Ortner, Sherry, 'Specifying Agency: The Comaroffs and their Critics', *Interventions*, 2(1) (2001), pp. 76–84.
Owen Hughes, Diane, 'Towards Historical Ethnography: Notarial Records and Family History in the Middle Ages', *Historical Methods Newsletter*, 7 (1974), pp. 61–71.
— 'Domestic Ideals and Social Behaviour: Evidence from Medieval Genoa', in Charles E. Rosenberg (ed.), *The Family in History: Lectures Given in Memory of Steven Allen Kaplan* (Philadelphia: University of Pennsylvania Press, 1975), pp. 115–143.
— 'Urban Growth and Family Structure in Medieval Genoa', *Past and Present*, 66 (1975), pp. 3–28.
— 'From Brideprice to Dowry in Mediterranean Europe', in Marion A. Kaplan (ed.), *The Marriage Bargain: Women and Dowries in European History* (New York: Haworth Press, 1985), pp. 13–58.
Pérez de Heredia, Ignacio, 'Sinodos medievales de Valencia: edición bilingüe', *Anthologica Annua*, 40 (1993), pp. 477–858.
Pérez de Tudela y Velasco, Maria Isabel, 'La condición de la viuda en el medievo castellano-leonés', in C. Segura Graiño (ed.), in *Las mujeres en las ciudades medievales* (Madrid: Seminario de Estudios de la Mujer, Universidad Autónoma de Madrid, 1984), pp. 87–108.
Peristiany, Jean G., *Mediterranean Family Structures* (Cambridge: Cambridge University Press, 1976).
Piles Ros, Leopoldo, *Estudio sobre el gremio de zapateros* (Valencia: Ayuntamiento de Valencia, 1959).
— *Apuntes para la historia económico social de Valencia durante el siglo XV* (Valencia: Ayuntamiento de Valencia, 1969).
Pitt-Rivers, Julian, 'Honour and Social Status', in Jean G. Peristiany (ed.), *Honour and Shame: the Values of Mediterranean Society* (London: Weidenfeld & Nicolson, 1965), pp. 19–78.

Poska, Allyson, *Women and Authority in Early Modern Spain: The Peasants of Galicia* (Oxford: Oxford University Press, 2005).
Queller, Donald E. and Thomas F. Madden, 'Father of the Bride: Fathers, Daughters and Dowries in Late Medieval and Early Renaissance Venice', *Renaissance Quarterly*, 46(4) (winter 1993), pp. 685–711.
Riemer, Eleanor S., 'Women, Dowries and Capital Investment in Thirteenth-Century Siena', in Marion A. Kaplan (ed.), *The Marriage Bargain: Women and Dowries in European History* (New York: Haworth Press, 1985), pp. 59–79.
Roca Traver, Francisco, 'La Gobernación Foral del Reino de Valencia: una cuestión de competencia', *Estudios de Edad de la Corona de Aragón*, 4 (1950), pp. 21–38.
— *El Justícia de Valencia, 1238–1321* (Valencia: Ayuntamiento de Valencia, 1970).
— 'La inmigración a la Valencia medieval', *Boletín Sociedad Castellonense de Cultura*, 52 (abril–junio 1976), pp. 161–191.
— 'La inmigración a la Valencia medieval', *Boletín de la Sociedad Castelleonense de Cultura* LIII (abril–junio 1977), pp. 198–248.
— *La jurisdicción civil del Justícia de Valencia, 1238–1321* (Valencia: Real Academia de Cultura Valenciana, Número 8, 1992).
Rogers, S.C., 'Female Forms of Power and the Myth of Male Dominance', *American Ethnologist*, 2 (1975), pp. 727–757.
Romano, Dennis, *Housecraft and Statecraft: Domestic Service in Renaissance Venice, 1400–1600* (Baltimore: Johns Hopkins University Press, 1997).
Rosaldo, Michelle Zimbalist, 'The Use and Abuse of Anthropology: Reflections on Feminism and Cross-Cultural Understanding', *Signs*, 5 (1980), pp. 389–417.
— and Louise Lamphere (eds), *Women, Culture and Society* (Stanford: Stanford University Press, 1974).
Rosen, Josef, 'Two Municipal Accounts: Frankfurt and Basel in 1428', *Journal of European Economic History*, 16 (1987), pp. 363–388.
Rosenthal, Elaine G., 'The Position of Women in Renaissance Florence: Neither Autonomy Nor Subjection', in Peter Denley and Caroline Elam (eds), *Florence and Italy: Renaissance Studies in Honour of Nicolai Rubinstein* (London: Westfield Publications in Medieval Studies, 1988), pp. 369–381.
Rosser, Gervase, 'Going to the Fraternity Feast: Commensality and Social Relations in Late Medieval England', *Journal of British Studies*, 3(4) (October 1994), pp. 430–446.
Rubio Vela, Agustín, *Peste Negra. Crisis y comportamientos socials en la España del siglo XIV: La ciudad de Valencia (1348–1401)* (Granada: Universidad de Granada, 1979).
— *Pobreza, enfermedad y asistencia hospitalaria en Valencia del siglo XIV* (Valencia: Institución Alfonso el Magnánimo, 1984).
— 'Infancia y marginación. En torno a las instituciones trecentistas valencianas para el socorro de los huérfanos', *Revista d'Història Medieval*, 1 (1990), pp. 111–153.
Ryder, Alan, *The Wreck of Catalonia: Civil War in the Fifteenth Century* (Oxford: Oxford University Press, 2007).
Ruggiero, Guido, *Boundaries of Eros: Sex Crime and Sexuality in Renaissance Venice* (Oxford: Oxford University Press, 1985).
Sahlins, Marshall, *Stone Age Economics* (Chicago: Aldine Publishing, 1972).

Sanchis Guarner, M., *La ciutat de València. Síntesi d'història i de geografia urbana*. (Valencia: Ajuntament de València, 1972).
Sanchis Sivera, José, *Vida íntima de los valencianos en la época foral* (Altea: Aitana, 1993).
Sanday, Peggy Reeves, 'Female Status in the Public Domain', in Rosaldo and Lamphere (eds), *Women, Culture and Society* (Stanford: Stanford University Press, 1974), pp. 189–206.
— *Female Power and Male Dominance: On the Origins of Sexual Inequality* (Cambridge: Cambridge University Press, 1981).
Scholberg, Kenneth R., *Sátira e Invective en la España medieval* (Madrid: Editorial Gredos, 1971).
Scott, James C., *Weapons of the Weak: Everyday forms of Peasant Resistance* (New Haven, CT: Yale University Press, 1985).
— *Domination and the Arts of Resistance: Hidden Transcripts* (New Haven, CT: Yale University Press, 1990).
Segalan, Martine, *Love and Power in the Peasant Family: Rural France in the 19th Century*, trans. S. Matthews and J.C. Whitehouse (Oxford: Blackwell, 1983).
Serrano, Gloria Lora, 'El servicio domestic en Córdoba a fines de la edad media', in Manuel González Jiménez and José Rodríguez Molina (eds), *Actas de III Coloquio de Historia Medieval Andaluza: La sociedad medieval Andaluza. Grupos no privilegiados* (Jaén: Diputación Provincial de Jaén, 1984).
Sewell Jr, William H., 'A Theory of Structure: Duality, Agency and Transformation', *American Journal of Sociology*, 98(1) (July 1992), pp. 1–29.
Shatzmiller, Maya, 'Women and Property Rights in al-Andalus and the Maghrib: Social Patterns and Legal Discourse', *Islamic Law and Society*, 2 (1995), pp. 219–261.
— *Her Day in Court: Women's Property Rights in Fifteenth-Century Granada* (Cambridge, MA: Harvard University Press, 2007).
Sixto, R., 'La contration laboral en la Valencia medieval: aprendizaje y servicio domestic (1458–1462)' (tesis de licenciatura, Universitat de Valencia, 1993).
Smail, Daniel Lord, 'Démanteler le patrimoine. Les femmes et les biens dans la Marseille médiévale', *Annales Histoire Sciences Sociales*, 52(2) (mars- avril 1997), pp. 343–368.
Strathern, Marilyn, *The Gender of the Gift: Problems with Women and Problems with Society in Melanesia* (Berkeley: University of California Press, 1998).
Stretton, Tim, *Women Waging Law in Elizabethan England* (Cambridge: Cambridge University Press, 1998).
Stuard, Susan Mosher, 'From Women to Woman: New Thinking about Gender, c. 1140', *Thought*, 64(245) (1989), pp. 208–219.
Swanson, Heather, *Medieval Artisans: An Urban Class in Late Medieval England* (Oxford: Basil Blackwell, 1989).
Teixidor, M.J., *València, la construcció d'una ciutat* (Valencia: Edicions Alfons el Magnànim, 1987).
Thelamon, Françoise, 'Sociabilitié et conduites alimentaires', in M. Aurell, O. Dumoulin and F. Thelamon (eds), *La sociabilité à table: Commensalité et convivialité à travers les âges* (Rouen: Publications de l'Université de Rouen, 1992), pp. 9–15.

Tramoyeres Blasco, Luis, *Instituciones gremiales: su origen y organización en Valencia* (Valencia: Domench, 1889).
Van Kleffens, E.N., *Hispanic Law until the End of the Middle Ages* (Edinburgh: Edinburgh University Press, 1968).
Vinyoles, Teresa-Maria, *Les barcelonines a les darreries de l'Edat Mitjana (1370–1410)* (Barcelona: Salvador Vives Casajuana, 1976).
Vinyoles i Vidal, Teresa-Maria, 'Ajudes a donzelles pobres a maridar', in Manuel Riu (ed.), *La Pobreza y la asistencia a los pobres en la Cataluña medieval: Volumen misceláneo de estudios y documentos I* (Barcelona: Consejo Superior de Investigaciones Científicas, 1980), pp. 295–362.
Visser, Margaret, *The Rituals of Dinner: The Origins, Evolution, Eccentricities and Meaning of Table Manners* (Toronto: Harper Collins, 1991).
Weiner, Annette B., *Inalienable Possessions: The Paradox of Keeping-While-Giving* (Berkeley: University of California Press, 1992).
Wessell Lightfoot, Dana, 'Family Interests? Women's Power: The Role of the Family in Dowry Restitution Cases in Fifteenth-Century Valencia', *Women's History Review*, 15(4) (September 2006), pp. 511–520.
— 'The Projects of Marriage: Spousal Choice, Dowries and Domestic Service in Early Fifteenth-Century Valencia', *Viator: Medieval and Renaissance Studies*, 40(1) (2009), pp. 333–353.
— 'The Power to Divide? *Germanía* Marriage Contracts in Early Fifteenth-Century Valencia', in Jutta Spurling and Shona Wray Kelly (eds), *Across the Religious Divide: Women, Property and Law in the Wider Mediterranean (1300–1800)* (New York: Routledge, 2010), pp. 109–121.
Wickham, Chris, '*Fama* and the Law in 12th century Tuscany', in Thelma Fenster and Daniel Lord Smail (eds), *Fama: The Politics of Talk and Reputation in Medieval Europe* (Ithaca, NY: Cornell University Press, 2003), pp. 15–26.
Winer, Rebecca Lynn, 'Silent partners? Women, commerce and the family in medieval Perpignan, c.1250–1300' (Ph.D. dissertation, University of California at Los Angeles, 1996).
— *Women, Wealth and Community in Perpignan, c.1250–1300: Christians, Jews and Enslaved Muslims in a Medieval Mediterranean Town* (Aldershot: Ashgate, 2006).
Yver, Jean, *Égalité entre héritiers et exclusions de enfants dotés* (Paris: Sirey, 1966).
Zomeño, Amalia, *Dote y Matrimonio en Al-Andalus y el Norte de Africa: Estudio sobre la Jurisprudencia islámica Medieval* (Madrid: Consejo Superior de Investigaciones científicas, 2000).

Index

Note: 'n.' after a page reference indicates the number of a note on that page.

Adubell, Francesc 166, 170-2, 174, 195
adultery
    dowry restitution and 153
    germanía and 106
    loss of dowry and 31
agency theory 1-4, 6-7
    agency of intentions 7-8
age of majority 27, 31, 114-15, 127
Agnes (creditor of Tomàs Dauder) 172, 195
Alcodor, Bernat 29, 46
Alfons IV, King of Valencia 106-7
Alfons V (El Magnànim), King of Valencia 31
Ametler, Jaume 82, 137
Amparo Baixauli, Isabel 23, 146n.17
Andrea, wife of Bertomeu Andreu 31
Andreu, Pere 172, 195
Angelina, daughter of Jaume Bella 137
Angelina, wife of Dominic Navarro 117
Angelina, wife of Pere Oller 68
antefactum see counter-gift
any de plor see widows
apochas 31, 113, 116-18, 132, 175-6
apprenticeship 123, 139
    female 17-18, 39n.27
    migration 20-1, 40n.42, 60, 167
arras see counter-gift
artisans 16-18, 19, 66-71, 77, 87, 89, 105, 122, 132, 159-60, 165, 169, 178
    family structure 28, 75, 82-3, 123-4, 139, 149n.101, 166, 167-8
    guilds *see* confraternities
    journeymen 51-3, 71, 82, 132
    marriage alliances 50-4
    women as 17-18
Aspiti, Joan 162
Aspiti, Miquel 162
augmentum see counter-gift

Aventín i Puig, Mercè 55
Aznar, Joan 48, 58

Barberà, wife of Pasqual Guerau 126
Bartolomena, wife of Berenguer Roig 84
Bartolomena, wife of Bernat Ballester 129
Beatrix, wife of Garcia Pereç 123
Belda Soler, M. Angeles 30, 32, 93-4n.57, 108
Benadusi, Giovanna 13n.19, 148n.76
Benedicta, wife of Garcias Pere 119
Benedicta, wife of Simó de Romanos 117
Bengut, Jacme 172
Bennett, Judith M. 6-7
Bensch, Stephen 87
Bernat, Jacob 27, 65-6
Bestor, Jane Fair 143
Blanqua, wife of Joan Dalearaç 169
Blanqua, wife of Pere Sanxo 137
Bonaventura, wife of Pere Roig 53
Bonet, Gabriel (notary) 156-8, 163, 174-5, 192-6
Bonnassie, Pierre 39n.29, 57
Bou, Miquel 36, 166, 170, 174, 194
brideprice 28
Brigida, wife of Gabriel Garbeller 104

Campos, Joan de (notary) 56
canon law on marriage 21-3, 25, 37, 44, 157, 169-70, 189
Caposa, Joan (notary) 166, 171, 192-3
Castellena, wife of Antoni Castellens 73
Castellens, Antoni 73, 78
Castile 5, 18, 19, 25-6, 46, 89, 102, 104, 108, 111n.41, 133

Castrella, Guillem 29, 46
Caterina, daughter of Antoni Speralbo 80
Caterina, daughter of Bernat Perez 134
Caterina, daughter of Lois Amoros 136
Caterina, daughter of Pastasius Malonda 119
Caterina, widow of Jacob Madriz 56
Caterina, wife of Andreas Martini 116
Caterina, wife of Antoni Carbonell, daughter of Bernat Cebria 82, 137
Caterina, wife of Antoni de Vilamosa 133
Caterina, wife of Antoni Eximarch 71
Caterina, wife of Antoni Garo 173
Caterina, wife of Antoni Speralbo 80
Caterina, wife of Antoni Trullos, sister of Clara Pardo 130, 144
Caterina, wife of Arnau Pujol (Jr), widow of Pere Enyego 86, 88
Caterina, wife of Bartolomé Solat 140
Caterina, wife of Bernat Martí 51
Caterina, wife of Jaume Fortea 126-7
Caterina, wife of Joan Alfons 61
Caterina wife of Joan Gerat 175
Caterina, wife of Joan Stella (Jr) 133
Caterina, wife of Nicolau Martí 74
Caterina, wife of Pere Ramon 98, 197
Caterina, wife of Pere Saragoça 35, 166
Celestina, wife of Bertomeu Olma 76
censals 74, 83–5, 132
Cerutti, Simona 51
Chabot, Isabel 4
Chojnacka, Monica 70, 169
Chojnacki, Stanley 5, 131
Clara, widow of Joan Stella 59
Clara, wife of Berenguer Romeu 158
Clara, wife of Gabriel Pardo, sister of Caterina Trullos 130
Clara, wife of Joan Aspiti 162
Clara, wife of Joan Portagelet 68, 80
Colomines, Pere 29, 46
community of goods *see germanía*
confraternities 17, 34, 44, 50–3, 68

charity and 131–2, 147n.65
llauradors and 17–19, 71
consent to marriage 27, 28, 44, 47, 56, 98, 175
  in canon law 21–2, 25, 37
  in Valencian law 22, 24, 28
Constança, wife of Pere Lazer 116
Coolidge, Grace 49, 94n.60
Corpus Iuris Civilis 25, 153
Costum de Tortosa 32
counter-gift (*antefactum, arras, augmentum, creix, donatio propter nuptias*) 10, 25, 29–30, 31, 87–91, 142–4, 173
  virginity and 28–9, 89
  see also widows
creix see counter-gift
curator 27, 66, 118–20

Dabella, Narcis 36, 162, 173
Dalarit, Joan 175, 192, 196
Dauder, Tomàs 1, 36, 47, 135, 155–8, 160, 162, 165–6, 170–2, 175, 177, 189, 192–7
Davis, Natalie Zemon 141
Dillard, Heath 5, 111n.41
Dolça, wife of Bonant de Heredia 169
domestic service 12n.6, 20–1, 39n.27, 46–7, 56–7, 58–61, 76–7, 116–20, 126, 142, 146n.27, 167
domestic violence 153
donationes inter vivos 81, 82–3, 88–9, 98–9, 103, 106, 114–15, 122–3, 125, 129, 134–5, 138–9, 142
donatio propter nuptias see counter-gift
Doto, Martí (notary) 24
dowry
  elite women and 8, 10, 73–4, 83–4, 116, 131, 146n.17, 168
  estimation of 75–6
  in Roman law 5, 25–6, 65, 77, 153, 184n.15
  surety for 30–1, 41n.79
  see also widows

INDEX

dowry inflation 68–9
dowry restitution 31, 33–7, 42n.91, 67, 128, 151–84, 189–90, 192–7
    appeals 152, 155, 177, 179, 182
    conjugal collusion 163, 174
    contracts of 178–9
    evidence 161–76
    and *germanía* 182–4, 188n.134
    reasons for 25, 76, 153–4, 157, 163, 172
    see also Justícia Civil; widows
Dulcia, wife of Guillem Ramon 197

Eiximenis, Francesc 7, 35–6
Eleanor, wife of Jacme Bonjoch 176
Elinor, wife of Lanzer Ballester 60
Elinor, wife of Sanxo Ferran 88
Elionora, wife of Joan Pruella (Jr) 81
Elvira, wife of Alfons Ferran 136
Elvira, wife of Martí de Mora 129
Enyego, Joan 20, 60
Estreller, Bernat (notary) 56
executors 9, 67, 132, 147n.50, 152, 155, 180–1
    wives as 80, 82, 94n.64, 114, 128–9, 136

fama 36, 167
Farr, James 52
Ferraro, Joan 168, 173
Ferrer, Vicent (Dominican preacher) 7–8, 23, 36
Florence 4–5, 85, 164
Font Ruis, José Maria 32
Francesca, widow of Bernat Vallseguer 133
Francesca, wife of Antoni Milla 103
Francesca, wife of Antoni Vicent 58
Francesca, wife of Clemens Dabella 88
Francesca, wife of Gabriel Fuster 178
Francesca, wife of Jacob Albesa 60
Francesca, wife of Joan Romira 33
Francesca, wife of Joan Vilar 50
Francesca, wife of Nadal Defort 85
Francesca, wife of Pasqual Perpanya 67

Francesca, wife of Tristan Gueralt, daughter of Joan Galiana 48
Francisca, wife of Joan Marti 47
Francisca, wife of Marti Rodriguez 59
Fueros of Aragon 26
Fueros of Teruel 25–6
Furió, Antoni 46, 55, 92n.20, 101, 105–6
Furs de Valencià 2–3, 10, 14, 22, 27, 75, 79, 86, 101, 113–15, 125, 152–4, 156, 161, 163, 165, 176–7, 180
    administration of dowries 25–6, 30, 130, 172, 186n.89
    regulation of *creix* 28–9, 87–91
    see also germanía

Garces, Pere 29, 127
García-Herrero, María 34, 93–4n.57, 146n.27, 149n.86
García, Honorio García 93–4n.57, 108
Gaudemet, Jean 104
Genoa 89, 167
germanía 3, 32–3, 44, 45, 97–110, 113, 121–2, 125, 126, 128–9, 133, 135–6, 137, 140–1, 144, 197
    restitution of assets 108–9, 182–4, 188n.134
    Valencian law and 106–7, 108–9
    see also widows
Gobernació (court of the Governor) 9, 152, 179–81
    see also miserabiles personae
Goldberg, P.J.P. 47
Gomiç, Bartomeu (notary) 183
Gostança, wife of Dalmau de Mir 181
Griselda, wife of Joan Marti 198
guardianship 48, 79, 127
    mothers and 49, 94n.60, 129, 137, 147n.54
Gueralt, Jacob 48
Gueralt, Tristan 48
Guillomena, wife of Ramon Perelada 172
Guismar, neighbour of Joan and Johana del Spital 174

Heredia, Bonant de 169
Herlihy, David 54, 59, 92n.19
Hilaire, Jean 104
honour 59, 64n.69, 69–70, 89, 128, 131, 162–3, 189
honrats ciutadans 19, 180–1
Hughes, Diane Owen 5, 28, 167
hypothec *see* dowry: surety

inheritance 32, 98, 100, 107, 114, 124, 130, 131–2, 134–5, 141–2, 148n.76, 148n.79, 152, 190–1
    disinheritance by parents 22
    from husbands 67–8, 72–3, 86–7
    from fathers 79, 81–2, 128, 136–7, 146n.17
    from mothers 85, 115, 126
    partible 20, 72, 75, 101, 121, 136, 138
Iradiel, Paulino 19, 28, 58–9, 65, 68–9, 71, 87, 92n.15, 122, 136, 149n.101
Isabel, daughter of Alfons Ferran 136
Isabel, daughter of Bernat and Jacmeta Martí 136
Isabel, daughter of Bernat Perez 134
Isabel, wife of Bartolomé Banada 51
Isabel, wife of Garcia Gomiç 34
Isabel, wife of Luis de Partasa 162
Isabel, wife of Michael Pujol 54
Isabel, wife of Pasqual Moreno 68

Jacmeta, wife of Bartolome Miquel 73
Jacmeta, wife of Bernat Marti 136
Jacmeta, wife of Joan Soriano 73, 88
Jacmeta, wife of Nadal Rosselló 179
Jaume I, King of Valencia 14, 17, 26, 32, 106
Jaume II, King of Valencia 177
Joan, Antoni (notary) 176
Johana, daughter of Bernat Sant 84
Johana, widow of Martí Alvaro 129
Johana, wife of Bartolomé Mazaret 58, 132
Johana, wife of Bartolomé Tolia 123
Johana, wife of Berenguer Catala 68
Johana, wife of Guillem Noguera, daughter of Dominic Martinez 90, 103–4
Johana, wife of Jacob Andreu 197
Johana, wife of Joan del Spital 173
Johana, wife of Joan Fanos 100
Johana, wife of Joan Mingot 183–4
Johana, wife of Joan Perez 33
Johana, wife of Lorent Nanyes 182, 184
Johana, wife of Narcis Dabella 36, 162, 173
Johana, wife of Pastasius Martí 46
Johana, wife of Pere Carbonell 135
Johana, wife of Pere Çoll 35
Johana, wife of Pere Marti 81
jurats 16, 38n.13, 152, 176
Justícia Civil 31, 33, 152
    Procedure 153–79
    Sentences 176–7, 179–80
    Witnesses 33–7, 42n.91, 161–9, 185n.39, 186n.74, 188n.134
Justinian 25

Kelleher, Marie 5–6
Kirshner, Julius 5, 155–6, 163
Klapisch-Zuber, Christiane 4–5, 45, 54, 59, 89, 142–3, 164
Kuehn, Thomas 5, 67

Ladurie, Emmanuel Le Roy 105
law, Visigothic 25–6, 28, 93–4n.57
law, Roman 5, 25–6, 28–30, 65, 77, 115, 128, 153
Liber Judiciorum see law, Visigothic
Llauradors 16, 38n.17, 46, 165
    family structure 20–1, 106, 138–9
    forms of landholding 18–20, 71–2, 75, 105
    germanía contracts and 101–2, 140–1
    marriage alliances 54–61
Lynch, Katherine 190–1

March, Ausiàs 14
Margalida, wife of Joan Domingo 179
Margalida, wife of Pasqual Marti 84
Margalita, niece of Joan Portagelet 80

INDEX

Margalita, wife of Daniel Mascaros 135
Margarita, wife of Michael Ruiro 56
Mari, wife of Alvares Peres 99
Maria, daughter of Pere Rossell 56
Maria, wife of Alvaro Pereç 123
Maria, wife of Antoni Pujol (Jr) 138
Maria, wife of Francesc Oviet 34, 135, 160, 163, 165–8, 171, 174–5, 193, 196
Maria, wife of Joan Alfons 135
Mariana, wife of Antoni Tarasquo 74
Mariete, wife of Joan Carbonell 127
marital behaviour 35–6, 168, 172–3
marital property of men 109, 122–4, 138–41
marriage
  age of bride and groom 69–70
  clandestine 22
  cohabitation and 34–5, 71
marriage ceremonies 23–4
  betrothal 24, 135, 166
  synodal legislation for 22–3
marriage contracts 24–33, 44–5, 66, 113, 154, 175, 196, 197–8
  absence of bride 45, 48
  breach of 29
  burden of marriage (*carregà matrimoni*) 30, 77, 108, 121–2, 126–7, 154
  domestic servants and 46, 47, 57–8
  elite women and 45, 88, 146n.17
  germanía 32, 97–100, 104, 144, 197
marriage feasts 23, 34, 135
Marti I, King of Valencia 106
Martinez, Dominic 90, 103
Mauss, Marcel 142, 144, 149–50n.113
Meyerson, Mark D. 173
Mingot, Joan 119, 182–3
miserabiles personae 152
  see also widows
Molho, Anthony 64n.69
Montalvo, Mariá Gámez 89, 96n.102
morgengabe 28–9
mortality rates 79, 190
  of children 62n.6, 70, 136

of labouring-status men 46, 128

Nanyes, Lorent 182, 184
neighbours 8, 10, 24, 28, 118, 190–1
  dowry donation by 134, 141–2, 148n.75
  as witnesses 35–6, 164–8, 173, 181
  see also social kin
Nicolana, wife of Andreu Casals 81
Noguera, Guillem 103–4

Orfisina, wife of Joan Bonfill 181
orphaned girls 117, 180
  dowry donations to 131–2, 134
Ortner, Sherry 7
Oviet, Francesc 1, 34, 135, 160–1, 163, 167, 170–1, 174–5, 192–6

parafernalia 79, 128, 162
Pasquala, wife of Joan Vianya 126
Pastasia, wife of Ferdinand Sanchez, daughter of Pere Rossell 56–7, 77
Pere II, King of Valencia 106
Pere III, King of Valencia 105
procurador dels miserables 180, 187n.124
procurator 156, 159, 161, 171, 174–5
Pujol, Ramon 80, 86, 138

Ramon, Guillem 98, 197
Ramon, Pere 98, 197
Ramona, wife of Pere Martinez 59
Ramoneta, widow of Berenguer Ripoll 127
Ramoneta, wife of Pere Garces 29–30
remarriage 87, 90–1, 130–1
  see also widows
Riudaura, Francesc 166, 171, 174, 195
Roca Traver, Francisco 152, 176
Roig, Jaume 14, 143,
Romano, Dennis 58
Romia, wife of Pere Colomines, daughter of Bernat Alcodor 29, 46

Rossell, Pere 56, 77

Sanxo, Joan 20, 60
Sanxo, Joanet 20-1, 60
Saragosa, Pere 35, 166-7
Siete Partidas 26, 102
Simona, wife of Dionis Dodena 168
slaves 25, 100, 165
Smail, Daniel Lord 137
social kin 134, 141-4, 190-1
   as curators 118-19
   dowry donation and 112
   neighbourhood conflict and 52
   as witnesses 164-8
   see also neighbours
soldata see domestic service
Soriano, Joan 73, 88
Sperança, daughter of Pasqual Alvaro 82
Spital, Joan del 173-4
Stretton, Tim 158, 170, 174
Suau, Manuel (civil court judge) 156, 174, 192

Teresa, wife of Tomàs Dauder 1-2, 8, 14, 36, 47, 135, 155-8, 160-3, 165-8, 170-7, 189-90, 192-7
testaments 59, 79-82, 84-5, 90, 100, 113-14, 121, 126, 128-9, 131-8, 146n.17, 147n.50, 148nn.75, 76
Tomasa, wife of Pere Exarch 72
tutor 117-18, 129
trousseau 25-6, 77-8, 93-4n.57

Ursola, daughter of Bernat and Jacmeta Martí 136
Ursola, widow of Berenguer Cortez 21
Ursola, wife of Bertomeu Pasqual 166
Ursola, wife of Francesc Ferrer 172
Ursola, wife of Francesc Scola 54
Ursola, wife of Jaume Ametler, daughter of Bernat Cebria 82, 137
Ursola, wife of Joan Mayues, widow of Antoni Bo 88

Ursola, wife of Lorent Comes 45
Ursola, wife of Pere Peres 99
Ursola, wife of Ramon Pujol 80, 138
usufruct rights *see* widows

Valencia 14-21, 69, 70-1, 82, 83, 152, 168, 173-4
   Horta 18-20, 38n.2, 75, 78, 80-1, 100-1, 105-6, 149n.102
   immigration to 1-2, 15-16, 167-8
   municipal council 16, 43, 51
   plague 15, 70, 104-5, 122
   textile industry and 16-17, 19-20, 50-1, 53
Venice 4, 58, 70, 131, 168, 169, 185n.27
Vicenta, wife of Bernat Doties 178
Vinyoles i Vidal, Teresa 102
Violant, wife of Joan Martí 48
virginity 25, 28-9, 87, 89
   see also counter-gift

widows 3-4, 18, 29, 45, 48, 49, 60-1, 87-9, 90, 91n.6, 127, 143-4
   any de plor 90-1, 149n.83, 180
   creix and 149n.83
   dowries and 67-8, 72-3, 79-80, 84-7, 125, 128-31, 135-6, 142
   dowry restitution and 9, 67, 91n.7, 155-6, 160, 164, 186n.53
   germania and 80
   as *miserabiles personae* 152, 180-1
   usufruct rights and 3-4, 86-7, 95n.91, 128-9, 135-6, 140, 149n.83, 149n.86, 180
Winer, Rebecca Lynn 2
Witnesses
   and gender 168-9
   to marriage contracts 24-5
   see also Justícia Civil

Yolant, daughter of Dolça Cerda 119
Yolant, daughter of Pere Sanxo 137
Yolant, wife of Lorenç Arnau 158
Yver, Jean 104

EU authorised representative for GPSR:
Easy Access System Europe, Mustamäe tee 50,
10621 Tallinn, Estonia
gpsr.requests@easproject.com

www.ingramcontent.com/pod-product-compliance
Ingram Content Group UK Ltd.
Pitfield, Milton Keynes, MK11 3LW, UK
UKHW041920140426
5217IPUK00014B/248